**WITHDRAWN**
UTSA LIBRARIES

BEHIND THE BAMBOO CURTAIN

# BEHIND THE BAMBOO CURTAIN

The Experiences of an
American Doctor in China

BY A. M. DUNLAP, M. D.

ILLUSTRATIONS BY EVA WYMAN DUNLAP

FOREWORD BY DR. DANIEL T. MacDOUGAL

INTRODUCTION BY JOHN LEIGHTON STUART
FORMER AMBASSADOR TO NATIONALIST CHINA

GREENWOOD PRESS, PUBLISHERS
WESTPORT, CONNECTICUT

*The Library of Congress has catalogued this publication as follows:*

**Library of Congress Cataloging in Publication Data**

Dunlap, Albert Menzo, 1884-
    Behind the Bamboo Curtain.

    1. Political prisoners--China (People's Republic of China, 1949-    )--Personal narratives.  I.  Title.
[DS777.55.D8 1973]    951.05    72-14086
ISBN 0-8371-6752-3

## TO MY SISTER ISABELLE

*Copyright 1956 by Public Affairs Press*

Originally published in 1956
by Public Affairs Press, Washington, D. C.

Reprinted with the permission
of Public Affairs Press

First Greenwood Reprinting 1973

Library of Congress Catalogue Card Number 72-14086

ISBN 0-8371-6752-3

Printed in the United States of America

# INTRODUCTION

The history of modern medicine in China is in large part the life story of Dr. A. M. Dunlap. Throughout his forty years in Peking and Shanghai he observed the Chinese as individual persons in a manner that few Americans have been able to do.

Dr. Dunlap and I were fellow witnesses to many great events in the Far East: the rise of Sun Yat-sen and establishment of the Nationalist Government; Western contributions to higher education (we worked closely together when he was Dean of the Peking Union Medical College and I was President of Yenching University); crises of plague and famine; confinement under the Japanese conqueror; the struggle for national survival in the late 1940's; and the take over by the Communists which soon developed into oppression. His measured conclusions coincide with my own faith that the Chinese people have not unalterably abandoned freedom as a way of life.

There is a lesson in this book which reaches far beyond China. The newspapers tell us every day of the subtle wooing of all areas within reach of Communist propaganda; the same promises are repeated over and over. Only after Communist control is complete do the people of "liberated" nations realize that they have been talked out of the right to direct their own lives. Those who want to remain free would do well to read this eye-witness account of what happened when Communism came to China.

JOHN LEIGHTON STUART

# FOREWORD

This book by Dr. A. M. Dunlap, based principally upon his letters from Shanghai, constitutes an invaluable contribution to our knowledge of the effect of the domination and usurpations of Communism upon Chinese life.

As his letters to Dr. Houghton were received, they were read to a group of mature colleagues whose activities had networked the globe since World War I; their reflective comments were greatly stimulated by Dr. Dunlap's reports. The experiences of this small group—known as the Clan, it came together for a social hour weekly—embraced military action and its consequences, diplomacy and world affairs, the development of natural resources, education, public health, and the like. To the members of this group it seemed that Dr. Dunlap's unfolding story of men and events in China was a significant picture, worthy of communication to a much larger audience.

In assessing Dr. Dunlap's letters with especial reference to our relations with Communist China, it will readily become apparent to the reader that the judgment of so many newspaper correspondents that "America has lost China" is somewhat naive. Dr. Dunlap makes it perfectly clear that the Chinese, from peasant to high official, from the illiterate to the scholar, are distinctly aware of their cultural eminence and do not consider themselves pawns that can be "won" or "lost."

The effectiveness of many of the early broadcasts of the "Voice of America" to the Orient was greatly reduced by failure to understand China and the Chinese in terms of their culture and their way of life. To be effective, counter-propaganda must be shaped as if originating in the country concerned; it must not only conform to language idiom, but also to social and cultural patterns.

Despite all they have said and done, the present rulers of China have not succeeded in their efforts to create an impression of favor toward Communism. They cannot succeed because the principles and practices of Communism can make little impression upon a people whose traditions have bound them to their land and to their families for a hundred generations.

Dr. Dunlap's book gives the reader the privilege of being present, as it were, at the spectacle of the reactions of a great people in an emergency—one of the gravest in its history and one of the utmost concern to the United States.

Dr. Daniel T. MacDougal

# TABLE OF CONTENTS

| | | |
|---|---|---|
| 1: | The Setting | 1 |
| 2: | City in Chaos | 5 |
| 3: | Communist "Liberation" | 13 |
| 4: | Honeymoon Phase | 23 |
| 5: | Uncertainty and Confusion | 29 |
| 6: | The S. S. General Gordon | 38 |
| 7: | Inflationary Trends | 44 |
| 8: | Days of Indecision | 47 |
| 9: | Bonds, Bonds, Bonds | 59 |
| 10: | Echoes of the Korean War | 63 |
| 11: | Anti-American Propaganda | 68 |
| 12: | The Ubiquitous Loud Speaker | 83 |
| 13: | Regimentation of Doctors | 90 |
| 14: | Day-to-Day Living | 101 |
| 15: | The Price of Austerity | 114 |
| 16: | Ideological Reform and Self-Criticism | 123 |
| 17: | The Five "Anti's" | 136 |
| 18: | Personal Pressures | 147 |
| 19: | Cowed Merchants | 157 |
| 20: | Closing the Office | 170 |
| 21: | Final Settlements | 183 |
| 22: | Dawn of the "Beautiful Future" | 193 |
| 23: | Last Days | 201 |
| 24: | Homeward Bound | 207 |

*Illustrations by Eva Wyman Dunlap*

| | |
|---|---|
| The Shanghai waterfront | 1 |
| Teng Lu, weekend house of the Dunlaps in the suburbs of Shanghai | 5 |
| Junks on the Whangpoo River | 13 |
| Mat-sheds of refugee farmers | 23 |
| T'ai Hu Lake | 29 |
| A Shanghai garden | 38 |
| Pei Chi Ko, Nanking city wall | 44 |
| Shanghai harbor; note absence of foreign ships | 47 |
| Traditional stone bridge, Pootung | 59 |
| Memorial Pagoda at Wusih | 63 |
| Wusih garden | 68 |
| Geese at village of Liu Ho | 83 |
| Gateway of Peking Union Medical College, early view | 90 |
| Soochow Creek, west of Shanghai | 101 |
| Greek Orthodox Church | 114 |
| Central Hall of Ginling College, Nanking | 123 |
| Street scene, Route Dupleix, Shanghai | 136 |
| Pearce Road, Shanghai | 147 |
| Shanghai skyline; note spires of Chinese department stores | 157 |
| Hangchow Arch (period of Marco Polo) | 170 |
| Chinese roof-detail | 183 |
| Scene at Ginling College, Nanking | 193 |
| Widows' Memorial Arches, Peking | 201 |
| Whangpoo River at dusk . . . sailing home | 207 |

## 1: THE SETTING

Since my return from the Orient, many friends and acquaintances have repeatedly urged me to set down my experiences. I have done so in this book with the hope that it will help promote a better understanding of the Chinese as I have known them. Would that it were possible to convey to the reader the yearnings for peace and freedom from Communist domination which I have witnessed behind the Bamboo Curtain. These yearnings have been expressed by Chinese men and women in all walks of life—by colleagues and students who have come to my office for private talks, by patients, by friends, and even by my barber.

To one who has lived all of his professional life in close contact with the Chinese people and has watched the reactions of intellectuals, merchants, pedicab men, stenographers, farmers and laborers as Communism flowed in, around, and finally over them, it is not credible that the majority of thinking and intelligent Chinese have personally accepted Sovietism. And despite considerable anti-American propaganda, there are few who harbor any ill will toward America.

After forty-one years as a resident of China, I have nothing but the deepest respect for the culture and industry of the Chinese people. In many ways Chinese and American attitudes toward day-by-day living are parallel. A keen sense of humor is common to both peoples. A distinct community of understanding largely accounts for the congenial atmosphere which has surrounded all institutions of learning and hospitals established by Americans in China.

I arrived in Shanghai in 1911 with a small group of Harvard Medical School graduates to assist in the establishment of the Harvard Medical School of China. This school had no organic connection with Harvard University, but carried the good wishes and moral support of the faculty of the Harvard Medical School in Boston. Charles W. Eliot, President Emeritus of Harvard University, was President of our Corporation and Chairman of our Board of Trustees. During the brief life of the Harvard Medical School of China, we helped to train a number of men who have become outstanding in their profession. Many of them are now held behind the Bamboo Curtain.

The Harvard Medical School of China later gave way to a more comprehensive program for medical education including the establishment, under the auspices of the Rockefeller Foundation, of the Peking Union Medical College. I joined the staff of this new school in 1918, after a year and a half of "refresher" study in the United States.

My long stay in China was devoted mainly to medical education. My professional posts have been primarily in otolaryngology (ear, nose and throat diseases), a field of specialization that had not previously been developed. As a result of my years of teaching, there are now twenty-eight fully qualified otolaryngologists in China who are either my graduates or students of my graduates. Aside from teaching, a wide consultation practice grew up since I was for many years the only physician in China who devoted himself exclusively to otolaryngology.

My clientele has been distinctly cosmopolitan. Patients have ranged from high Chinese officials to the coolie on the street, from the Panchen Lama of Tibet to Communist fanatics—both Russian and Chinese. Nationals of various countries who visited in China were frequent callers, including Count Ciano, Mussolini's son-in-law, important Soviet and Japanese representatives, and members of the American diplomatic corps.

A physician anywhere in the world has special access to the hearts and minds of his patients. My memory goes back to many family councils over a seriously ill son or daughter and to demonstrations of grief as death has come. When modern medicine has been instrumental in saving the life of one supposedly doomed, I have been the recipient of a great outpouring of gratitude. No one who has had these experiences and who has observed the steadfastness and great good sense of Chinese friends and colleagues can believe that they have really been won over by Communism.

# THE SETTING

Mrs. Dunlap and my son John shared most of my experiences during the period covered by this book. In the course of our early years in China Mrs. Dunlap taught courses in music at two missionary schools for girls. Later she gave lectures on music in the Peking and Shanghai areas. Her interest in Chinese art began in 1921 in Peking where she joined a number of other artists in painting of the Forbidden City and of ancient temples. Shortly before the Communists entered Shanghai, she had a fall which injured her back, compelling her to lead a restricted life during her last few years in China.

My youngest son, John ("Sandy"), was born in Peking and spent most of his early life in China. During World War II he was interned by the Japanese together with his older brother, James, who died in camp a month before peace was declared in the Far East. (I escaped internment only because I was hospitalized for many weeks following a major operation and Mrs. Dunlap was permitted to remain with me as "nearest of kin.") In the early fall of 1943 John, Mrs. Dunlap and I were repatriated and returned to the U. S. Following his graduation from a Chicago high school in 1945, John was inducted into the Army and sent to the Philippines. Several months after Mrs. Dunlap and I returned to Shanghai in December 1946 he was transferred to the American Military Attache's office in China. About a year after he received his discharge, the Communists seized power there. At the time of Shanghai's "liberation" he was advised not to attempt to secure an exit permit since in so doing his connection with our military would have to be revealed and might lead to his arrest as a spy. He therefore remained quietly with us and finally came out in 1952 as a member of the family without difficulty. In the letters which follow, the "S" stands for his nickname "Sandy."

For several months before Shanghai was "liberated" by the Communists in May 1949 and during the years following that event, I wrote weekly letters to my oldest son, Donald, and his wife (the "D" and "H" of my letter-diaries). Since Donald was born in China and spent his youth there, he had a special background for reading between the lines of my cryptic communications. As a growing boy he was always very friendly with Chinese lads of his own age and became quite proficient in spoken Mandarin. During his senior high school year in Shanghai he had an attack of poliomyelitis resulting in mild paralysis of one foot. After graduating from Pomona College, he worked in an airplane plant during World War II. He is now living in Detroit. His wife, Helen, is a registered nurse; she came originally from the Swedish community in Jamestown, New York.

Dr. Henry S. Houghton and I have been associated in medical education in China since 1913, when he became the Dean of the Harvard Medical School in China. We joined the staff of the Peking Union Medical College together, where in the course of time he became the Director and I became the Dean. When the Japanese Army took over the Peking Union Medical College in 1941, Dr. Houghton was held as a political prisoner, along with Trevor Bowen, the Comptroller, and Dr. John Leighton Stuart, then President of Yenching University and later our Ambassador to Nationalist China. At that time I was in Shanghai in private practice and it was during this period that "H.S.H." and I began to exchange notes. Our long association and unbroken correspondence over the years led naturally to my letters to him in California, giving a day-by-day account of the changes which were taking place under the Communists. Without any pre-arrangement, my letters to him, although frequently couched in terms which would be opaque to the average censor, were readily understood. Later they were read and interpreted to a small group of men who were keenly interested in world affairs. Dr. Daniel T. MacDougal was the leading spirit of this group.

Throughout the letters, initials are used to identify colleagues and friends. For example, "Sir R." refers to Sir Robert Calder Marshall, for many years the head of the British Chamber of Commerce in Shanghai, in whose house we were living when "liberation" struck Shanghai.

Originally it was not intended that these letters should be other than private communications. Since, however, I have decided to tell of my experiences, I have collected as many of my letters as possible; excerpts from them appear in the pages that follow. It should be noted that frequent mention is made of golf games and social activities. This was for the purpose of reassuring friends and relatives who were receiving alarming tales of our life under the Communists.

These letters start with one written three weeks before the Communists entered Shanghai. Whenever necessary italicized comments are added to clarify the situations referred to. In this day-by-day account it will be seen that the residents of Shanghai—foreigners as well as Chinese—passed from a period of hope that the new regime meant a new and brighter era in China, to one of confusion and despair as the Communists imposed first one pressure and then another upon them.

## 2: CITY IN CHAOS

Terror gripped Shanghai as the Communist forces approached the city in the spring of 1949. The whole metropolis seemed to live on the very edge of a precipice. No one knew whom to trust and contradictory rumors spread confusion and uncertainty. Material values dropped sharply as inflation ran rampant and moral values were steadily being undermined. Hysteria, mild but definite, was evident everywhere.

APRIL 29, 1949 (TO D. & H.)

It was good to hear your voices last night over the telephone. I have an instrument just beside my bed and you must have had quick connection after getting through to Shanghai. Your voices were clear and I recognized both in spite of the fact that the radiophone distorts voices a little. This is a good time to call me should you need to do it again. It was 12:40 a.m. Shanghai time. I would always be within inches of my phone. As I said over the phone, we are all right though things are in a bit of a mess, but we are not thinking of getting out. I said we do not expect much fighting. Great preparations have been made to defend Shanghai and some sort of fight may take place. Just beyond our Lincoln Road property trenches are being built in addition to "grave mound" pillboxes and some heavy guns have been placed in position a mile or so beyond. Trees are being cut to make tank traps but as yet we have been able to save ours. Three times the soldiers have come but Doctor B., who is living in our small house, has been able to turn them away. Today I have given him a placard from the American Consulate which states that it is American property. If there is fighting out there everything including the house is likely to go.

Our most immediate need is money with which to pay staff and servants, as well as to buy food. We would have enough in the bank if patients could pay, but everyone is in the same predicament. The money has depreciated so fast that even if you have a few millions it is worth only a few U. S. dollars.

An hour ago Sir R., S., and I were eating supper while listening to the "Voice of America" come over NBC, New York. For once there was no Russian jamming of the broadcast and we could hear it just as clearly as you hear local broadcasts at home. The "Voice of America" comes via San Francisco. Their broadcasts are mostly correct about our situation except for their statement that the Communists are within ten miles of Shanghai. If they are, we would hear firing. But all is quiet here. As a matter of fact, Dr. T. of Soochow phoned a friend at eleven o'clock this morning that while the Nationalists had departed, there were no Communists in the city. *(Soochow is 50 miles west of Shanghai.)*

There is some talk here that the Communists may by-pass Shanghai for the time being, as they have Tsingtao. In some ways, this would be a good move but it would keep us on the anxious seat for an indefinite period. All sorts of rumors are flying about, but beginning as of now people will be careful of what rumors they spread as two were shot only this morning for spreading untrue rumors. The editor of the North China Daily News has been in jail for two days for publishing statements of Communist advances which were not true. The paper is not to be published for three days and other papers have been warned.

It is late at night and I must bring this to a close. Today one dollar U. S. will buy 900,000 gold yuan.

MAY 3, 1949 (TO D. & H.)

I am writing this letter to go by hand to San Francisco and then by mail. If in the next day or so I can get enough gold yuan together to buy stamps worth a million and a half, I will send you an air mail letter, providing the planes are still running. *(Postage for one air mail letter was the equivalent of something over $1.50 U.S.)* Since I am writing a letter which will not be censored, I can say that yesterday we had a general committee meeting of the American Association to which I now belong. A number of confidential proposals were made.

First of all, as our money goes off so rapidly, it was proposed that our Consulate bring in some American bank notes for our personal use. We should know if this is to be done shortly. Second, definite plans are being made to provide all Americans with enough flour to carry through almost any emergency. Some Navy stores have been left behind, and these will help. Third, in case of riots or trouble within the city, Americans are not to go to collection points but are to remain off the streets and in their homes.

It hardly seems worth saying anything about the political and war situation as much will have changed in the three or four weeks before you get this. As of today it appears that the Communists do not intend to take or "liberate" Shanghai for another two months. They say as much from Peking, but this may be a bluff. In any event, the general impression here is that nothing is likely to happen to the present state of affairs until perhaps the last of summer. Some wish they would come sooner so our money would straighten out.

On April 23rd, my newspaper sent me a bill for two months for 480,000 gold yuan. My secretary found it yesterday she says, and tried to pay it at that rate. "Sorry," they say, "the bill today is 12,000,000 gold yuan." How our money is slipping!

The future of my practice is most uncertain. If we can continue to get by without bringing in any outside money, we shall be happy. The eight people who are dependent upon me are constantly on my neck for money. They all have the idea that the foreigner can always get money. It will be interesting to see how this show turns out.

MAY 7, 1949 (TO D. & H.)

It is Saturday morning and I will start this letter hoping to be able to get it off by air mail on Monday. I will try to give an up-to-the-minute account of our situation and ask that you circulate it as before. If and when we are cut off by mail it is probable that I will still be able to get through by phone, if necessary. At present Shanghai can talk with Peking and Tientsin. Of course, people have to be careful of what they say.

You probably know as much about our war as we do. We listen every evening to the San Francisco and Los Angeles stations and they are not badly informed as we know the situation. On several occasions I have heard news about Shanghai from New York that was repeated later from our local station. When we had our big fire the other day in the area which I pass in going to St. John's University for golf, I did not know how much of a fire it was until I heard the nine o'clock NBC broadcast from New York via San Francisco.

Reception here at present is excellent despite the attempts of the Soviets at jamming. San Francisco and Los Angeles use at least three frequencies which give us a chance to get away from the interference. Toward ten p.m. the Russians are usually lax and then programs come through as clear as on any local station. We listened to a concert from NBC last night which was better than anything we can get from the half-worn records of the local stations.

The Nationalist army in Shanghai is making great preparations to defend the city. Small houses and most of the trees out in the western residential area have been leveled. As yet our small house on Lincoln Road has not been disturbed, but the soldiers have come repeatedly to cut down the trees. Up to last night they were still standing. Doctor B. continues to live out there even though everyone has been ordered from those houses. To leave a house at this juncture would probably mean it would be looted.

This afternoon I go across town to Bishop R's house, the house we lived in during the Japanese war. We will go by jeep through a Chinese village to St. John's where we hope to get some uninterrupted golf on our small nine-hole course. The road which I usually take has been blocked for defense purposes. I will try to add a bit more this evening or tomorrow. *(An interesting part of the Nationalist defense of Shanghai was the building of a log stockade, reminiscent of early American forts during the Indian wars, which paralleled the road for over two miles. It disappeared as kindling wood immediately after "liberation.")*

Sunday, May 8. After a hospital visit this morning I went over the railroad tracks to the small house on Lincoln Road. With my license to practice issued by the Health Department of this city, I was able to pass all the Chinese sentries. Some were mere boys; I think the first probably could read the Chinese of my license but I am sure that the second could not. In any event, I had very little difficulty getting out to the small house, even if I did have to go on a slightly roundabout road. This gave me a better view of the fortifications being built in that area. They are mostly of soft brick and mud and I should think a good tank could easily push them in. Barbed wire in most places is strung on posts similar to cow fences in the Middle West.

Every family in the city and countryside must send at least one person every four days to help dig trenches and place dirt and sod on pillboxes. Our cook and coolie have been ordered to report, or give eight pounds of rice each time if they don't go. Of course, they think we should provide the rice so they can keep on at their jobs, but Sir R. and I have agreed that a little outdoor work may be good for both. This morning I saw hundreds of civilians at work. Most of the soldiers were merely bossing. Some of the pillboxes are dressed up as grave mounds and will make fine mausoleums after this war. It would appear that each group is attempting to make the best looking grave mound pillbox without paying much attention to its primary function.

Everything at the small house is in order. Doctor B. is staying on as long as possible. There has really been no evacuation order. Several attempts have been made by the military to get our trees, but up to today only one or two have been cut. We have an official American Consulate notice that it is American property. This has saved our trees twice. I was able to bring in a fair number of vegetables from the garden which will help the family and the servants. The past two days, the green vegetable situation within the city has been better as the authorities are allowing the farmers in. I saw many coming and going.

Yesterday all owners of motor cars were ordered to pay a special levy of 100,000,000 gold yuan within the next four days. Fortunately, I was paid 250 millions on Friday, so I can do it if I can get the money out of the bank, but there are many who cannot get that amount quickly. I can see where the banks are going to be empty of any cash again immediately before the next pay day which comes on the fifteenth of the month. *(100,000,000 gold yuan was equivalent to only $10 to $20 American money.)*

You may think from your news report that we should be hearing gunfire constantly these days. As a matter of fact, it is only an occasional big gun boom which comes through during the quiet of the night. I think I have not heard such booms more than half a dozen times.

The E.C.A. has a great deal of flour in the city and a fair amount is already in the American School to be used by Americans in case of need. We don't expect to starve, and as I have said in another letter to you, the risk of life for us is probably considerably less than for any of you using the American motor highways.

MAY 13, 1949 (TO D. & H.)

Friday the 13th is a good day to start most anything. I wonder what will be started today. I will get this letter under way and finish it this week-end at home. It will be in the nature of a progress report on our general situation which is far from healthy at the moment. At any time we may have our mail to the outside world cut off. Letters are still coming in by air mail . . .

The noise of big guns was heard in Shanghai for a long time last night. We know there is some fighting around twenty miles from the city. Sir R. was sure he could hear small arms firing, but I did not think I heard it. In the meantime, there is a general tightening up within the city. Sand bags are being placed around hotel doors where soldiers are being lodged. Some of these places are well within the city and are probably more for the protection of the military from local disturbances than as a general defense measure. The extensive boarding up of all department store windows and similar establishments with large plate glass windows is probably for the same reason.

11 p.m. Saturday, May 14. At the 10 p.m. NBC broadcast sent through San Francisco tonight, we learned that gunfire can be clearly heard in Shanghai today. As I sit here writing there is almost continuous sound of heavy gunfire to the North. Yet, it is only an occasional burst of machine-gun fire that is heard. Today when I was out at St. John's playing golf I heard a few bursts.

Everyone looks for a showdown very soon. When I go to the office Monday, I expect to see no ships in the Whangpoo River, as it appears now that the "liberating" army is moving toward the mouth of the Yangtze River, and intends to block the Whangpoo at Woosung. I think that we have seen our last trans-Pacific ship for some time. I hope that planes will still be going until at least the middle of the week as I want to get this letter and several others off.

Doctor B. still remains in the Lincoln Road house, but told me over the phone tonight that he does not know how long he can stay. The Nationalists have big guns placed back of him on Chung Shan Road. The attack does not seem to be coming from that direction at present.

Many Chinese villages and houses out in Hungjao have been destroyed for defense purposes. Today two foreign owned houses were burnt down. Doctor B. said our trees are about the only ones standing in the whole Hungjao area. This wanton destruction is much resented, of course. Many villages were set afire about the same time three nights ago farther west. People are asking how much destruction of the city is being planned by the authorities.

I will add a little more tomorrow as our picture changes. At least one can say we rarely have a dull moment. If the guns will let us sleep, we can stand a lot.

May 15, Sunday. It begins to look like this letter may have some difficulty getting out. As of today, no ship is likely to enter the Whangpoo, and planes may refuse to land at any time. The drive now is toward Woosung to cut off the City by sea, but as yet no activity has occurred to indicate an advance on our air fields. This morning I made visits to three hospitals and found the city fairly normal.

Here is hoping I can get this letter off Tuesday morning. The cannonading is heavy this evening. Occasionally one shakes the house. It is mostly to the north and I do not think that this part of the city will come under fire.

MAY 18, 1949 (TO D. & H.)

An occasional plane with mail is getting out, so I will chance another letter. We live a day at a time with every expectation that each day will see the last link with the outside world broken. Many people thought that today would be it, as last night was noisy. Our windows and at times the whole house vibrated with the cannonading. Sitting at my desk here at the Bund office, I can see fires or rather the smoke from fires across the Whangpoo in Pootung. These are probably fires the Nationalists have set to hold back the Communists. There must be a sizable battle going on as there is constant booming of big guns... Down in front, the Whangpoo is being emptied of shipping as the mouth of the river is in danger of being blockaded. Since this morning no one can cross the river.

Sandbag nests are being placed all over the city. When the shooting starts, we shall hope to be inside. As a matter of fact, our hutung is closed every night at eight o'clock now and if anything is likely to happen it will probably be during the night time. *(A hutung is a narrow street—in this case the entrance drive into a terrace of houses.)*

The head of the Northwest Air Line was just in and tells me that his company is going to try and bring one more plane in on Friday, if they think they can get in, or rather down, without being fired upon. The Communists are within six miles of the air field even now. The cannonading appears to have let up for the time being. It is just lunch time and that may explain this quiet period.

Under present conditions our foreign checks are being discounted 20 to 25%. Everyone wants silver dollars or U.S. bank notes.

May 19. Some change is taking place in our city today but we don't know what it is. There are many rumors; some go so far as to say that we may expect a change in the next few days. It is certain that troops are being moved in and out of the city in a most peculiar way. I phoned Dr. B. who is still living out at the Lincoln Road house, and he told me last night that all the soldiers had left that area. If they have gone permanently, that is hard to understand, if the City is to be defended.

MAY 20, 1949 (TO D. & H.)

This morning we have come down to the Bund to find it swept clean of all traffic excepting the military and tram cars which must turn around at this point. We had to get out of the car some distance from the office because of the traffic jam. It is not clear just what is happening . . . Everything is very quiet here this morning—too quiet! Something is likely to break loose at any moment. It is most difficult to tell what the plan of defense may be. Fighting may be very near, probably just across the River. At the moment the Bund and the River remind me of the Japanese war period.

## 3: COMMUNIST "LIBERATION"

The days immediately preceding the capture of Shanghai by the Communists were tense and expectant. Hundreds of concrete pillboxes were built around the city, usually with connecting trenches. An important battle was considered imminent.

Two days before the approach of the enemy, the Nationalist Government staged a big "victory" parade composed of hundreds of open trucks filled with students shouting slogans and throwing out leaflets. Both proclaimed that Shanghai was to be "defended to the last man."

On the following morning I stood at my office window overlooking the waterfront and watched thousands of Nationalist soldiers marching north toward the Garden Bridge. It was assumed at the time that they were to take up positions for defense, but we now know they were retreating from the city.

In the letter which follows an account is given of the Communist Army's approach to the city and their entry. It should be noted that there was no evidence that the pillboxes to the west of the city (the route of entry) had ever been used. There was much firing of guns but little fighting.

MAY 24, 1949 (TO D. & H.)

I shall start this letter tonight *(Tuesday)* but it will probably not get out for many days to come. It is 9:30 p.m. and the Shanghai battle is in full cry. Guns big and small can be heard on all sides. At the moment we are in one of the battle areas and as I write an action is taking place down the road some five hundred yards away. It sounds like a Chinese wedding celebration. But we know it is not. Every so often a bullet sings overhead. Nationalist troops have been retreating all day and the Communists are now over the railroads to the west and in some places are moving into the city.

S. just came running in from the gate to this big compound, saying he was beating a retreat. Too much firing in the street. Perhaps a wise procedure and one I might follow as I am on the exposed side of the house.

11 p.m. I'll add a little more tonight. The "storm" is over for the time being. But off to the North and East the big guns still rumble. The firing is probably at the old Civic Center out North near the junction of the Yangtze and Whangpoo. It is possible that the Nationalists are making a last stand out there.

After the heavy firing had ceased which had made us move to the other side of the house I phoned Mr. W. of the American President Steamship Lines. He lives over in the Picardie, a high apartment house on Avenue Petain a little west of the American School. He advised me that the fight was beyond him at Zikawei and it looked as though a stand was to be made just below him at the corner of Win Ling and Petain. For some three hours he had watched Nationalist troops streaming past the Picardie in what he thought was a retreat.

The Communist advance today has been so rapid that every one has been taken by surprise. Out Amherst Avenue to our west there is an occasional short burst of gun-fire. (*It was at this point that Dr. B. was almost caught between opposing forces when he was trying to return to the Lincoln Road House for lunch.*)

We learned this morning that the Hungjao Golf-course was occupied by the Communists and by noon they were at the railroad. Behind the Communist lines all is quiet.

An interesting sidelight on the speed of radio communication was demonstrated tonight. About 9:45 p.m. Mr. W. told me over the phone that the fighting appeared to be at Zikawei. Over the ten o'clock New York news broadcast, S. heard that Zikawei had been captured by the Communists. My guess is that a reporter had sent in a wire earlier in the afternoon that Zikawei had been captured but we did not know it, although it is only a mile and a half away.

May 25, Wednesday, 9:30 a.m. Well, we were "liberated" about 3 a.m. today. It was a very noisy night with machine-gun firing everywhere. One advantage of being in a compound with fairly high apartment buildings about us is that the machine-gun and rifle bullets have

## COMMUNIST "LIBERATION"

not reached us. H.L. was just in about an hour ago and tells us that the Communists came in about midnight. He lives near the railroad, a half mile from here, and was in a direct line of fire for a short time ... Apparently the city is about half "liberated." Since our phone is out of order this morning, we can't find out what the situation is. In any event, we are being good and remaining quietly at home for the day. Fortunately, I have no patients needing attention.

Yesterday noon I called Mrs. D.R. at St. John's to see how things were, as we had heard there was fighting at that point. She replied that all was quiet. Within an hour all was *not* quiet. The Nationalists blew up the railroad bridge and the regular road bridge. We felt the blast here but at St. John's two-thirds of all window-panes were broken and a large piece of the steel framework of the railroad bridge landed forty feet from the R.'s house. No one was hurt in St. John's University.

Now that we are in Communist territory, the Nationalist planes are "the enemy." Just now there is one overhead and if it gets in the right position a heavy machine gun around the corner will start up. Twice this morning two long bursts were sent after a small plane. All the firing we hear now is in the distance. By the end of the week we should be a completely "liberated city."

12 o'clock, same day. I have just returned from making an outcall with Sir R. acting as my chauffeur. He was anxious to go to the city to see how it had stood last nights' fighting, and what the Communist soldiers looked like. After visiting my patient, we drove into the city in Sir R.'s small Austin. The streets were almost deserted and only a few soldiers were to be seen. Their uniform is greenish yellow and the soldiers we saw appeared to be young country boys.

And did we see any signs of battle left from last night's din? We did not. All the noise last night could just as well have been firecrackers driving away the serpent eating up the moon at eclipse time.

6:30 p.m., same day. Over the 6 p.m. New York "Voice of America" I learned that "Communist forces entered Shanghai via the old French concession and moved down to the Bund with hardly a shot being fired." This is not the way we heard it! At some periods during the night I don't think anyone could sleep in this part of the city. But New York had a pretty up-to-the-minute picture.

The C's are only up to the Customs House on the Bund. At 4 p.m., both the British and American Consulates had not been "liberated." It is highly probable that some time tonight the bridges over the Soochow Creek will be destroyed to give the Nationalists time to evacuate.

It will probably be two or three more days before we can get downtown. This will make little difference as there are practically no patients. I was in touch with Dr. B. at 5 p.m.; he has been out to the Lincoln Road house today. He brought back some vegetables and reported that all is well there. The house and garden are in good condition and it looks, now that the place is in a "liberated area," like nothing will happen ... As night comes on the big guns are tuning up. Our guess is that whatever Nationalist troops remain in the city will make their escape tonight. It is rumored that all top officials have already gone out by plane. There are a few nests of Nationalist soldiers still about, and every now and then a single rifle-shot is heard. One of the streets over which Sir R. and I went this morning was closed off this afternoon, so that some of these remnants could be cleared away.

9:30 p.m., same day. It begins to look like a quiet night for a good sleep for a change. The big guns are pounding down Woosung way, but there is nothing very loud. On the Bund there appears to be some machine-gun firing. We are all hoping the Nationalists will move out tonight without blowing up the bridges. *(The bridges were not destroyed.)*

Thursday, May 26, 10:30 a.m. Thinking that the road to the hospital would be clear this morning, I attempted to go over an hour ago, but was stopped by Communist soldiers. We are told that all foreigners are to be kept off the streets for a few days. As a matter of fact there is still some sniping even in this area. Downtown it is fairly active. The Nationalists still hold the bridges over Soochow Creek and I suspect will continue to do so until they can evacuate some of their forces through Woosung.

May 27, Friday. Our Shanghai battle may be drawing to a close. The resistance of the Nationalists at Soochow Creek appears to be melting away. It is a most peculiar situation. Our gas and much of our electricity are coming from the area still in the Nationalists' hands. Friends and newspaper editors are in touch by telephone with foreigners living in buildings right on the Soochow Creek. As far as can be learned only one foreigner has been seriously injured, a German. There have been some narrow escapes which will become more narrow as their stories are repeated.

St. John's University grounds, my second golf course, had their "liberation" day before yesterday after two days of explosions and fighting. Mrs. R. phoned me last night and gave me some of the details. They really had some close calls but no one on the place was injured even by flying glass. The Communists arrived just in time to save them from being looted. Boatmen on Soochow Creek, which runs through the grounds, had pulled down some of their fence and were all ready for looting when they were driven off by Communists.

We are told that we can get out in our cars this morning, but I must wait until a patient arrives who made an appointment to come to the house yesterday but could not get through the barriers. Sir R. has just gone out in his small car, and apparently had no difficulty in getting through. You would think that at 72 he would be willing to sit quietly at home and wait until the storm had completely passed, but not Sir R. He wants to see what is going on downtown. His office is not very near the line of fire, so he should not be in danger. This morning we have heard only a few loud explosions, possibly indicating that the Nationalists are blowing up ammunition dumps or bridges. It is to be hoped they will leave the Garden Bridge alone. The trams go over that bridge and some service conduits underneath. Up to the moment we have had no difficulty with any of our utilities.

Last night was our first good night for sleeping in days. There was little firing and a heavy rain which covered up other sounds. It is still raining but there are signs of clearing. My one concern is, will it clear sufficiently to permit golf out at St. John's tomorrow afternoon, assuming that there will be no road blocks preventing us from getting out there.

7 p.m., same day. I was able to get out to the hospital or rather three hospitals where I saw a patient in each one. The last patient was the mother of the number two General defending Shanghai, who must be somewhere at sea just now, if he was able to get out with the Nationalist troops. Or he may have gotten on one of the transport planes which left here last Monday night.

Communist soldiers were entering the city and taking up their positions as I moved about tonight. There was no limitation on our movements today, as there was yesterday. With all Nationalists virtually out of the city there will be no further fighting. However, we at times hear loud explosions on all sides of the city. Land mines are probably being destroyed.

Sir R. found this morning that all resistance at the Soochow Creek bridges had ceased and tonight our evening paper tells us that the Nationalists gave up during the night. The foreigners in the area got in touch with Communists by telephone and arranged the surrender of Nationalist officers.

Sir R. found that about a dozen ships had been scuttled in the Whangpoo. Some should not be hard to salvage. As I went around today I noticed that many of the sandbag road-blocks, built by the Nationalists and in perfect condition two days ago, had virtually disappeared. The good bags have been removed by looters and the sand left behind. Fortunately there has been very little looting within the city this side of the Soochow Creek due to the rapid advance of Communists into the city. It is feared, however, that there may have been looting out in the Northern side of the city.

May 28, Saturday, 5 p.m. We have heard no explosions today. This must mean that all the mines or most of them have been found and set off. Since this has been a very rainy day, perhaps the military has taken a day of rest . . . I was out seeing patients this morning and had no difficulty in going about. By Monday the city should begin functioning again in very much the limited manner it has been doing in the past.

This has certainly been a week of quick changes. A week ago our inflation stood at 50,000,000 gold yuan to one U.S. dollar. (I don't know why we continue to call it a gold yuan as there is nothing gold in it.) One U.S. dollar is of less value than one Chinese silver dollar! Much is changed now. No one wants to take gold yuan and 10 U.S. dollars will buy 15 Chinese silver dollars. (U.S. dollar up in value.) Peoples' Bank notes are already with us, we understand their value is $450 JMP to $1 U.S. *(Upon arrival, the Communists discarded the much depreciated Gold Yuan of the Nationalists and brought in their own paper money, the Jen Ming Piao [JMP], which was pegged to the pound sterling and the American dollar. The exchange rate of this new currency was only what the authorities wished to make it, and it had no real backing.)*

At the end of a hectic week the Shanghai American School is holding its Commencement exercises at this moment. It is raining cats and dogs so they will have to be held inside. S. is chief usher I understand.

Later, same day. They had a good attendance, with thirteen graduating.

May 29, Sunday, 12:15 p.m. Our rains continue. I have just been out to the hospital. There are very few soldiers on the street. Those I've seen are going about their own business, asking no favors of anyone. By tomorrow we should begin to get a line on what is before us. We know from the New York broadcast at eight o'clock last night and our morning newspaper, that the gold yuan is to stop on June 5. A new currency, the Peoples' Bank notes are to be used, and each dollar of

# COMMUNIST "LIBERATION"

such notes is to exchange for 100,000 G.Y. Chinese silver dollars. U.S. bank notes probably will continue for a time. We don't know quite where we are with wages coming due the middle of next week, but having had a fair amount of experience with slippery currency, this city should be able to adjust very quickly.

May 30, Monday, 11:30 p.m. It has been a day full of a number of things. This morning I went to the Bund office where I was able to see all the boats scuttled in the Whangpoo. Then this afternoon I went to St. John's University where the blasting of the railroad bridge on Tuesday last had smashed over half the windows on the grounds. Some two thousand Communist soldiers were in the dormitories of the University, but behaving themselves.

May 31, Tuesday, 7 p.m. I am just in from a Governors' meeting at the Country Hospital. We are attempting to carry on in spite of many obstacles. Patients are few and overhead is high. Money from British and American sources is helping to keep things going.

9:45 p.m. Daylight-saving time, but tomorrow it will be 8:45 p.m. as an order went out today to return to Peking time or ordinary time. We are likely to have many changes shortly. Yesterday it was said that we might expect soon to get letters out by ship. Some American President liners are due in, but they may not be allowed up the river. And if they are, will Communist stamps carry out letters into the United States? We'll simply have to wait and see and I'll continue to add a word to this from day to day.

June 1, Wednesday, 12:45 p.m. We are told that in a few days we'll have to change back to driving on the left side of the road. Apparently we must do everything just the way it is done in Peking. No doubt there will be other changes, but one would think there would be more important things to do, such as getting the piles of garbage off the streets. *(The change to driving on the left was not made.)*

There are more rumors of shipping expected in the River. We learned from New York last night that exports and imports were to start as of yesterday. Some of my Chinese friends tell me this is quite right as notice to this effect was made in the Chinese press two days ago. We learn most of our first news about Shanghai from New York these days.

6 p.m., same day. Our evening paper tells us that our harbor is open as of today and the P.O. is receiving letters for overseas. As soon as we can get some money to buy stamps we'll send letters on the way. If all looks favorable, I'll send this rather prolonged epistle.

Of course everyone is keeping his fingers crossed, but up to the present, things appear to be going very well excepting that no one has any money. None of our bills will be sent out until next week at the earliest, as the foreign banks are not really opened yet. I was talking to S. T., a former student, who is now in private practice in the city, and he feels that the present Communist group in Shanghai is the conservative wing. He points out that whereas anti-American and anti-British posters appeared within a day of entry of the Communists into Peking and Tientsin, none has appeared here as of this day. Also the eight points in a proclamation put out a week ago when the Communists came in state that all foreigners and their property must be protected.

If present signs hold we may be in for a turn for the better in many things. If for instance we can keep away from serious inflation a big step forward will have been taken. If the black market can be put out of business we shall be happy. Prices are still high but should be coming down in another week or so. But in terms of home-side prices food-stuffs are low. S. is doing the housekeeping and rarely must he go over the equivalent of $1.50 U.S. for this family of four per day. Of course some of our canned goods stored against the present emergency are being used. At the American Club I rarely pay more than 60 cents U.S. for my lunch.

June 2, 8:40 p.m. I'll add just a line before going up to listen to the radio in mother's room to find out from New York what has happened in Shanghai today. I do know from looking out my window at the Bund office, that work is being started on raising our scuttled ships in the harbor. If the Nationalist bombers will leave us alone, I think it will not be long before the city is in order again. According to our evening paper, six foreign ships will enter the harbor within the next week. Two are American and already the P.O. is receiving mail. I'll send this over on Monday at which time I hope to have money enough to buy stamps. There is some talk also in the evening paper of possible resumption of air-mail service to America. That may come before we know it.

My old farmer came in from the Pearce Road property today and told us that he was allowed to keep his mat house. The squatter's factory at the South end of the property had been burned down by the Nationalist soldiers and from my point of view that was a good thing. Unfortunately they want to build a small place to live in on the same site, and that I can't prevent at present.

June 4, Saturday, 10:30 a.m. We are having our first sunshine in **ten days, and if all goes** well I intend to get some golf at the Race

Course this afternoon. We usually play at St. John's but Mr. H., my Hungjao golf-course partner, wants to do down to the Race Course today as there is some uncertainty as to how long we may be allowed to use the place.

Our important news as of yesterday is that all foreign exchange must be given over to the Peoples' Bank. You may remember that we did the same thing when the Nationalists were here back in August '48. I don't think we would mind if there would be no depreciation of our new currency. The Gold Yuan started at four for one U.S. dollar and today, which is almost the last day it can be used, the rate is G.Y. 70,000,000 to $1 U.S. Don't tell us we don't know all about inflation! We live in disturbing times when it is necessary to keep one's fingers crossed much of the time. *(Foreign money did not have to be surrendered.)*

June 5, Sunday, 6.45 p.m. Mr. H., S. and I went out to see the Hungjao area and our little house on Lincoln Road this afternoon. We were all agreeably surprised to find that while there has been a great deal of wanton destruction of twenty to twenty-five year old trees and burning of Chinese and foreign houses, the area which this destruction covers is far less than we had been led to believe. At the Hungjao Golf-course many trees have been cut, but still many are standing. There are trenches in some places. The Number One Boy told us that the Course would probably be playable in another three weeks. I hope so as a game of golf helps to make the week go a bit easier. Yesterday we had a game at the Race Course. I was not too hot with my woods but did manage to get off a few good shots, and I suppose that is all I can expect.

Today the optimists have it. There may be a definite turn for the better in these parts. Perhaps the entry of the first foreign ship into the harbor may have something to do with this attitude. Then there is a vocal school of thought which tells us that socialism similar to the British pattern is to be the order of the day for the next few years. It might be the making of China, if such could be the case.

June 6, Monday, 9:30 p.m. I have just come down from mother's room where we heard the "Voice of America" from New York, followed by "Press Opinion, U.S.A." The sun spots, and not Soviet jamming, made reception rather poor tonight. Ordinarily it comes through as any local station. "Press Opinion, U.S.A." is a valuable program for us out here. A review of the editorials in the leading newspapers throughout the U. S., it gives us a clear picture of what is in the minds of Americans. From where we sit, it would appear that there are forces at work which are gradually and surely making things better, a certain country to the contrary.

Very little new has happened to us today. In general, one can say things are looking up in Shanghai. Regulations for export and import trade came out today and Sir R., who is in that line of business, thinks they are workable. There is certainly a desire on the part of the authorities to get business started again. I hope, among other things, that they will import some good bank-note paper as the present notes are wearing out rapidly. Some I have at present certainly cannot last more than a month longer, and as one of my Chinese friends said today, we would have to be careful not to be caught in a rain with them in an exposed pocket.

We had a meeting of the General Committee of the American Association today and everyone was most hopeful of the future. There will be problems, of course, but as things are opening up at present, some American firms are talking of bringing back families of the men now in the field. I sat beside Mr. W. of the American President Lines who told me that two of their ships are due in this week and are expected to take mails out. I'll take this letter to the office in the morning and get it on its way. I suggest that you have it printed and distributed to those who you think might wish to see it.

## 4: HONEYMOON PHASE

There is no doubt that the Communists went out of their way to reassure the populace of Shanghai that all would be well. There was little interference with private business concerns and it was announced that exports and imports were to be continued just as soon as all China was under a single administration. Some merchants, especially British ones, placed sizable orders for imports which, as a matter of fact, never were received.

Public opinion regarding the new regime was divided, but there can be no doubt that a majority believed a change for the better was taking place. Among our friends, many who had been critical as the Communists worked their way south to Shanghai, came to the point where they felt a good thing was happening. They were disillusioned by subsequent events.

Among the foreigners who were not at all deceived by the soft line taken by the Communists were the "White Russians." Most of these people had fled Russia to get away from Communism and they knew about all the methods used. At one time we had over thirty thousand White Russians in Shanghai, but they were the first to leave as the Communists approached the port city. Many left during this "Honeymoon Period." Today there are probably not more than eight hundred of these people left in Shanghai and most of them are aged.

In the first few weeks of the new regime considerable attention was given to the registration of all properties and the establishment of new taxes. The registration was the first hint that while the Communists might be ignorant regarding some municipal affairs, they knew how to tax.

JUNE 22, 1949 (TO D. & H.)

It is a hot June morning and I am sure no one will come down town for nose, throat and ear treatment on such a day. I will start a letter to give you a day-to-day account of our immediate situation, but by the looks of things it may be weeks before any mail will be going out.

We continue to live in stirring and disturbing times. We live in a city which at one moment may be peaceful and the next may be physically and psychologically in utter confusion. Yesterday was such a disturbed day, but up to this moment all is peaceful. Since it is after the time, usually 8:30 a.m., when Nationalist bombers come over, we may assume that nothing may happen until afternoon around 2 p.m. which is another favorite time to put us on the spot.

We are not near any point where bombs are likely to be dropped unless it is here on the Bund. But what we do not like is machine gun-fire originating from every non-foreign flat-top roof in the city, and the rifle shots and even revolver fire from soldiers in the streets. One has to remember that all that goes up must come down, and already some civilians have been killed and injured by descending missiles. Yesterday morning as I was going to the hospital a plane came over at nine or ten thousand feet and the machine guns near the Country Hospital began blazing away. My chauffeur pulled over near a high house and waited until it was over, or we thought it was over. We got around the corner to the Husi Hospital, a distance of a hundred yards, just in time, when the bullets started flying again. Later, as I was entering my Bund office building, there were short bursts at this point, with people clearing off the streets in short order.

To complete a most unusual day, but what may be commonplace with us soon, Mr. H. and I went out to the Hungjao golf course for our usual Tuesday afternoon game. All was peace. Only nine holes had been cleared and the grass is long in many places on the fairways, but we did not have to spend too much time looking for balls.

As you can guess, possibly from reading your papers, there is a great deal of resentment in these parts over the bombings and the proposed blockade of the port, which comes into effect on the 26th of this month. With no fuel and gasoline coming in, we may be in difficulty, especially if any more company oil tanks are destroyed by bombing. Our local situation, were it not for the outside interference noted above, would seem to be getting under way in a satisfactory manner. While

# HONEYMOON PHASE

the "People's Administration" has a long way to go in perfecting its machine, there are many signs of progress. Everyone is hoping for better business conditions and a revival of exports and imports. With the country under a single administration a great step forward might be expected. Of course the important point which foreign business men want to know is, are they going to be able to carry on their businesses and recover some of their profits for home use. Time only will tell. *(Time told us that this was a forlorn hope.)*

June 24, Friday. No bombers yesterday due to fog or world reactions to Tuesday's bombing; none today to this point: 9:45 a.m. All foreign ships have left the harbor in view of the blockade which comes on day after tomorrow. Whether or not it will be enforced remains to be seen. I hope that letters already mailed to you will get out or have already been sent out.

JUNE 27, 1949 (TO D. & H.)

I will keep up a running account of our day-to-day situation, in spite of the fact that our letters will probably not be going out for many days. Our typhoon over the week-end has kept all planes away and as the storm is still with us no bombing is likely today. We have been warned, however, by the Nationalists that they have three hundred military planes and they intend to bomb Communist held cities. We may be in for something a little more uncertain than anything to date. If these boys could bomb where they intend, perhaps we should not be too concerned. But they fly so high that their aim is not too good.

We certainly live in the midst of flying tempers and much talk. In our present surrounding words take on the function of bullets. We are hoping that some straight talk can originate in Washington and London. It is possible that if pressure could be made in the right quarters, much might be accomplished. It is difficult to believe that the Nationalists have sufficient come-back to alter the present trends. To us sitting here, it seems perfectly useless to continue the wanton destruction of ships and oil installations in the port, to say nothing of human lives.

Shanghai is a dead city from a business point of view, with no ships coming in or going out. All trucks have virtually disappeared off the streets. The Bund down in front of the Hong Kong and Shanghai Bank Building is as inactive as a midwest town on a hot summer day. When I come down to the office now, we make the run without the repeated stops we usually made because of former heavy traffic. As a matter of fact, the Nationalists took many cars out of the city and many others are being kept inactive because of the small amount of gasoline available in the city. I am getting what I need to this point simply because I am a physician. I am staying down at the American Club for lunch today, among other things, to see what gossip I can pick up regarding our current situation. I shall not see many men there, however, as many have been sent home to England or America, and others are giving only half days to business during the summer.

June 28, 10:45 a.m. It is Tuesday and the end of five days of typhoons, so our golf is out. We will have to stay home and meditate on our sins. I hope to get a little sleep in between my meditations. It is still overcast so I don't think we will be disturbed by bombers. We are watching the international reactions to our so-called blockade and hoping that the situation will crystalize soon. The Chinese National Government states that the action taken regarding the port is "merely closure," but can one close something which is out of one's control? In the meantime, our harbor is as free of shipping as I have ever seen it. Even in Japanese times there was a fair amount going on. Now there is nothing!

My visit to the club yesterday was not productive of very much. One man who knows a great deal about the Nationalist Air Force thinks there is very little likelihood of any very heavy bombings since planes and equipment are not in good condition, to say nothing of the scarcity of trained pilots. Of course it only takes one bomb dropped in the right place to do a lot of damage. Our big concern is our power plant.

June 29. Perhaps our greatest anxiety in Shanghai today is labor. They are making such unreasonable demands, that it is doubtful if business firms can meet them. Just why the present authorities are not doing something about this situation is hard to understand. *(Even this soon after "liberation," the Communists probably encouraged the labor groups in making their demands.)*

June 30. At this point yesterday a patient came in and before he left the bombers were over us. In spite of our overcast sky they attempted to reach their objectives and managed to kill several hundred civilian Chinese. One bomb yesterday was dropped in the Bubbling Well Cemetery at about 1:30 p.m. I had passed that point about 12:30 p.m. It is clearing now and I suppose we shall have planes over again today. I should much prefer it to be clear when they come; then the center of the city will not be mistaken for their so-called "objectives," whatever those may be.

Again last night, as on previous occasions, we had to wait for our nine o'clock New York news broadcast to get information as to where the bombs were dropped. They had it, as usual, and fairly correct as judged from our newspaper reports this morning. I don't know what we would do without our short wave to tell us what is happening, not only in the world at large, but in China as well.

July 5, the Bund office. Due to the July Fourth holiday (for Americans) I have not been down here since last Friday. During that time we have continued to have our usual bombings. One was dropped fairly near about 5:30 this morning, before we were out of bed. I suppose they thought they would get an early start as it is becoming fairly hot today.

On Saturday, when bombs were dropped, leaflets were also showered on the city to say that we are now isolated from the rest of the world. They did not have to tell us that as we already knew it. Of course, the wireless is still working in spite of the fact that attempts were made on Sunday to knock it out. At the moment we can see no light. With the port closed and rice prevented from coming in, the situation is not pretty. Anything can happen when the Chinese cannot get their rice. They cannot or will not use any other substitute in this area unless they come from North China where wheat is widely used. Since the country around Shanghai even in normal times does not supply enough rice to feed the city, the situation becomes acute when nothing can come in by sea. Rice riots and labor troubles of a fairly serious nature may take place at any time.

I have just been talking with one of our Chinese workers here at the office and he tells me that there is a great deal of resentment in the city over the killing of so many Chinese civilians yesterday by Nationalist bombers. It is said, and with considerable truth, that not a single Communist soldier was injured. You can imagine how popular former President Chiang is in Shanghai this morning, and you may be sure he is blamed for what took place here yesterday. It probably will be repeated within the next few days. My secretary just tells me that over two hundred people were killed near the railroad station and that the Chinese are saying, "Why does Chiang Kai-shek do such things?"

July 6. It is clearing so that we should have bombers over today. If they know of the great resentment of the Chinese populace as set forth in our morning paper, they will hesitate to return. In the meantime, our labor problems become worse and worse. If this is a method of breaking the so-called capitalist, it may be successful. Many firms are just about at the end of what they are able to pay when there is no business. Our inflation is now in the price of rice. With the port closed and no rice being harvested, the stocks are rapidly becoming depleted. So the price goes up. It is three times what it was when we were "liberated."

July 7. Tomorrow is Shanghai's big "liberation" day! How big it is to be remains to be seen. All offices including all physicians' offices will be closed. It would be a good time for all cars, and I suspect for all foreigners, to be off the streets. The Nationalists have promised they will give the city a severe bombing on the "big day," which is again a good reason for staying off the streets.

Since early yesterday we have had no planes over; perhaps they are saving all their gas and bombs for tomorrow. This running account will give you our news providing we don't become involved with the bombs. Fortunately, there are few real anti-aircraft shells to explode over us. Otherwise shell fragments would come down about us, to say nothing of a plane or two dropping on the city. From that angle I suppose we have something to be thankful for.

July 8, Friday. The big celebration came off Wednesday afternoon and continued through yesterday, all with overcast skies, and at times very heavy rain. There have been no planes over due to the weather. It is raining today, so we shall continue to wait for the severe bombing we have been promised.

This morning we arrived at the Bund office to find all the servants in the place on strike. No lifts are running, so we had to walk up to the fourth floor. All bank employees are included in this strike. Every organization is having labor trouble. It is not that labor is starving, but they are all out to get all they can during the turnover. Since no funds may now be brought in from the outside, most foreign firms will be unable to pay anything after another month as there is absolutely no business. As the *North China Daily News* has it in their morning editorial, "the chicken which lays the egg will soon be dead." Then where are we? . . . Riots are expected but just what form they will take and how well they will be controlled by the present administration is not clear at this time. I had a letter from Peking this morning and they are having very much the same sort of thing up there, with no solution in sight.

## 5: UNCERTAINTY AND CONFUSION

The growing demands by labor, together with what most firms felt was excessive taxation, combined to dampen enthusiasm for the new order. Committees of accountants were sent into all Chinese and foreign firms for the purpose of searching out any irregularities for which a fine might be imposed. A British merchant described these "irregularities" as normal transactions under usual trade conditions which might go back ten years and more, but could be labeled as improper under Communist law. Of course, "Communist law" was anything they wished to make it, and what they wanted to make was something "irregular" enough to squeeze money out.

JULY 15, 1949 (TO D. & H.)

I shall start another note and hope an opportunity may present itself so it can be gotten out before too long. We are expecting to get some letters already written out by way of a sailor who will leave within a short time on the British ship which was bombed here some time ago.

Our floods up the Yangtze are giving us great concern primarily because rice fields have been destroyed. It is being said that it is the worst flood in many years. Famine is certain to follow. In times like this America has usually come to China's aid with large shipments of rice, wheat and flour; but what can be done now?

Our rains continue and with them cool nights. A light blanket is needed. We had bombers over yesterday but as far as we can learn only leaflets were dropped. Sir R. took one to his office this morning for translation. I will find out all about it when I go home at lunch time. On hearsay, I understand that the Nationalists are coming back. I don't know that we want them back unless they change their ways. *(Sir R.'s translation stated Nationalists were to return October 10, the anniversary of the founding of the Republic of China, but I suspect the year was not mentioned.)*

It is most difficult to see any light ahead. The present administration probably can hold Shanghai as long as it wishes and the Nationalists can keep the port closed with a single gun boat and the threat of bombing. No one is willing to take a chance.

This city is far from at peace with itself. Soldiers are on every corner and all streets are patrolled at frequent intervals. I have never seen so many armed men around, most of them with fixed bayonets. The number of small machine guns and automatic rifles one sees about is really remarkable. Also, the number of very young soldier boys, say, fifteen years old, is noticeable.

Our Chinese friends are very confused about the situation. It looked better at the start than it does now. There is a great desire for return of the old order, but not some of those who made the situation difficult. Of one thing everyone is certain, China is thoroughly sick and tired of war and would do most anything to see it stop.

July 18, Monday. The rains have apparently stopped for the time being, and our heat is starting. Our east wind will probably give us some relief for a few days and then with little or no wind, it will be really hot, but we have not done too badly thus far as we have been sleeping under blankets most of the time, right up to the present.

You may have seen in your papers or heard over the radio that Americans in Shanghai have asked for a ship to take them out. This came over the Armed Forces Radio Service from Los Angeles on Thursday night. I know there has been some talk of such a move here, from something which was told me last Wednesday, but I am surprised that it has become public property so soon. In some quarters serious consideration for such a move has been made, but this is not generally known among the Americans of the city.

We would find it most difficult to leave, primarily because of the fact that I am the only British or American nose, throat and ear man in Shanghai. I talked with A. W., who hopes, but does not wish to give advice, that I should find it possible to stay. As he expresses it, one out of every hundred Chinese in the city knows my name, and while they may not come frequently for advice, they know I am here

# UNCERTAINTY AND CONFUSION

in case of need. I feel he is "putting it on," but some of my friends and patients are very faithful and I should like to stand by them if possible. The reason for this evacuation move can be seen in the deterioration of the labor situation. Every fifteen days when pay day comes around the situation becomes tense. It is felt that few effective measures are being instituted to bring labor under control and that anything can happen. Anti-foreignism is seen by some. *(At no time did I witness the slightest anti-foreignism among the people with whom I associated.)*

July 19, Tuesday. I have just been told that my license for the car for the next six months is to be three hundred thousand JMP, or the equivalent of a hundred and fifty U.S. dollars. If this administration does not get on it will not be because they do not tax well! It is assumed that anyone able to have a car is well able to pay. On top of this we pay thirty-five hundred JMP for a gallon of gasoline. Today's official rate is two thousand JMP to one U.S. dollar. So I can hear you say, "and still you want to stay in China."

July 20. Last night our London radio told us that Leighton Stuart was leaving Nanking in a day or so for the U.S. I learned this morning that several other Americans are going with him. You'll probably know all about it before you receive this letter. It will be interesting to hear what these people report when they get home, and believe me, we shall know within a matter of hours just what they have said, both from New York and London. *(John Leighton Stuart was U. S. Ambassador to Nationalist China.)*

July 21, Thursday. I learned last night that our car tax of three hundred thousand JMP, that is a hundred and fifty U.S. dollars, is only for three months. At this rate then we would pay six hundred U.S. dollars in JMP equivalent per year. I don't know where this thing is leading, but it does not look good.

A telegram has just come in from Dr. H.S.H. to say that he has received my letters, so you must have had some of mine. He states that his letters have not beeen accepted by the U. S. Post Office for forwarding to China.

JULY 28, 1949 (TO D. & H.)

We have just passed through what is said to be the biggest typhoon in seventy years. The city certainly shows the effect of the big wind. Now, three days after the storm, we have to avoid certain streets because of high water while we go through others with less water rather slowly. Here in the bank building the water was so high that many of the vaults were flooded and the elevators were out of commission because of wet motors. At Columbia Circle our big fence was blown over but not down. Two days ago when S. saw it, a few pieces of bamboo had been stolen. Yesterday when the chauffeur went out with a fence man to see about putting it up again, practically all the fence was gone. *(Bamboo makes good fire wood.)*

The local authorities may get my property for taxes. They are placing such high taxes on properties that few can afford to pay. Dr. S. told me this morning that a friend of his with three acres out on the Hungjao Road was being asked to pay the equivalent of nine hundred U.S. dollars tax for six months. These people seem to have gone completely unreasonable in their charges for everything. Many people are putting up their cars because they cannot afford to pay the high license fee. If I did not need my car for my rather poor practice I would do likewise.

August 3. We learned that our physicians' cars are to have the license rate reduced from three hundred thousand JMP to a hundred and fifty thousand, but every member of the practitioners' association (we are all compelled to be members), must pay two hundred and fifty thousand JMP as a contribution to the "liberation" army. Here goes my neutrality!

There was more talk yesterday of an American President Lines ship coming in about the middle of September. There are many obstructions yet to be cleared away if this becomes a reality.

August 4. We have had rather heavy bombing of the dock yard just south of the Chinese city yesterday and early this morning.

The sun spots are interfering with our radio reception even more than the Russian jamming these past two nights; so we don't know too well what is going on in the world. A notice has come out in this morning's paper that all letters for abroad must have names in Chinese. The city and country must also appear in Chinese. I'll have Mrs. C. put our family name in Chinese, "Mr. Teng," on my letters to you.

An attempt is being made to get the refugees who have come into the city during the war to return to their homes. This will not be easy as many came from areas now flooded and where there is likely to be famine this winter.

Over the week-end I talked to a number of old Chinese friends, among them a judge of seventy. I wish I might convey to you what they have said. Some day it may be possible. They all want peace above everything else. All they want is to be left alone, to go about

# UNCERTAINTY AND CONFUSION

their own businesses and be able to make enough to have a decent home. The leveling off process going on now is very hard on them.

More and more motor cars are being put up as licenses and gas cost too much. From the 25,000 cars operating six months ago there are probably not more than 5,000 at present. Many doctors are giving up cars, especially as the medical association to which we all belong is making a heavy levy from all members to pay a fifty million JMP association tax. It is likely that there will be competition soon to see who can become completely broke first.

August 9, Tuesday. A patient from one of the oil companies has just come in. When his company pays his fee, it will cover my next three and a half gallons of gasoline.

August 10. I am having a summer cold, probably passed on to me by a patient, and the whole world looks dark today. I suppose one thing which makes it look dark is that nearly every day a new tax, payable "within three days," is levied. *(Taxes not paid on the day stipulated increased by one per cent a day. Later this was reduced to one-half per cent a day.)* This week I must pay out almost 1,000,000 JMP or close to 500 U.S. dollars equivalent.

August 11, Thursday. My laryngitis is better today and things don't look so dark. I wish the political situation might improve as fast. In the meantime, Shanghai is slowly going down. Yesterday I saw a farmer doing a brisk business selling potatoes on the street. When the Chinese come to eating potatoes, you know things are bad. I am sitting here at my window of the Bund office. Only an occasional motor horn can be heard. Last summer with the windows open we could hardly hear ourselves talking because of the constant blowing of horns down below. With so many thousand motors laid up because of the heavy license fee, you can understand our Sunday morning quiet.

We continue to have bombings. There was one this morning about seven. I understand a warning of some kind is usually given by the invaders so that people can vacate the place where bombs are to be dropped. (These warnings have on occasion been in the form of leaflets dropped from the planes a day or so before.)

August 12, Friday. Since yesterday morning certain things have happened in this tax affair so that I am paying only 100,000 JMP instead of 250,000 JMP as my portion of the medical association comfort fund to the "liberation army." Also, after giving a check for 693,200 JMP for taxes on three of our properties and one of Dr. H.'s, my agent called to say that everything was being held up pending a new meeting when taxes would probably be reduced. Many people have been unable to even think of paying.

Our golf club has finally decided to carry on by asking each paying member to pay one picul (133½ lbs.) of rice a month. At present that will cost between 20 and 25 U.S. dollars. Expensive golf but we need it.

AUGUST 18, 1949 (TO D. & H.)

I'll start another letter but there is no immediate possibility of getting it out. As things look at the moment I can't see much hope of a ship coming in. I doubt if the Nationalists will give a safe conduct and if they don't it is risky as we are having bombings almost every day, and some of them are on the river. At this end, exit permits are becoming hard to get. We don't know just what is going on but the number who have already had permits is extremely small.

We have definitely decided not to try for this ship. Your mother is really not in good condition for travel. She is making progress but moving up and down stairs is not easy. S. refuses to go without us in spite of the fact that the American school will probably have to close this winter because of the high taxes. China is passing through a most difficult time but one which I feel is not hopeless. The great hope of the future lies in the fact that the Chinese are tired of war and want peace. I cannot feel they are going to be satisfied with anything short of complete freedom. My friends talk freely and an explosion is likely to take place providing current policies are not altered. Already there have been clashes, both here and up country.

As I came down to the office this morning, I noticed the bleached out appearance of the present "liberation" army in the city. When the first group came in last May the deep olive green of the uniform was very noticeable. Now the army has faded uniforms and only here and there a real olive green can be seen. Perhaps this is what may happen to the Communist ideas back of the present crowd. There are some indications to suggest that this may eventually be the case.

August 22. There seems to be more hope of an American evacuation ship over the week-end. This is Monday morning and the radio yesterday from New York seemed to think progress was being made. The evacuation of the majority of British and Americans from Shanghai at this juncture, I believe, would be a mistake. Out of about 1,400 Americans in the city, perhaps 500 might go without weakening our position ... The Whangpoo River down in front of my office is smooth

## UNCERTAINTY AND CONFUSION

as a mill pond this morning with only small craft moving in and out. With tugs and larger boats almost non-existent, the river is becoming a fishing ground for small boats. I have just been watching two small boats doing net fishing. They don't seem to be pulling in very much . . . Lately, we have been having a few bombings directly across the river from this building. Friday there was an alarm given as a plane appeared and you should have seen people streaming out of small river steamers lying along-side the Bund. They rushed to get as far away from the shipping as possible and then no plane came this far up the River. As a matter of fact, we have had no bombings for three days.

August 23. I hope it will clear enough so I can get out to St. John's for a little golf. The grounds there are higher than the surrounding areas and so the place dries up rather quickly. Speaking of St. John's, I have not learned as yet whether or not I am to be allowed to teach my class in the English language this fall. I certainly will not consent to teach through an interpreter. As a matter of fact, were a rule to go into effect to have only Chinese used, not a few of the Chinese staff would have to drop out. *(A number of Chinese teachers came from abroad. They had little training in the Chinese language.)*

It is hard to tell how many are trying to get away on the evacuation ship. I saw the line of people waiting to get in for an exit permit as I came to the office this morning. It did not look like more than twenty people in the line.

I have just had a telephone call from a Chinese asking if I would sell the Pearce Road property for a Chinese cemetery. The price offered is 1,200,000 JMP a mu, which would mean a little over 23,000 U.S. dollars if one could get it out. Which is impossible! It is interesting to think of putting a Chinese cemetery there. As a matter of fact, there are very few modern cemeteries around Shanghai, but what there are are about the same size as this property, about seven acres. There is not much doing in land just now because no one has any confidence in the medium of exchange.

August 24, Wednesday. I arrived at my office this morning to find some magazines from home, all for May. I think these must have come in via Tientsin. At least we shall have a little fresh reading for the next week or so. No letters have come in.

August 30, Tuesday. Mrs. R. and her son were in to dinner last night and were telling us of their experiences in getting an exit permit. They went nine times and spent an average of an hour and a half each time.

As I have said before, we are in the midst of a big gamble. My belief is that there is a better than fifty-fifty chance that our political situation may clear in another six months to the point where a fair amount of business will revive. *(We lost.)*

August 31. Today is the last day when exit permits can be applied for to go on the "General Gordon," September 16th. It will be an overcrowded ship as it leaves and with it will go many of my patients, but I hope not all. One mastoid and one esophagus case will be staying behind that I cannot leave.

Of course we should like to get out of this mess but at present it just cannot be done. We are likely to be let in for some rather difficult times and living conditions. After today no foreign press reports can come into the city, but as yet we can use our radios. If we are to be cut off from the "Voice of America" we shall certainly be in the dark as to what goes on abroad as well as in the Orient. Our English language newspaper is not permitted to give us too much news.

Yesterday the board of governors of the Country Hospital met to consider ways and means of carrying on the hospital. With the number of patients so greatly reduced it is costing us about 10,000 U.S. dollars a month over and above our income. Since we have only 50,000 U.S. dollars in the reserve you can see we are anxious regarding the future. In ordinary times we would be able to go to the foreign firms and ask for grants, but this is out of the question now as all foreign firms are losing money.

Dr. W. is having the same difficulty as is every other hospital in the city. The servants and nurses are on a high wage scale because wages are estimated on the price of rice. The U.S. dollar and JMP are being held at 1 to 2,250. This is not a realistic exchange. It would be better for us were it 1 to 5,000.

September 1, Thursday. Our one English newspaper is asking for permission to close as there is virtually nothing to print. Gradually we see things closing in and before long we will probably not be able to use short wave radios. *(As it turned out, short wave radios were not prohibited during our entire stay under Communist rule.)*

September 2, Friday. Planes were over this morning and dropped some bombs on the outskirts of the city but I hope they will stop for a day or so while the "Gordon" is in port. It would be pretty sad if an "accident" were to be pulled off.

September 5, Monday. We have had some fairly long bombings the past few days. There is a plane over just now and we can hear the bombs but can't locate them. Saturday, one man was killed and five injured on a street which I take every morning just to the east of the Grant Theatre on Nanking Road. It was anti-aircraft shells which came down. Ordinarily we keep inside when a raid is on.

September 6, Tuesday. We are told that should the President Line ship come in it may not be possible to get letters out. The only chance will be to send out by hand which is illegal. Here is hoping there will be some way of getting this out. Yesterday at the American Association General Committee we were informed that it was pretty sure that the "Gordon" would come in on or about the 24th of this month. Each passenger is to be allowed to take three trunks and his household freight. There will be only 450 Americans.

I am hoping to have a foursome at golf this afternoon. It is pretty hot so we may not do more than nine holes. Bishop R. and his brother D., together with my usual partner, H., will make up the foursome. Our course is being put in better condition so we don't lose too many balls in the high grass. It is a pretty expensive club just now with dues and high gas prices, but it is worth all we pay. We get away from bombs and politics.

September 7. We continue to have some of our summer heat these days but our nights cool off fairly well. I wish we might can some of this heat for use this winter. From where I sit, it looks as though we are going to have severe limitations of fuel unless the port is opened. Coal is up to the equivalent of $80 U.S. a ton and fuel oil about the same. We have a ton and a half of fuel oil for the furnace but this is only about a third of our winter's need.

September 8, Thursday. Many rumors are about regarding the taking of mail out by hand, so unless there is some clearing of such matters we may be prevented again from sending letters out. I am inclined to simply post my letters and hope at the last moment public opinion will compel the President Lines to carry them out even if they are not paid to do so.

Mother got out in the car for the first time yesterday following her return home from the hospital. *(Mrs. D. had been hospitalized for three months following a fall which fractured one of her vertebrae.)*

## 6: THE S. S. GENERAL GORDON

As restrictions with regard to the activities of foreigners became more intense, missionaries and business people made an attempt to leave China. All Americans who had no "compelling reason for remaining" were urged to go if they could secure exit permits. After much negotiating and some delay, it was finally arranged to bring in the "General Gordon," a passenger vessel with a capacity of approximately 700 passengers. Several small freighters under British and American registry ran the blockade in the early months of Communist occupation of Shanghai, but they were not permitted to take out passengers.

SEPTEMBER 12, 1949 (TO D. & H.)
Eight letters including two cards for Father's and Mother's Day came together on Friday morning via Sir R.'s office here. Apparently they were all held in Hong Kong until a ship going to Tientsin could bring them. The most recent one dated August 21st was most welcome.

On Friday morning just a half hour before your letters were handed to me, I sent off a fourteen-page letter via the ordinary post. We have been told that no letters will be taken out on the "General Gordon" as there is no way to pay passage for them. Ma, my office boy, learned at the post office that foreign mail is being sent off every day but they will not say how it gets out. It probably goes out by way of Tientsin.

September 14, Wednesday. Your birthday, D., many happy returns. We are having a Chinese doctor and his wife in tonight and you may be sure your mother will have a birthday cake for you. In this case we shall be eating while you are asleep, so you won't miss it.

We have just had a plane over with the usual machine gunning but with no bombs being dropped as far as we heard here at the office. Our morning paper tells us now that the "General Gordon" is expected to take out letters so I shall keep this one for a few days longer in the hope that it will be taken out in this ship.

September 20, Tuesday. All conversation these days centers around the coming evacuation ship. It seems pretty certain now it will be in, so certain, in fact, that many farewell parties are being given. There is to be a big missionary tea this afternoon.

September 22, Thursday. The "General Gordon" gets in tomorrow and in case it is taking mail out I must get this posted today. There is no official word as yet that they will take it.

We have just passed through the heaviest bombing raid that I have heard to date if one were to judge from the intense anti-aircraft machine gunning. Some bombs were dropped on the water front down the River, but away from the side where two American freighters are unloading. I suspect they are trying to bomb a Chinese Nationalist destroyer whose crew mutinied and brought it up the Whangpoo under a white flag following the wake of the American freighters. It is said they killed their officers before coming in. *(Presumably the destroyer followed the freighters so closely in order to be sure of the narrow river channel, since their own officers were either dead or "unco-operative," and the regular river pilot service had been discontinued.)*

SEPTEMBER 23, 1949 (TO D. & H.)

The "General Gordon" is due up the river in the hour and there is still time, we are told, to get letters into the post in the hope of having them go out. If the ship sails without taking American letters I shall be tempted to write to my congressman!

SEPTEMBER 28, 1949 (TO D. & H.)

From my window this morning I can see that the two blockade-running American freighters are still here. Since we are told that no ship will be given clearance unless she takes out overseas mail, I'll get this note to the post office this morning and hope it goes out fairly soon.

Your telegram of September 23rd came last Saturday stating that five June and July letters had arrived, and that you were attending to the various matters mentioned. The "Gordon" got off without incident. There were no planes over during the period she was in port nor have there been any since. Perhaps they are waiting for these

American freighters to leave port. In another ten days we are to have a French ship in to evacuate a thousand or more foreigners, mostly French, Russian and British.

Our weather has turned into fine fall days and yesterday we had one good game of golf. If the gasoline problem were not so difficult, I think many men these days would be spending them on the golf course, since there is absolutely nothing to do for many. We doctors are fortunate in having a few patients. A fair number of foreign doctors, however, got out on the "General Gordon," some of whom we did not know were leaving.

OCTOBER 4, 1949 (TO D. & H.)

The last letter or letters which went out to you may be in the hands of the Nationalist Navy as I think they went out on an American freighter captured last week and were taken away to one of the islands controlled by the Nationalists.

These few days we are having prolonged celebrations for the new "People's Government," but it has rained hard almost the entire time. So much rain has fallen that our streets are flooded. *(It was remarkable that most of the early and frequent parades of the "People's Government" were carried out under heavy rains. Some took this to be an ill omen.)*

We are all watching with considerable interest to see what happens with regard to possible recognition of the new government by the Western Powers. It goes without saying there must be some guarantee regarding treaties now in force before steps can be taken. We hope there will be early agreement on such matters as prompt recognition would greatly ease the situation now facing us. The next two weeks should be interesting ones from an international point of view. With Russia recognizing the new government, there may be some complications in the United Nations. *(In retrospect it is hard to believe that those of us living in the midst of Communist changes in China could have thought that recognition of the "People's Government" was desirable. We were following local Shanghai opinion very closely and had concluded that the only way of preventing China from turning away from the West was to give full recognition. It is clear now that it would not have made the slightest difference.)*

At home we are carrying on without too much difficulty. Food is not too high and as yet we have not had to meet the fuel problem. Unless the port is opened so oil can come in, we are likely to have a real shortage of oil for the furnace. Coal is to be had, as I said before, at $80 equivalent U.S. a ton, but no one wants to buy very much at that price . . . Starting this month we are to have another cut in our gasoline allowance. I now have 25 gallons a month, but we have been warned that this will be reduced. I see my golf "going west" if this keeps up.

I just looked out of my window to find that the third American freighter which had been left at the mouth of the Yangtze yesterday has come up river and is tied up at the Hongkew Wharf. This is very funny business, this blockade running! These freighters even advertise while in port to take out cargoes and passengers. Within a few days we shall have the French evacuation ship in.

October 11, Tuesday. Since writing the above the two freighters have been freed and we conclude our letters must be on the way. Since the third freighter is still in port I'll get this in the mail this morning and hope it gets off . . . B. and J. called us last night at about 10:30 p.m. and got through very clearly. Mother had just gone to bed and I was already asleep. All three of us had a word with them but mother had the most time. It makes you all seem so very near to be able to talk with you in this way. Bombs had been dropped earlier in the day near the radio receiving station but fortunately no damage had been done.

OCTOBER 13, 1949 (TO D. & H.)

I am beginning my fall lectures to the St. John's Medical School this afternoon. This is my usual medical school work and the coming of the new administration has not changed things. This year I have a class of 27 . . . At this moment I am being visited by the police to get data regarding my status in the city and my professional life. They sit on the other side of my desk gathering their information while my secretary interprets for them. Everyone is very polite.

October 14, Friday. I wish we might have some of your gas for our furnace. At the present I have some fuel oil but this will not run us through and even that amount may be taken away from us if no more fuel oil comes in to keep the power company turning over. Our nights are turning rather cold just now and I suspect we shall have to start some grate fires pretty soon. I have about 3,000 pounds of wood in the basement together with three tons of soft coal . . . News this morning indicates that Canton will soon be in the hands of the "People's Army." We continue to have air raids. Yesterday a plane was over and dropped a single bomb.

OCTOBER 21, 1949 (TO D. & H.)

Our situation, politically, remains very uncertain. With more and more of China being taken over by the "People's Government" it does not seem possible that recognition can long be delayed. There is no doubt but what our local situation would be greatly improved with full recognition. It would mean the opening of the port to shipping and probably to imports. We need oil very badly . . . Some imported foods have become expensive. Powdered milk, for instance, is being sold at the equivalent of 20 U.S. dollars for five pounds. Fresh milk is out of sight for the ordinary individual. By using stores laid in some time ago I think this family of four is getting by on the equivalent of three U.S. dollars a day for the day-to-day food. Electricity and gas are costing us from four to five times what they would at home. This is because of the blockade and high price of oil and coal. *(Our increase from $1.50 to $3 U.S. per day food costs for four people was due to higher local food prices.)*

There have been some very poorly controlled bombings in the city recently. It looks more like spite bombing; no military objectives were attacked. In one instance a bomb was dropped in a fairly populous area and many people were killed or wounded. I hope one does not drop through the roof of this bank building while we are here. This top floor does not have too much protection from above.

October 24, Monday. We have an unconfirmed report this morning that the Butterfield and Swire ship "Tsinan," which was probably due in here yesterday, has been sunk by the Nationalists. If this proves to be true, and if it happened on the high seas, there are likely to be serious repercussions . . . The new tax for motor cars is out this morning with virtually no change. Unless the doctors can get a special reduction as we did in July, I shall have to pay three hundred thousand JMP for three months which is the equivalent of $75 U.S. They don't let us alone. We no sooner get one thing paid off than another one comes along. *(The change in the U.S. dollar equivalent of the three hundred thousand JMP is due to the fact that the currency was being depreciated.)*

October 26. Over the "Voice of America" this morning we learned that the Western Powers will act together if there is to be recognition. Of course they cannot wade in unless there is some assurance that the usual treaty obligations will be observed.

We understand that the B. and S. "Tsinan" has not been bombed but she is taking a fair amount of time coming to Shanghai. I have just been looking over the River with field glasses and there is no sign of her. We want to get letters off by ship rather than have them go to Tientsin as considerable time will be saved, so will not put our letters in the post until the ship comes in.

For several days now there have been no planes over and it may be that they are moving planes farther south. This will not make us unhappy. A note in the morning paper tells us that Dr. T.'s hospital at Ningpo and his house were partially destroyed by a bombing some two weeks ago. This was the one hospital, a missionary one, serving that city. We do not know whether there was loss of life.

October 27. One of the signs of the present situation in Shanghai is the large number of trucks which have been converted to charcoal gas. Out in front of my office here at the Bund I can see the big black tanks on the back of the truck cabs putting off white smoke. Then every now and again someone gets down and does a bit of cranking along the side. I don't know the system but it takes them a half hour to get gassed up every morning before they can start.

Our river out front continues to be a placid pond with no steamers going out or in. Chinese junks under sails are making the most of the situation and just now with the good wind from the north several hundred sails are in sight. I suspect that some of these junks have taken the place of coastwise small steamers as they can get in and out over shallow waters without having to run the blockade. I know of a doctor's daughter who was taken out on one of these junks to an island down the coast which is under control of the Nationalists, from which point she took a plane to Formosa and then to Hong Kong.

October 31, Monday. We are looking up! This morning we have three or four ships in the harbor which have run the blockade. This may be a sign that the blockade is breaking down. Yesterday we had a bomber over which dropped two bombs, but not on the water front ... This morning our paper tells us that the British are thinking very seriously of giving recognition to the "People's Government."

## 7: INFLATIONARY TRENDS

After living through the severe inflation which took place under the Nationalists, inflation under the Communists was "mild." For several months the exchange slipped rapidly, as will be shown in these letters, but later it firmed up at 23,000 JMP to $1 U.S. and remained there for months.

NOVEMBER 1, 1949 (TO D. & H.)
This is my day for the General Committee of the American Association. We have lunch together once a month at the American Club. There is not a great deal for us to do but we do have a chance to exchange ideas. There is also a bit of gossip about.

There has been a fair amount of excitement in the city the past 24 hours over the news from Hong Kong that the Nationalists intended to bomb British ships entering the harbor of Shanghai. Yesterday evening the "Voice of America" told us that the Nationalist Government's spokesman in Chungking had denied that they had made such a statement. Now we don't know where we stand. It would appear that the Nationalist Government groups are not together. In any event there is not likely to be any bombing today in this storm.

Prices on all sorts of things are going up again. Unless something is done we may be in another inflation. The exchange on the U.S. dollar is also changing. Saturday we could get 5,300 JMP for one U.S. dollar. It started last June at about 450 to 1. What a relief it would be to live in a country where such changes do not take place!

# INFLATIONARY TRENDS

There are also a few other things which we could do without . . . We are being hit again for our motor car license. For the next three months I must pay, with a doctor's reduction of 25%, the equivalent of 55 U.S. dollars.

November 9, Wednesday. At the mouth of the Yangtze just now are two British ships held by the Nationalist Navy but watched over by a small gun boat from the British Navy. It is a tug-of-war and we are all watching to see how it ends. Much depends on this affair because the British have made a determined effort to break the blockade. I believe the time is near when a showdown is likely to get our port open.

November 10, Thursday. And now we pay 14,000 JMP per gallon of gasoline. This is almost three U.S. dollars. Unless this blockade is broken pretty soon we are all going broke. Something is disturbing the situation with regard to prices as they are all going up, some doubling during the past week. Gas last week was 8,000; now it is 14,000. A pound of imported powdered milk was 13,000 as of yesterday, but it can be anything today.

This morning it would appear that the British navy is determined to stop the Nationalist navy from taking ships and removing cargoes. If this can be done it is likely that one or two Chinese Navy ships cannot prevent free entry into the harbor. Recognition of the "People's Government" and the lifting of the blockade will help to clear away some of our problems. As long as the authorities must have large lumps of money to carry on the war we are due for these high taxes and charges . . . We had our first plane over in several days this morning but I did not hear bombs.

November 11, Friday. We now learn that the plane which came over yesterday morning machine-gunned the British ships at the mouth of the Yangtze. Things appear to be getting a bit thick! These happenings together with the fact that both commercial plane companies have gone over to the "People's Government" leads one to conclude that the collapse of the Nationalist Government is not far off . . . This is a rainy day with plenty of fog on the river. There are eleven ships at the mouth of the Yangtze trying to get in. I should think this is a good time to get in if they have pilots who know the channel. It looks like no golf today.

November 14. The tug-of-war at the mouth of the Yangtze still continues. We had heard that some of the ships had gotten out on Saturday but that apparently was untrue.

With our rains over we have colder days upon us. Now we have to worry about fuel. We have some fuel oil for the furnace, as I have said, for when it gets cold, and some coal and wood for the fireplaces, but it goes pretty fast. My grey hairs are increasing daily.

November 17, Thursday. These days are most difficult as our money goes off again and everyone feels he is underpaid. In the meantime we have difficulty getting enough money from patients to pay salaries. I'd like to get rid of at least four people, but if I try to do so I must pay from three to six months separation pay. The order of the day in this area is for the staff to extract every last cent possible from the master. We live a day at a time, and from pay day to pay day which is every two weeks. It would be wonderful to be in a country where one could tell them to go to ——! (You can supply the last word, though I am perfectly capable of doing so under some of the periods of provocation I run into.)

While talking with R. two days ago, I learned of some of his problems and how he had had great difficulty holding on to his temper the day before. H.M., owner of the *North China Daily News*, had been in that morning and had given him a quotation which he says he will frame and hang before his eyes for daily use. Here it is:

"When you are in the right,
You can afford to keep your temper.
And when you are in the wrong,
Why, you can't afford to lose it."

November 22, Tuesday. Getting squared away with all this money has been a headache. Our currency has been doing a nose dive. Last week we were seven thousand JMP to one U.S., now we are ten thousand to one in less than a week. Unless something is done soon this JMP will go "the way of all flesh." In the meantime we are facing some pretty heavy payrolls. Any money which we took in the first of the month has depreciated fifty per cent. It is the old game now, trying to catch up with devaluation and the increased cost of living.

November 24, Thursday (Thanksgiving Day). This will be no holiday as I must hold office both this morning and this afternoon. I am trying, however, to get over to the special service at the Cathedral at eleven o'clock.

December 1, Thursday. A ship, the "Sir John Franklin," which came in yesterday, was struck twelve times by small shells as she made a run for it. I can see her lying down at her wharf from my window but she does not appear to be greatly damaged.

## 8: DAYS OF INDECISION

An American journalist who interviewed Communist army officers outside Peking when General Fu's Nationalist army was defending that city, emphatically denied that Communist China was connected with the Kremlin. Whether by veiled intent or sincere belief many in the new regime gave the impression that it was an agrarian movement.

During the early days of the new order's occupation of Shanghai many gained the belief that what we were seeing was a nationalist movement built around the Communist idea. It was felt that if the China group could be kept aligned with the West and withheld from becoming dependent on Soviet Russia, a suitable government could be expected.

The reflections on the movement as demonstrated by the letters in this chapter indicate that much serious thought was given to this matter of U. S. recognition. There was an honest belief that recognition might be effective in keeping China open to the West. In the light of subsequent events it is extremely doubtful if recognition would have altered in the slightest the course which Communism has taken in China. England's attempt at recognition which has been consummated only after four years with a representative in Peking would seem to bear this out.

DECEMBER 13, 1949 (TO D. & H.)

Out here we are all hoping for early recognition, not because it will make life a little easier for us, but because we feel it is the only way to put a damper on what is happening in China. Delay is bound to push the Chinese more and more to the left.

December 19, Monday. We have been having a great deal of bombing these past few days. It would appear that the Nationalists are out to do as much damage as they can before they must give up the struggle.

December 20, Tuesday. We had a birthday party for Sir R. last night which pleased him no end. Bishop W. of the Methodist Church was one guest. He had recently been in touch with some of his mission people up country. It would appear that there may be a fair amount of starvation this winter where there were floods last summer.

Our New York broadcast this morning tells us that our port, along with others, is to be mined tomorrow. If they get as far as Tientsin with their mining there will be no way of sending letters out and this may not reach you for a long time. This move on the part of the Nationalists may bring about a serious situation with the Western Powers. As Great Britain is just on the point of recognition, a clash may take place there. In any event, I suspect we are in for a spot of trouble until the Nationalists are completely out of the running. If only all foreign powers might act together things out here might be righted in short order.

Please thank Mr. B. for his interest and say we are still sitting it out. He assumes from what you say that we are to be completely Sovietized. We may be wrong, but there are a goodly number here who are betting, some with higher stakes than mine, that this will not happen. *(Subsequent history showed that we were entirely wrong in our assumptions.)*

It is like going to see a sick man. From a distance all symptoms may point to a very serious situation, but not infrequently a close look at the patient may tell you that things are not too bad. So it is with China. We grant that symptoms you are getting abroad make a serious picture and as we see some of them close, they are also serious, but we also see signs that certain symptoms are not indicative of deep-seated disease. It is possible that we may read some of the signs incorrectly due to wishful thinking, but when a number of people come to the same conclusion (that some of the red is not as red here as it appears abroad), then I believe our diagnosis and prognosis must be given weight.

One of the things which gives one hope for the future is the current deep down thoughtful consideration of their affairs by our thinking

## DAYS OF INDECISION

Chinese friends. The individualism of the Chinese is beginning to assert itself and one of these days you may hear of changes which, while not unseating the present group, may greatly distress some people we could mention to the northwest. I have had a number of these thinkers say to me recently that above everything else they want to see American recognition of the new government as soon as possible. There are forces at work behind the scenes which would be much more effective should such an event take place. These people have no hope of a come-back by the Nationalists and most of them would not be in favor of such an attempt.

Last night we were told of a factory owner who believes he can operate and make a suitable income under the new order, and that a change for the better may not be too long delayed. He represents a group of capitalists who are being wooed by the new order just now, in the hope of bringing greater prosperity to new China. This probably comes from a realization that friendship in the northwest does not carry with it financial aid. *(Subsequent history clearly demonstrated that our early optimism as well as that of our Chinese friends was entirely unfounded.)*

December 21, Wednesday. I don't think anyone is looking forward to Christmas in Shanghai this year. Everyone feels as poor as church mice. I'll do well if I can meet all my obligations. The utilities have gone up four times this month which is far more than anyone had reason to expect. It is the same old game where we can't get our bills out at a rate which will help us meet the inflation.

December 27, Tuesday. It was a beautiful Christmas day but the day before and yesterday were wet and cold. No golf! We had a comfortable Christmas with a small tree and enough gifts to go around. Sir R. is still pretty much a boy and enjoys a tree and gifts. Many of his Chinese friends remembered him, some with food which went into general stores. At 10:30 in the evening your Uncle B. and Aunt A. finally got through by telephone from America and your mother had a real thrill ... I have just had a phone call from the Dean's office of the St. John's Medical School informing me there would be no more classes for two months as the Government is taking all medical students into the field for some kind of instructions. Imagine our Government emptying all the medical schools on twenty-four hours notice!

December 28, Wednesday. Last night, I learned that the students are being called out to help treat schistosomiasis in the army about

Shanghai. These men have come from the north and have been infected in the lake region to the west. This can be a very serious matter if large numbers have been infected. *(This disease, caused by a blood fluke parasite, is epidemic in the lakes and canals to the west of Shanghai and incapacitated large numbers of Communist troops.)*

December 29, Thursday. Sun spots have prevented us from getting good reception from New York the past few nights, but judging from what comes more clearly from Australia, there has not been a great deal doing. With BBC, the "Voice of America" and Australia, we don't miss much. On Christmas we had music from all three places. In the evening the King's speech came over via Hong Kong and this pleased Sir R. very much.

Our harbor continues absolutely dead, the worst it has been to date. The threat to mine entrances has effectively kept the blockade runners away. We are anxious to see what happens when recognition by the British comes.

Shanghai is having an epidemic of parades these days. We got mixed up with one coming down this morning. Now a big one is passing along the Bund. They take themselves very seriously and all normal traffic must give way to them. Some of our Chinese friends feel that the outlook is much worse than under the Japanese. At the moment many dfferent labor unions are being organized.

December 30, Friday. The big question is whether or not an extra month's pay is to be given at New Year. Soon there will be no more "blood" to be squeezed out! *(This has reference to the usual New Year bonus which every laborer and servant in China considered his right under the older orders.)*

JANUARY 16, 1950 (TO D. & H.)

With the American Consulate here closed as of today we don't know just where we stand. *(During this period a number of letters apparently failed to reach their destination. The interruption of shipping in and out of Shanghai as well as Tientsin served to make all outgoing mail very uncertain.)*

JANUARY 24, 1950 (TO D. & H.)

Your Christmas evening letter came two days ago and was most welcome in these days of gloom, days when we don't know whether we are coming or going. The withdrawing of U.S. Consulates from China is making a situation, and if a ship were to be brought in at this time many people would leave if they could get exit permits. Things are so involved for us that I cannot say at the moment what we can do.

My practice is going down almost to the vanishing point and I can't afford to carry my present overhead for long. What is happening to me is happening to every other doctor in the city. The Chinese physicians are especially hard hit and hardly a week passes when I don't talk to some of my old students who are in difficulty and are beginning to use up their savings.

January 26, Thursday. Yesterday we had a heavy bombing in which some five hundred civilians were killed and hundreds were injured. This is such a senseless thing to do as no military objective was attacked. I had just left the bank building before it started, but Mr. S., the bank manager, one of my golf partners, told me the entire bank building felt the concussions. One building across the Whangpoo from the office was struck and burned to the ground.

China just now is sitting at the parting of the ways. As a result of the Moscow talks now going on she will go behind an iron curtain or a split will take place and it will be China for the Chinese. The latter would mean a new day and one which would give relief from many ills now surrounding us. There is no doubt about the seriousness of the present situation, not only for the Chinese but for the world. It is possible that it will not be long before we know just which way the wind is blowing. Then it may be more clear what move we must make.

The Consular people are talking about getting out of here in about five weeks, but I don't think that is possible. If the Yangtze River has been mined by the Nationalists, as we have been told, then I think it is not likely there will be a ship in here for many weeks. Some radical change in the situation must take place before there is any move to sweep mines out of the River. It may be that the Consular people are attempting to get out by some other port but I don't think that will be easy because of the red tape.

FEBRUARY 9, 1950 (TO D. & H.)

If my writing is irregular or rather more irregular than usual it is because I am writing in a cold office. Day before yesterday we had our power plant bombed badly by Nationalist planes and it is not back in working order yet. This is the most severe bombing we have had to date but we are promised much more. Protests are going out from the city to the U.N. but I doubt if anything will come of it. Locally, Communist propaganda has it that these American built planes had the backing of the U.S. With that supposed backing it is the height of irony that an American-owned power plant should have been bombed. The French power plant, which gives us most of our power at home was missed, with the killing and injuring of hundreds of people, but because this plant gets some of its power from the American plant we have had no light for two nights.

February 13, Monday. For one week we have had rain and more rain! The only good thing about this has been the low ceiling which prevents the bombing planes from coming over. We are glad to find a warm office and electric lights this morning. Walking up to our fourth floor only to find a cold office is not conducive to comfortable thinking, and these days it needs to be comfortable as so much of it is difficult. Tearing up one's home is difficult in ordinary times but when one adds all the complications of exit permits and getting rid of staff it is one severe headache. Every Chinese who is dependent on you for a living, hangs on for dear life because he knows that when you leave there is no place for him to turn.

China is fast building up to something and it is not clear just what that can be. The unrest goes deep into all walks of life, and there are signs that the mass of the people will not stand for the new order. Just what they can do about it remains to be seen. Then, things are not too happy at the fountain head in Peking. There are many rumors and all point to Moscow. Many questions are being asked as to why China's number one and number two are staying in the latter place so long. *(China's "number one" and "number two" were Mao Tse-tung and Chou En-lai.)*

Some of my Chinese friends beg me to stay but at the same time say that if they were in my place they would get out. The difficulty lies in our properties and unless we can find an agent who would take care of them I don't think I would be given a permit to leave.

February 21. It is Tuesday morning following the Chinese New Year holiday. We have taken four days away from the office, expecting during this period to see the heavy bombing of the city promised by the Nationalists. As a matter of fact we have had only two short raids and not more than half a dozen bombs dropped.

Now all of a sudden we have air raid alarms which disrupt our coming and going even more than the bombings. When our alarm is sounded all motor traffic must stop. All power and water is cut off. We are without power and light in the bank building this morning because as much power as possible is being used for factories. It is probable that we will be without light and power during the day for some time. *(Air raid sirens had just been put into operation in the city.)*

Now that a treaty between the People's Government and the Soviets has been signed and China's number one and two are returning to Peking in a few days everyone is watching to see what happens next. There are divided thoughts here regarding this matter. We may be in for a rougher time than at present. Our cost of living, taxes, and staff salaries are getting beyond us. It does not seem possible that things can go on much longer as at present. One of my big problems is the motor car. With high license charges and gas almost two dollars a gallon, and with an end coming to gasoline in the city unless the port is opened, the prospects are not bright.

FEBRUARY 27, 1950 (TO D. & H.)

We are over some three days of good bombing weather and still no big raid such as we have been promised. It may be that protests are having some effect. The last raid some four days back resulted in a bomb fragment entering the room next to mine here at the bank building, and a larger fragment, some ten inches long, went into the front door of the bank. These bombs were dropped into the Whangpoo about two hundred yards away. South of us and nearer the bomb, the Shell Oil Company building, the Shanghai Club, and a foreign bank lost most of their windows from the blast, but no one was hurt. Some Chinese on the water front were injured.

Since people are afraid to come to the Bund during the raid periods my patients are again reduced. If planes come from islands about a hundred miles distant we usually see them before 10 a.m., but if they come from Formosa they do not arrive before twelve noon. No planes have come this morning and as it is now 11:30, the Formosa crowd may still show up. We have been without electricity in the office for a week but Mr. S., the bank manager, put on the screws this morning so we have our power and light again. I have been running on flash lamps and a battery box.

We learn that an LST may be brought in here within two weeks to take out the Consular staff and as many others as are prepared to go. They are to go, we understand, to Japan where they are to be transferred to more suitable ships for the trans-Pacific trip. I cannot learn how many Americans plan to leave. I think some of the missionaries, those due for leave, will go.

There is no doubt but what some of us are in the biggest gamble of our lives. Ultimately we may be relieved of everything we own but there is always the chance that a turn for the better will take place. Some of my Chinese friends believe that this change may come during the next year. In the meantime there is no doubt about the depth to which Shanghai is sinking. Levies in various forms are cleaning out not a few. There must come a point of explosion pretty soon!

1:30 p.m. The air raid alarm has just sounded. Seen from my office window the boat people rushing across the Bund make an interesting picture. There are no planes to be heard and no anti-aircraft guns. As a result some men are beginning to go back to their boats in spite of the fact that police on bicycles with small triangular red flags on their handle bars are trying to keep them off the water front. All traffic is at a standstill ... I had opened my windows to avoid having them smashed by concussion but as there does not seem to be a real raid, I have closed them again as our temperature is around 40°F. It is nearly half an hour since the first warning sounded and still all is quiet. You asked if it is dangerous to sit here in the offices with only four inches of concrete above me. (There goes the all clear signal so it must have been a false alarm. Now the city comes to life with the charcoal-burning trucks getting under way and as they do so they make clouds of smoke as their gas generators are cranked up.) Of course it is dangerous but perhaps not as much as modern motor roads at home.

February 28, Tuesday. It is 10:45 a.m. and as I sit down to write the air-raid alarm is sounding. They are a bit nervous about their warning this morning as a half hour ago one sounded followed almost immediately by an all clear. This may be a real one and we should know shortly. There was an airplane over about 3:30 a.m., our first night raid, but I did not hear any bombs.

March 1, Wednesday. We had four air-raid alarms yesterday but did not hear or see any planes. They must be getting phone warnings from a fairly good distance about planes that do not intend to come to Shanghai. My guess is that the Nationalists are running short not only of planes but of bombs as well. This does not mean that I can't have a rude shock one of these days. We have been promised a bombing with upwards of a hundred planes ... Out on the Whangpoo River I can see the results of the usual nightly shifting of small ships. This is done, I suspect, to keep the Nationalists' air force guessing. I notice one fairly large boat very near the place where a bombing took place last week. It has recently been about a mile and a half down the river. Now I suppose they think bombs will not be dropped twice in the same place. At present I am leaving my car at the back of the bank building since it came so near catching a piece of bomb last week.

It is overcast this morning and may not be too good for bombing, but I hope it will clear enough so my Wednesday golf partner, Dr. S., may feel like taking a mild nasal infection out for an airing. The sun is really trying to come through just now so I think we will be all right.

March 2, Thursday. We are having a meeting of the Board of Governors of the Country Hospital today to attempt again to find ways and means to carry on. The prospects are not good as we are having no help from the authorities, primarily because they want to take over the place.

Over the "Voice of America" this morning we learned that nearly everything is arranged to take the Consular people out of Shanghai. Other Americans will go, too. Until I have arranged to have someone pay for my land tax there is not the slightest chance that I could get an exit permit. In other words, like many others here, I am a hostage.

With more and more people getting out of the city the practice of all of us is being pushed down almost to the vanishing point. I am just able to meet my obligations this month after receiving a loan from the bank. The future is more uncertain. Of one thing we are sure— all of us will be fleeced of every cent we have as long as this crowd is here. It is the same for the Chinese. A Chinese doctor friend in last night cannot see any light. He feels that the only hope for the future lies in a turning to the right of the people now in authority.

My office boy has just come in with a big pile of money to pay for my next 10 gallons of gasoline. It is back up again in terms of local currency and now for 10 gallons I pay 560,000 JMP, or the equivalent of almost two U.S. dollars per gallon. It is just one thing after another! The head of one of the big American firms told me several days ago that he would settle for three exit permits and passage out to Hong Kong in exchange for equity in the business here of 20,000,000 U.S. dollars.

MARCH 3, 1950 (TO D. & H.)

It is a good day for bombing but nothing yet. Yesterday afternoon we had a short raid down the Whangpoo River but nothing close. Throughout the city many preparations are being made for possible raids. The shop windows are being taped and sand bags placed around the municipal buildings. Some of the windows are rather attractive with distinctive designs. I can't believe the center of the city will be attacked except by accident. Our water front is another matter and when planes come over I get next to my thick outer wall which is just behind my desk chair. It is remarkable to see how quickly a city of noise and outward activity is turned into one of suspended animation at the sounding of an air-raid alarm.

Something new is happening in the city but we don't know yet what it means. Some foreign houses in Hungjao have been taken over on twelve hours' notice. It is said they are being prepared for people coming from another country. *(The taking over of part of Hungjao Road became a reality. Over a mile of the area was sealed at both ends and "advisors" and Russian aviators were housed in the area. This particular part of Shanghai has been known as the "Forbidden City.")*

It looks as though we may be in for some warm weather and may be relieved of one of our problems, heating. We are greatly restricted as to electricity, being allowed only twenty KWH a month.

MARCH 23, 1950 (TO D. & H.)

We are in the midst of some foul weather, which while not pleasant, does keep the bombers away. While we have not had too many raids recently there have been alarms which have tied up all traffic for two or three hours at a time. There is nothing to do but sit and wait.

March 24. There is no doubt now in our minds but what we are caught up in the general fabric of world politics. We see things happening here which are reported from East Germany and other places under Soviet control. There are many predictions as to what we may expect in the near future and none of them good. One prediction is that all doctors are to be nationalized as of July 1st. If this is carried out no foreign physician will be able to carry on. If the present taxes continue no one will want to carry on! If one could sell land or anything to meet the situation, some relief might be obtained but no one can sell because no one can buy. All up and down Nanking Road are big sale signs on shop windows and some are having auctions of everything in their shops. This is all being done to get money for taxes and to buy "voluntarily" Victory Bonds. Where will it all end?

March 29. We learn this morning that the "General Gordon" is probably turning back to pick up passengers from Shanghai. Final word was to be received by eleven this morning. I wish we were ready to go.

March 30, Thursday. It would appear this morning that new plans for the evacuation of about two thousand foreigners from Shanghai may be going through. I understand an agreement has been reached and the "General Gordon" is on the way back.. If this method of evacuation is carried through it may clear the way for further small evacuations later this summer. At such a time we may get away.

March 31. All arrangements are off for the evacuation of foreigners

## DAYS OF INDECISION

from Shanghai. They hope to be able to fix something up within the next two weeks. In the meantime some people are going to wear out their welcome for last meals before departure.

April 3, Monday. Things continue to happen with us. It looks from where we sit this morning that we will have to give up our car. It is believed that the next three-months license will be five to eight times what it was last time. This will mean that we would have to pay JMP equal to $250 U.S. for three months. With gas also virtually at an end there seems no other way but to put the car up and use the trams and pedicabs. Again one sees the signs of a city gradually coming to a complete standstill.

Many people attempting to leave China are going by train to Tientsin and out by boat from there. There is no news as yet regarding when arrangements will be made for those who are left to get out by ship from Shanghai . . . Over the week-end I have been talking to some of my Chinese friends. It is interesting to find that a number of them are expecting some kind of a show-down within the next three months. This may be wishful thinking but again there may be something in it. There is no doubt but what the situation generally could not be much worse. . . Sometime ago I suggested that you hold these letters which get through so I can use them as records later on. There is no point in keeping a diary as it would not be allowed to pass out of China. There are some funny ideas as to what one can and cannot do as one leaves the country.

APRIL 25, 1950 (TO D. & H.)

A "boat train" goes off tomorrow to meet the "General Gordon" at Tientsin and my guess is that letters will be sent off on her. I'll get a note into the mail today, therefore, just in case.

I have finally put my car up as being too expensive to run. We do not know what the license is likely to be but the least we think it can be is between $75 and $100 U.S. equivalent a month. On top of this I must carry insurance of $100 per six months. To this must be added gas at a little more than $1.50 per gallon equivalent and all the extras. I have set the clock back 39 years and am taking the trams. I suspect the French tram I came down on this morning may have been in operation 39 years ago. It jogs along much as of old and as I pass shop windows nothing seems to have changed. I think one wicker chair shop which I passed must be the same one where we bought chairs when we first came to China nearly 40 years ago.

Our big news here today is that the British are thinking very seriously of getting out of China. This would mean that they would abandon an investment worth several hundred million pounds sterling. They are getting fed up because they continue to pour 350,000 pounds per month into China to protect these interests without any income. This is a situation which has been developing in a very tense manner since there seems little hope that the British offer to recognize the People's Government will be favorably received.

A situation is building up here as foreign firms refuse to bring in more foreign exchange to meet salaries and wages. They have little income and the authórities will not allow the reduction of staffs. It is becoming clear to many wage earners of the city that they have been directly or indirectly dependent on money controlled abroad.

Our two American banks, the National City Bank and Chase **Bank,** are attempting to close. This will be a big blow to the American interests as well as to many Chinese who have used these banks. Our clubs are also trying to get together in a single international club. **This** will shock our British cousins as the old Shanghai Club is a very sacred affair. If Chinese, Americans, and women members are allowed in, some of the "old timers" are likely to have a fit. The present move is to close the American Club and join up with the British Club as an International Club. Our Golf Club would also join this International Club. We are in difficulty with the Golf Club as a tax far in excess of our ability to pay has been levied. Since we have refused to pay, the Club may be taken over. We shall continue to go out for play just as long as possible. There has been so much rain the past few weeks that there have been few playing days.

MAY 10, 1950 (TO D. & H.)

Your air mail letter of April 23rd made excellent time out and it is good to have such recent news. We find it difficult and expensive to send back by air mail and will not attempt it unless we want to forward something in a hurry. . . Some time before deep summer local changes may take place so the future will be more clear. Just now there are many things occurring in China including a very severe famine. We see something of this in the great number of homeless people in the city. As I come down on the tram every morning I see many hundreds of them camped along the old Rue du Consulat under the overhanging store fronts. One cannot walk a block without being asked for assistance.

You might pick up a car in Shanghai just now at a bargain. For 500 U.S. dollars you can get a practically new Packard. Mr. R. at Bill's Motors told me the other day that he would be willing to sell any one of four new Fords for $800. No one wants a car with taxes what they are.

## 9: BONDS, BONDS, BONDS

In May 1950, a year after Shanghai had been "liberated," the authorities were feeling the need for more funds to run the city, a situation which was prevalent throughout the country. It is doubtful if they found any solid currency in the banks upon their arrival: from the vantage point in my office window overlooking the Bund, I had watched a few days before "liberation" as heavy boxes of currency, probably Chinese silver dollars, gold bars, and U.S. bank notes, were carried across the Bund from the Bank of China and loaded into barges on the water front. It is believed that this money was carried away to Formosa.

While the People's Bank notes had no backing other than the guns of the Communists, it was the currency of the country, and more of it was needed to run the affairs of state. Consequently a big "Victory Bond" drive was staged in which firms and individuals were urged to "voluntarily" purchase as much as and more than most could afford.

Our Medical Practitioners Association was assigned a total number of bonds which the officers were told members should "volunteer" to purchase. Small groups of doctors in the various districts of the city were given the chore of making an estimate of how much each physician might be expected to buy. The Association then notified each member as to the number of bonds he was expected to take. Resistance on the part of any physician had to be reported to the authorities, and such individuals were persuaded, if necessary, by a form of "brain washing," to change their minds. Some, who objected to buying the amount which their colleagues had felt they could buy, were finally compelled to purchase many more bonds than had been set aside as their share.

At first foreign firms and individuals had been told that they must "volunteer" to buy bonds. It was pointed out, however, that this would be violating the foreigners' neutrality; consequently, they were not pressed to do so.

MAY 16, 1950 (TO D. & H.)

As yet I have not had my new tax bill for our land. There has been some hitch due to resistance to these excessive taxes. Many people are not paying because they can't. There is no question but what these people have over-reached themselves and something is likely to explode soon. It is difficult to understand how a city of this size can go on under such pressure.

As I come down on the tram every morning all the shops are trying to make the people be patriotic and buy so they can secure more Victory Bonds. Shanghai people are as poor as I have ever seen them. About all many can do is to buy food. On our streets are many from the famine area. As I go out now to take my tram home for lunch I shall pass many of these people. A few will be begging and if you give to one more will be upon you in no time.

May 17. Our "Voice of America" told us last night that the Nationalists have withdrawn from the Chusan Islands some hundred miles south of Shanghai. It was from this point that their navy blockaded our port. It remains to be seen whether or not they can continue to make it effective from Formosa. It may be that our harbor will be opened in the near future . . . We may have to give up our golf course shortly. The authorities are pressing for the land tax, an equivalent of 100 U.S. dollars from each member for six months. I would have to resign rather than pay; my funds are not that fluid. The foreigner is certainly being taken for a ride these days! We hear all the time that this is the last big tax but they still keep coming.

I should think the next few months will be deciding ones for us all. Either there will be a complete smashing up of everything in Shanghai, in which event we must get out; or there will be some attempt at saving the situation and the productivity of the city. I must say, it does not look very hopeful. As I look down on the Whangpoo River this morning, it still resembles a country mill pond. A few small fishing boats are about but nothing else moves. And this was one of the busiest harbors in the world! The outlook is really worse than it was

## BONDS, BONDS, BONDS

during the Japanese war and certainly the city is much less active than during that period.

MAY 26, 1950 (TO D. & H.)

With the evacuation of the Chusan Islands by the Nationalists there is hope that shipping will become more free. There is talk of two British ships on the way from Hong Kong and preparations for renewing shipping trade between here and the north. There is more activity on the Whangpoo River this morning than I have seen for weeks. It may be that we are in for a change. Something will have to be done pretty soon for this dying city. In the meantime taxes are extremely heavy without any means of earning to meet them. Members of the Golf Club have just had to pay a sizable amount. Mine was 1,600,000 JMP, or a little over fifty dollars U.S. We must now decide what to do with the Club as there is no hope of getting members to pay a second land tax. I had to borrow to pay this one.

MAY 31, 1950 (TO D. & H.)

It is getting hot and I don't think I am going to enjoy my tram trips down to the Bund too much. It is a great relief, however, to be without the expense of a motor car. Two days ago a Hong Kong ship entered our so-called blockaded harbor. Today another ship is due and down below me on the River, I can see two small boats lying in wait to welcome the seamen who bring the ship in. You will note I say nothing about welcoming the ship or its officers. They belong to an imperialist nation and it is wisest to ignore them. There is a feeling here that our blockade is almost over and that soon shipping will be entering freely. This will make it much easier for us to get out by ship when the time comes. Whether or not the Nationalists will attempt any more bombings remains to be seen. There are some Communist jets and fast fighter planes in this area and probably some radar directed anti-aircraft batteries. It is now not a very healthy place for slow bombers to operate. A night raid some three weeks ago resulted in the Nationalists losing one bomber.

There is some talk of lowering taxes but nothing definite as yet. Motor car licenses are more than three months overdue and there is some indication that a softer attitude is being taken regarding licenses. Certainly Shanghai is getting near the end of her money reserve. A Chinese secretary came into the house last night with a story of trying everywhere to get a job. It is getting to the point where families formerly with plenty of funds are running short.

June 1. I was wrong about Hong Kong officers not getting a reception. Those who arrived yesterday were given flowers and had their pictures taken. I can see this second ship from where I sit writing. Shanghai may get a new lease on life if this continues ... I had my second game of golf of the week yesterday. Our road out to the course is getting to be almost impassible. Many trucks are going out with stone and sand to the landing field beyond the Club and the roads are being badly cut up. This field is being very much enlarged. You should see these trucks. They are all charcoal burners and with the rough treatment they are getting, many are on the point of falling to pieces. It is remarkable how they get over the road with these charcoal burners, big black stove-like containers using ordinary wood for fuel and with fenders and hoods held together with bits of ordinary tin and wire.

JUNE 6, 1950 (TO D. & H.)

We understand the invasion date for Formosa has been set and with all the ship-repair activities we see around here it may not be far off.

At the start of the changes we have seen during the past year, many were very hopeful but after they have been in operation for a time no one is pleased and all hope of a new day has gone. Even some of those involved in the administration are far from happy. If it were not for outside influence, which is more than influence at the moment, one of the quick over-night changes which China has seen so often, might take place.

The brief entry of our port by two British ships has given some people a bit of optimism. The British shipping people have hopes, but much depends on what changes if any take place when China is entirely under the control of Mao's government. Those of us who are in the midst of things feel that the Chinese will not ultimately give over all contacts with the West. Shanghai is too important to their industrial and commercial life and it does not seem possible, in spite of what is going on now, that it can be destroyed.

We were out to a dinner last night where I met a missionary who told me the authorities have given consent for famine aid to be brought in from America. If this food really comes out some changing of present attitudes may take place. It may be one very good way to combat what is going on today. I think they will have to wait until the port is really open before American ships come in with such supplies. *(This proved to be an untrue rumor.)*

June 8. It is the opinion of many here that an invasion attempt on Formosa is not far off. I just saw a well fitted out LST going down river and there is another near the Pootung side. We think they must make the attempt before typhoon season starts and that is likely to come in another month.

## 10: ECHOES OF THE KOREAN WAR

A number of us were having tiffin at the American Club in Shanghai on the day the news of the war in Korea first broke. At the table were two Chinese who had graduated from military academies in the United States. Each, in almost the same words, declared that Korea was lost and the free nations would not come to the aid of the South Koreans. They reversed themselves with pleasure the next day when it became known the United States troops were on their way to Korea.

Following the action taken by the U. S. Government in sending the Seventh Fleet to the Formosan Straits all bombings of Shanghai ceased. Life in the city became a little more normal and shopkeepers began removing the paper strips which they had placed in fancy designs on shop windows for protection during air raids.

JUNE 29, 1950 (TO D. & H.)

It is too early to tell you just what effect the American and U. N. actions of yesterday with regard to South Korea and Formosa will have in Shanghai. This morning the *North China* and one English language newspaper were withheld because of the foreign news they contained. As long as we have our radio, we can keep informed but we may have to turn them in as we did with the Japanese. All Americans and British, as well as many of our Chinese friends, are much encouraged by the action.

Whether or not it means concentration camps again for us, we are proud of the stand the U. S. has taken. I'll write you after a few days to give you an idea of how things are developing locally. At this writing the stock of the U. S. has gone up a great deal among many of my Chinese friends who had been saying the U. S. officials were only "good for talking."

We heard Senator Scott Lucas over the "Voice of America" last night giving his endorsement of the President's action. His voice was clear and he might have been in the same room with us. For the time he was speaking no "dentist drill jamming" by the Russians was coming through. Mr. Lucas' comments were very favorably received here.

The Chinese stamp in red on the outside of my envelope to you, which you have returned for translation, merely says, "Mr., please write more letters so the post office will have more revenue."

With the stopping of bombing and Nationalist Navy action from Formosa it should not be long before our port is wide open. Two ships were sunk here last week due to mines but now they should have a chance to clear them out. Two ships are caught in harbor and must wait for the clearing.

JULY 7, 1950 (TO D. & H.)

We are getting a little more the general feeling of the people about us regarding the Korean and Formosa situations. It is the action with regard to Formosa which is disturbing their thinking. Some who are anti-Chiang think we are helping protect his show while those in the present government think we are interfering in the affairs of China. In Formosa they think our attitude regarding the keeping of their navy and air force at home is giving the People's Government time to prepare for the invasion.

July 10, Monday. You, of course, are keeping up with what goes forward in Formosa. We, behind the Bamboo Curtain, get both sides. America's name is mud out this way! Believe-it-or-not, "John Foster Dulles gave the signal for this aggressive move on the part of South Korea"!

The real thinking Chinese are more than pleased at the turn of events. Many feel that while this does not mean a "Third World War" there is likely to be considerable loss of face by some people to the Northwest. There are some who feel they can detect already some changes in attitude in some of those around us. The response of all the free world over the action in Korea is making people sit up and take notice.

Should there be a swing to the right in China it will be a good time to be here and to try to recover on our properties. With the temper of the people what it is, a change here could take place over night. So we continue to gamble with the course of events. We may be happy finally to get out only with our shirts; but again it could be much more.

JULY 18, 1950 (TO D. & H.)

If the U. N. effort in Korea can result in putting a crimp in aggression, we may see some changes in the Far East. There is much hope here that a favorable outcome of the Korean situation may considerably alter the one in China. Her new guests from the Northwest are hated even above the Japanese. A Chinese friend told me last week that the Chinese would never mix with these people. If you were to see some of them riding around in motor cars you would not like them either. Everyone is just waiting for the day when they can be pushed out. *(A lapse of two months occurred at this point when letter writing was virtually impossible. Every moment that could be spared from the office was used in a community effort aimed at the collection and listing of medical and surgical supplies which were to be used as a reserve as Shanghai became more and more isolated from the free world.)*

SEPTEMBER 26, 1950 (TO D. & H.)

As I see the world situation from where I sit, I am inclined to feel that another few months will show considerable improvement in our Far Eastern situation. The average Chinese in these parts does not want to see the old Nationalist group return. Of course they do not wish to have the extreme group of the present government carry on. A turn to the right is what they want and if the cards are played correctly in the U. N. all should be well.

It looks good in Korea and we should see a different picture there soon. We want to know what happens now with the 38th parallel. Do we go beyond it? I think it would be a mistake if we do not clean up the entire country. *(This letter reflects the first impressions and wishful thinking in connection with the Korean situation and reflects as well the favorable attitude on the part of the Chinese population toward the action which the U. N. had taken.)*

OCTOBER 5, 1950 (TO D. & H.)

Your letter of September 16 came in yesterday. I must leave shortly for my lecture at St. John's Medical School. My class there is made up of thirty-one boys and girls, more girls this year than I have had before. At the moment I am the only American on the staff and my teaching is in English regardless of the fact that only Chinese and

Russian are supposed to be used. As a matter of fact not more than a rare student would be able to take instruction in Russian; studies in the language have been started but I am told they are "wash outs."

I have just had a call to an important meeting tonight with all the current Consuls General in the city on the subject of the Country Hospital. I'll be glad when this affair is finished. We have hopes of getting rid of all our staff in another week and then the future of the hospital must be considered.

October 11. Much water has run over the dam since I started this letter. On Saturday p.m. the local authorities suddenly seized the Country Hospital and we have had endless meetings to decide how to meet the situation. We have expected something of the sort but not in the form which it finally came. We are protesting that this foreign property is private but they think otherwise. It looks like the old "grab game," and there is little we can do.

We are all well and fairly busy. I have a few patients but many of them are virtually gratis. I hope to collect my reward in the next world!

OCTOBER 19, 1950 (TO D. & H.)

As the Korean thing draws to a close we are wondering what next. In spite of all the talk in Peking about going to their aid, no move has been taken. It is the belief of some that certain individuals may be turning slightly to the right. There is no doubt, however, but what the leftists have pretty strong influence even now. On the other hand foreign exporters are being given more consideration this past three weeks. I should not think this would extend to drugs at present as these people have some grandiose ideas regarding what China can do about manufacturing their own. My guess is that they will not find it too easy. Someone told me the other day that they were manufacturing chloromycetin, but I don't believe it. They have been having some difficulty with penicillin in Peking where they are making it or trying to do so. *(As a matter of fact the small plant in Peking had been preparing a fair amount of penicillin but not enough for the army's use.)*

A White Russian friend was just in for a chat. His advice was to stay put as everything would be all right. He feels the strong stand taken by the Western Powers should have been taken months back and that it will have a good effect. He has often told me that the only thing his country can understand is force.

NOVEMBER 7, 1950 (TO D. & H.)

It looks as though we are in a hot spot again! It is too early to say how serious the situation may be but with Chinese troops moving into North Korea and all the propaganda against "imperialist" U. S., things can get out of hand. Many think that Shanghai may not feel the blast too much but it is any one's guess. My Chinese friends are very much disturbed over this new move but at the same time hopeful that it may mean a "Third World War" to the end that China will finally be truly liberated. *(Chinese "volunteers" entered Korea at this point.)*

The threat of war in the past few days has sent prices of food up. Here is hoping I can get a few more paying patients to meet the overhead. There is a great deal of resentment in these parts that China is becoming involved in Korea.

November 9. I think the feelings in Shanghai are a little easier the past twenty-four hours. There is much talk and propaganda but the Chinese are a sensible people and not easily led around by the nose. One Chinese thought that the Communists' anti-American propaganda did them more harm than good as they give out such obvious untruths. As the days go on, there is more resentment building up locally over the possibility of getting China into war with the United Nations. Since the People's Government has been invited to the Security Committee for talks, it is hoped a different attitude may be forthcoming. The next week should show which way things are likely to go. In the meantime we sit and wait for what may come along.

November 10, Friday. Nothing has turned up in our city to change the picture. People are not as worried as they were two days back. With action going forward in the U. N. perhaps things may be better. Much depends on whether or not the country to the Northwest is ready to strike. Certainly no one believes that China is ready to wage a war at this time. *(There is a one month interval here when letters failed to get out for some unexplained reason. During this period Shanghai blew hot and cold over the Korean situation. Intensive anti-American propaganda was started as the Chinese populace was urged to assist "volunteers" for Korea. It was the beginning of "volunteer" groups of physicians and nurses to care for the wounded coming out of Korea.)*

## 11: ANTI-AMERICAN PROPAGANDA

With the moving of "volunteer" Chinese divisions into Korea in support of the North Koreans, anti-American propaganda was launched and was most intense for about a year and a half.

In songs and posters the Chinese were urged to hate America and support Chinese volunteers in Korea. The first anti-American propaganda appeared in the *Shanghai News,* a newspaper completely controlled by the Communists. Soon the entire city blossomed out in lurid posters depicting the evil deeds of the Americans. Many ingenious mechanical sets in shop windows along Nanking Road were used to demonstrate the cruelty of American soldiers. A typical one of the "rocking horse" type showed an American soldier kicking a Korean child. *(In spite of all the anti-American propaganda, no antagonism toward individual Americans was shown by the Shanghai populace.)*

DECEMBER 12, 1950 (TO D. & H.)

Our situation outwardly is unchanged. Deep underneath the surface there are currents, and as a Chinese friend said to me months back, anything can happen here. Of course all eyes are on Korea and the U. N. I can say to you without any hesitation that there is little sympathy in this city for what the Chinese are doing in Korea. Our Chinese friends want us to stay with them. This is especially true of my professional colleagues. Those who are "beating it out of here" to Hong Kong or some place "more far" think we should also get out.

The family is well and making a few preparations for Christmas but they will not be many. The Christmas tree is growing in the yard where it was planted last year and will be brought into the house for the holiday season to be returned later to its place beside the fence. Gifts will be limited. I believe the Chinese shops will go in for their usual Christmas decorations regardless of "pressure." Season's greetings to you all.

DECEMBER 21, 1950 (TO D. & H.)

Our overseas radio last night informed us that only post cards and letters were to be allowed to come out to China from the U. S. As a matter of fact that is all we have been receiving for months. This letter will go without a return on the envelope and I shall be glad to have you tell me if it gets through. There is a definite reason for doing it this way. *(It was rumored that all out-going mail must have a "return address" but it was our desire to have nothing on the envelope which would identify the sender. Starting with the Communist "liberation" we did not use any return address.)*

We thought for a time there would not be much Christmas in Shanghai this year but since early this week, some of the streets are filled with Christmas trees for sale. I suspect that some of the shops are not being encouraged to play up the season but others are going ahead just as usual. It is good to see that some people have "what it takes" to meet the situation.

December 26. We had a very satisfactory Christmas. I don't think our Chinese friends have ever been as thoughtful. It has seemed that they have gone out of their way to be nice at a time when there is so much anti-American propaganda.

The Korean situation does not look too good at the moment. To the Communists it would appear that all they have to do now is set the day when all U. N. forces will be driven out. You can understand how people with this point of view are not interested in a cease fire. I trust they are to have a rude awakening one of these days.

JANUARY 11, 1951 (TO D. & H.)

Last Saturday we had a long Peking Union Medical College Trustees meeting here in Shanghai. The majority of the men came down from Peking and we were able to get a line on how things are going there. The big problem for the college is funds. There is enough for two months, then something must happen. The freezing of funds in America and the attitude of authorities here that they don't want any more "subversive money" for colleges and universities in China makes an almost impossible situation. The only alternative is for the authorities to take over the college. I don't think they are prepared to put in the $600,000 U.S. yearly required to keep it up to its present standard. We were supposed to elect new Trustees at this meeting, in which event I would go off the Board according to the by-laws, but we made it an "adjourned incomplete annual meeting" so there were no elections and I stay on. My guess is, as Trustees, we shall not function much longer, unless there is a clearing of the international situation. *(The Peking Union Medical College was very shortly taken over by the Government.)*

During the past week we have seen some pretty ripe effigies of MacArthur in shop windows. There are many cartoons about but only in places where they can be protected. There is much revulsion to this sort of thing and in some places they are torn down almost as fast as they go up ... We are still scratching along as far as money is concerned. No way has been found to bring out funds and my local account, which is very small, is also frozen. A few patients have paid cash and if we had more patients we could get along. A golfing friend, British, has offered to stake me if things get too hard ... It is just possible that we may be seeing a slight swinging away from the Northwest in some of the recent happenings in Shanghai. The picture of the number one of the Northwest did not appear in a recent important meeting, there were just two Chinese, the present number one and the "father of his country," Sun Yat Sen. This may (?) be good news.

FEBRUARY 19, 1951 (TO D. & H.)

We still cannot get any United States money into China. An American died here this morning and it is going to be a job to find funds for the funeral. He was married to a Chinese and out of a job. There are a number of such men around, retired men from the U. S. Army, Navy or Customs, like this man, who have been living comfortably here on pensions or savings. Now with funds frozen, they are in a bad way.

February 22. At the British Consulate this morning, I talked with the "number one" who is trying to arrange for a small group of doctors to stay here for the time being. He feels that the British Government, and possibly the U. S. Government as well, should help some of us to keep things going medically until times are better.

MARCH 5, 1951 (TO D. & H.)

Yesterday we had a big parade here. One does not cross streets when a parade is on, and S., who is a vestryman, could not even get to

## ANTI-AMERICAN PROPAGANDA

the church. It was S.'s birthday, and we had a missionary friend and his wife in for the evening meal and birthday cake. I think S. feels his years sometimes and I wish we might get him home soon. If all goes well it should not be too long now.

Every day seems to bring up something new. We are being asked to surrender our deeds for the Pearce Road property now. Under the present order of things this land will be taken away from us. Many pieces held by big real estate companies are going the same way.

MARCH 16, 1951 (TO D. & H.)

Your combined letter of February 27th came several days ago but moving has upset all letter writing. We are now getting settled in our new home in a Shell Oil Company house located in the old Rue Retard. On the 26th of the month I am moving my office out there as well. I shall be glad to have everything under one roof. We sold our four-year old refrigerator for about twice what we paid for it and this has helped us in the moving.

The seeds have come just at the right time. This is a nice package and came through in good shape. We have a fair sized garden with places around the sides where vegetables can be planted. Our old Peking cook's brother is here taking care of a property on Hungjao Road and has free time. He wants to come in and help us with the garden. He has been helping us move. He is the man who brought us food when we were caught in the old Jessfield compound during the Japanese war.

World affairs would seem to be looking up everywhere excepting out here. There may be things stirring which we know nothing about. Let us hope so!

MARCH 28, 1951 (TO D. & H.)

This is my first letter from my desk in my new office here at the house. Everything is working out very well and this bedroom with its own bathroom adjoining is a very good combination. Since this is an old Shanghai house with a big hall down stairs there is plenty of space for the receptionist and her desk, as well as a few chairs for patients. We have no central heating but there is a small stove in the hall which heats the entire stairwell. Fireplaces in every room are the main source of heat.

April 1. And that was as far as I got when I was visited by an officer connected with the foreign affairs department of the Government. He was just checking up and all sorts of questions had to be answered. Three times the man said he was sorry to have to bother me. This was simply a routine call to explain our moving our household. If one stays put he does not get attention.

APRIL 3, 1951 (TO D. & H.)
I have just this moment had to give up my papers on the Pearce Road property. In the land reform this property is being taken away. Later my deeds will be burned at a public celebration along with hundreds of others. Then the land will belong to "the people." If I could ever get reparations from the Japanese for the hundreds of trees they took away from this property I would be able to save something. The future of things out here is not too clear. Some think it is the dark before the dawn, but as yet there is no indication of light. Much may depend on the outcome of what is happening in Korea.

APRIL 23, 1951 (TO D. & H.)
It may be true that I am having a few more patients out here in this new place but there is no increase in the number of paying patients. People just have not got sufficient funds to go to a specialist. I estimate that seventy-five per cent of my patients are free and some of these cost something on my part to treat. But what is happening to me is also true of every other private physician in town. None of us can meet our overhead.

Tomorrow afternoon I must lecture to the students at the medical school. My class of 54, half girls, is the best I have ever had and very responsive. I can see no anti-Americanism there.

We are continuing to have fairly cool weather. It has been sunny the past two days but still cold for a Shanghai April. I hope they are having clear days in Korea. With this offensive on they will need all the air support they can get. If this affair which is going on now can be satisfactorily held there may be some hope for a change. Things are becoming a bit depressing around us. Fear is the order of the day.

APRIL 30, 1951 (TO D. & H.)
Dr. B., my British colleague, died very suddenly last Thursday. His house boy found him unconscious when he went to give him his morning tea and called his partner, Dr. S., and the latter called me at about eight o'clock. It was immediately apparent that he had had a stroke and nothing within our power was sufficient to bring him back to consciousness. He died in the afternoon.

This tragedy poses a problem for the British community as Dr. B. was the one remaining British physician. I am trying to secure an informal group of Chinese doctors who would be willing in case of need to take care of foreign patients. In the meantime, I am acting in an advisory capacity with regard to community medical problems.

Tomorrow is a big day here and all roads and streets are to be blocked except for marching thousands. It will be a big May 1st celebration where all organizations must take part, "or else." It is hoped that this will be the biggest show ever.

May 1. This has been a day of drums! We were awakened early this morning by drums beating on every side of us as small processions got under way for the main show and they did not let up until about four p.m. Fortunately for the marchers there was no rain today and tonight as the sun goes down the sky is clearer than it has been for days. *("Bands" consisting of large and small drums were much in evidence in all parades.)*

May 2. We held Dr. B.'s funeral this morning and since Mrs. B. is in England and there are no relatives here, Dr. S. and I acted as chief mourners with the British Consul and his wife doing the official honors. The funeral was held in the Cathedral and the nave was fairly well filled by the remnants of British and Americans still in Shanghai. It is remarkable how many men have fallen by the way during these recent years of stress and strain. It would be wonderful if one could see ahead to clear skies and freedom! I was looking at some photographs of American scenes this p.m. and wondered if such freedom and wide open spaces were being properly appreciated.

MAY 11, 1951 (TO D. & H.)

The house we are living in belongs to the Shell Oil Company and some days back it was taken over with all the other property of the company by the authorities. We were fearful lest we be asked to move out. Two days ago the Chinese in charge of the foreigners at the Bubbling Well Station sent word for me not to worry as I would not be asked to move and today at the golf course the head of the Shell Company told me that they had an official word that those living in the houses would not be disturbed. So our minds are at rest as we are nicely settled in with what I feel is the most convenient office I have ever had in Shanghai.

MAY 25, 1951 (TO D. & H.)

One of the things which one has to learn to take in a land of controls is unexpected and rather disagreeable surprises. Two days back we were told that our house would have to be given up for the use of the authorities. This came as a surprise because we had been assured as I wrote you we would not be disturbed. The recent U. N. resolution regarding strategic materials for these parts is having repercussions and this property which was recently taken over from the Shell Oil Company is to be used for "special purposes." I have been looking for a place where I can have my office as we have it here but as yet I cannot find anything we can afford. We think we have a month in which to find a place. I am sorry to have this arrangement disturbed as I have been having a few more patients lately, enough to meet my present overhead. I was playing golf on Wednesday when the head of the Shell Company gave me the bad news and you should have seen what it did to my golf!

Some say that the trials and tribulations make character but for my part I have had enough. One always hopes that this will be the last bump but it is a part of the Communist system to keep the knocks coming.

May 29, Tuesday morning. Nothing doing yet regarding a house. Already guards are on the outside compound gate and just now they refused to let a pedicab come in to take your mother out.

One hour later. Now another blow! We are ordered out of this house within the next three days! This is the usual stunt and where do we go now? I hope something turns up before the end of this day. Again, later. Good news! Mr. H. called up this minute to say that everything has been arranged for us to move into the Grosvenor House where I can also have my office. What a letter!

*(Letters to a colleague of earlier days in China are now to be introduced. In many of them, cryptic terminology is used to circumvent censorship which was becoming more strict.)*

MAY 29, 1951 (TO H. S. H.)

The blows fall thick and fast! This morning we have been ordered out of this house within three days. This is the usual way of doing it, first the word comes that a month will be given to make a move, then without warning, "get out immediately." Some people have been given only five hours. Since none of my expected patients have arrived this a.m. I assume they are being turned away by guards at the gate. It is wonderful to have power! If we could have more time we would try for an exit permit even if there is little hope in that direction. It seems so futile to keep on fighting.

Later. Here at this office we have had more patients and it looked as though we would be having enough to meet the overhead. Just what another move may bring forth is most difficult to see. People are being most kind and I am sure we can work something out. We have some six people in helping with the packing while I sit here writing to you and getting ready for my Tuesday lecture at the Medical School. There is one place where a labor of love brings some reward. My students have continued to be most responsive.

JUNE 4, 1951 (TO H. S. H.)

During the time of moving I have been pretty much out of touch with what has been going on out in the world not so much because of time consumed in moving but because our radios have been out of commission due to changed voltage.

In your letter of May 15 it is suggested that flaps had been opened on my letters. Certainly none of yours had that appearance. I am wondering if the appearance on mine may not have been caused by the fact that I put my flaps down with home made parts. No repercussions at this end. *(Because of the high humidity, envelopes and stamps are usually sold without glue in the Far East.)*

JUNE 9, 1951 (TO H. S. H.)

This is a slow Saturday morning in my office high above the city where on a clear day I can look out to the west and see the only land elevation in this part of China, the Shanghai Hills. Two crosses are prominent, one on the five-domed Russian church and one on the square steeple of the German church. The latter place is no longer used for the purpose for which it was intended but is now a meeting place for "our new thought." Our apartment also looks down on the French Club and their former tennis courts. These courts are now converted into a parade ground where colorful pageants are sometimes held. It is probable that the Club will soon have to close as membership is considerably reduced and taxes cannot be met.

At the request of the East Asia office of UNESCO I have been reviewing a recently published book on the early foreign missionary doctors in China, *Lancet and Cross* by Dr. K. C. W. It is truly remarkable that such a book should come out in times like these when no good of any sort is supposed to have originated in the West. The author is expecting to talk to our Medical Society soon. This is the only foreign language medical society operating at the moment and much to our surprise has become rather popular with the natives. This may be because we devote our time entirely to medicine (as well as to eating and drinking) and an opportunity is afforded for many to speak English, the language which they use most readily in discussing medical problems. One of my colleagues in the medical school told me two days ago that the students in our upper classes were demanding that they be taught in the only foreign language they know, that is English. Attempts to bring in a different language from the Northwest have not prospered. He also explained that there was a great shortage of medical school teachers to handle the stepped-up program and that is one reason why they are so anxious to have me continue my lectures.

A part of my morning has been devoted to destroying old papers which have accumulated in my files over the years. I am surprised at the great number of insurance policies for one thing and another which I have carried in years past. It seems to me I must have very largely supported a number of companies! I can remember collecting from two.

In one of the places I sometimes visit, the men have found time hanging heavily on their hands during office hours for want of patients who are able to pay, so have become very much interested in Chinese checkers. A day or so back I made inquiry regarding their daily tournaments only to learn that the group had been broken up because some of the men had left home for an indefinite period. *(When any Chinese left home for "indefinite periods" it signified that they had been imprisoned or had even been executed for so-called subversive acts.)*

June 10, Sunday. I don't know what some of us would do if we did not have the release which we get out at Hungjao golf course. It is one place where most cares can be laid aside and those of us who are left behind are playing more than in normal times. On the surface things do not change much. A recent clearing of walls of anti-American propaganda did not last very long and what has come back is "bigger and better." *(The clearing of the walls refers to the scraping off of anti-American cartoons and slogans. This was done periodically but usually new posters appeared almost over night.)*

We keep very much to our own Anglo-American crowd and rarely go into native homes. In fact, I go to A's only because I have some patients there. Some Chinese visit us in the evening and there are not infrequent phone visits. I know from what I have been told that our friends know how things go with us most of the time.

JUNE 10, 1951 (TO D. & H.)

In moving over here a week ago Thursday we lost all the accessories for my Maico audiometer and Kloman coagulating unit. We searched high and low and even alerted the police, but without results. I was sick over the whole affair as I had made Mrs. C. responsible for the moving of the office equipment. Yesterday the things turned up in a box mother had packed and forgotten all about. I am certain Mrs. C. must have given the package to her for safe keeping and then had forgotten what she had done with it. My office is in a room a little larger than the one at Kulu Lu (our previous home and office). It is perhaps one of the nicest I have ever had and I believe it is the most completely equipped in the Far East.

It is getting on toward 9:30 p.m. and time for us to go to church in New York. This comes over each Sunday night. Tonight it will be a Catholic service, only singing and a sermon. The Community Church here in Shanghai does not have an English language service now. After the sermon will be the news and then to bed with cool nights up here on the ninth floor requiring two blankets.

June 11. At just this minute I have been called up by one of my old students asking if I would like to sell my audiometer. He had not heard that I had lost and recovered my accessories. Under the new order hospitals are going in for everything modern and they would pay me anything I might ask for my apparatus. I told him it was not for sale.

JUNE 18, 1951 (TO H. S. H.)

Your letter of June 4 came in last week-end making a fairly quick and an uneventful passage. My guess is that the envelope still contained California air. I wonder how free air and "controlled" air like being mixed? I was not aware of any commotion!

In my present state of mind I should like nothing better than to join you in your carpentering. I know I would be good at painting especially if you would let me use red and add a picture now and then. At the moment there are many examples of what I might use in many places. *(This also refers to the numerous and elaborate anti-American posters which were covering many of our walls.)*

You would not recognize the old Race Course with its many billboards reaching all along Nanking Road. We have plenty of paint with which to produce all the hemorrhagic tints. Shop windows all down old Nanking Road have wonderful mechanical and set pieces, the central theme being, Uncle Sam is a bad boy. For a time our walls were free but now "anything but."

The taking over of the Race Course represents the process of creeping absorption so common among us. My impression upon looking down on the old French Club from where I sit is that the absorption process has been completed over the week-end. *(This was found to be untrue.)* We saw signs of the same process out at the golf course yesterday when a fairly large number of families with the father in semi-uniform invaded the grounds for picnics. They were rather offended when warned to keep out of the way of balls. My feeling is that we will do well to keep the place another six months.

Did you ever have the experience of living in a city of loud speakers? And I mean loud! We have certainly gotten it down to a fine art (?). Think of it, while riding down Nanking Road in the tram you could get your news of the day or the story of the moment from the same voice without missing a word. All speakers tie into the same station. I commend this system to you as an effective means of getting something across. You would only have to mount a loud speaker on every lamp post. (This is only a mild exaggeration!)

June 19. We continue our uncertain weather. Yesterday an east wind and rain and today clear with a south wind. It is clear enough this morning to see the Shanghai Hills. I think no one visits them any more since cars are not supplied with sufficient gas to go that far.

Our patient is no better. The symptoms are much the same but I must not elucidate as there may be resentment if too many details are given. One is free to say that the temperature is still very high with not infrequent convulsions. It is too bad we cannot bring in some of the new medications from the West. If we could only get the temperature down there might be a chance. *(The patient referred to in this instance was old sick China with all her convulsions and political upheaval at that time.)*

This is my day for teaching. My big class of 54 is asking that I give them an extra lecture instead of an examination. The last two classes have had similar treatment. I have no desire to read fifty-four papers. Under the present system most of the newly reorganized medical schools have several hundred students in each class, good, bad and indifferent, and all get the same grade in each section. No one fails and examinations are more for the purpose of telling whether or not the instructor is "producing the goods." In some respects this is not a bad system. It makes teachers prepare carefully in spite of the fact that it gives the indifferent student a way out. The end result is that all students entering a medical school are graduated, providing their serious thinking is right. *(For "serious" read "political.")*

Later. When I went into my class at the medical school today, one of my students told me that my Chinese colleague, Dr. L. K., had committed suicide last Saturday. This is a great shock and deprives Shanghai of its foremost Chinese otolaryngologist. You remember that he was Y. T.'s son-in-law. He studied under me at the Peking Union

Medical College and later in the United States. About three weeks ago he was in my office and a week ago I talked to him on the phone. I am told that certain "pressures" were imposed recently and A. believes this was the last straw. His act is an indication of how severe these "pressures" may be. I had hoped to turn my patients over to him should I be allowed to leave. Man's inhumanity to man!

JUNE 26, 1951 (TO H. S. H.)

I am just in from my lecture to the medical school students. They were a crowd of eager beavers today and I can't remember ever having a class more attentive. I have three more lectures to go, the last to be in place of final examinations. Judging from the hospital and my lecture room, you would never guess there is so much anti-American hate being generated within a stone's throw over on Nanking Road. As I walked into the hospital grounds today you might have thought I was a long absent son returning home, judging from the greetings which I received from the students who were waiting for me.

We are hanging on our radios since the Malik speech. The local reaction among the natives is that it doesn't mean a thing but certainly the world seems to be taking it seriously as well as cautiously. It is interesting to listen to the reactions coming from different parts of the world. Just now we're getting perfect reception with little jamming. A strong stand at this time is most desirable. The word goes round that "volunteer" activities overseas are all that could be desired and the people of your nationality break and run when faced with real opponents. Page Mr. Ripley! *("Volunteer" activities overseas refer to the Communist Chinese Army in Korea.)*

Tonight is one of drums for some reason. These seem to be down by the French Club which by the way has not been taken over as yet. Incidentally the house we were booted out of still stands empty along with all the rest which were vacated. What goes forward is anyone's guess. I wish it might be possible to paint the pictures of our days with more frank colors but they must be done by the indirect method. And speaking of colors I have never seen such paintings on hoardings as are springing up all over the city. It must be one grand time for the sign painters. Many of them are real works of art, from a distance. Can you imagine the state of these billboards after the first man-sized typhoon comes along?

June 27. There does not seem to be any indication of the free state being "led up the garden path" in this new cease fire effort. The next few days should tell us something. One of the questions being asked here is what would be the local effect of a real settlement?

I have sometimes wondered if dilantin might be used to reduce the attacks of our patients. I am inclined to think that nothing short of something pretty radical will do the slightest good. The left side of the body seems to be the only part functioning at present. Paralysis on the right seems virtually complete. Some doctors think they can see some nerve recovery on the right but this may be wishful thinking. Most will not hazard an opinion even in the bosom of their own families due to the possibility of having a report made to the authorities. This might lead to an indefinite stay away from home. *(The above indicated that there was no turning to the right in political circles. People were becoming cautious in expressing an opinion from fear it would be reported and they would either be imprisoned or executed.)*

Later the same day. Now with supper over and the eight-thirty broadcast behind me I'll add a bit to the tune (?) of the drums which are going strong again tonight. July 1st is the thirtieth anniversary of the founding of the party and we are "practicing" in preparation. There is to be a big parade and already trees over on Avenue Joffre are being wrapped with colored bunting and strings of electric lights line each side of the streets. I have never seen Shanghai so lighted up.

I appreciate being a member of the Clan in absentia and I hope one day to put the absentia out of business. For the time being my place is here, especially now that L. K. has gone and virtually all the other well trained men are so busy with institutional work that they have no time for the few remaining private patients. There is no change in the state of affairs which keeps the few remaining Americans in these parts.

It is not unusual to find an English speaking pedicab boy, someone's former house boy. Competition within this group is severe and one has the urge to help them as much as possible. They do not appear to be getting enough to eat.

Watch the red and blue pencil mark on the flap of these envelopes. Yours was not disturbed. Original California air was present.

JULY 3, 1951 (TO H. S. H.)

On the eve of the Glorious Fourth in the "land of the free" I'll get this started. How far I shall go is not too certain as I am casting about for all possible leads from foreign radio stations regarding "cease fire" proposals in Korea. While there is general restrained optimism among foreigners most natives are just down-right pessimistic. My guess is that this stems from a deep down belief on the part of these people that only an all out Third World War will correct the situation as far as they are concerned. It is a pretty black time for many.

It is the general belief here among foreign friends that a satisfactory solution to the overseas problem will make our own local situation better. That may be so, but I am not so sure unless there is a great deal of backing down in some quarters and that is not the usual story.

Thirty minutes later—I have just "come" from New York and some of the radio comments have been very heartening. I hope some of these men are right and we are on the point of turning the world more to the right. The next two weeks should be very interesting. For one thing, our local picture may have some of the colors slightly reduced even though colors are being piled on lavishly at the moment. Most of our main streets are lighted up like Christmas trees. It is all very beautiful in its way and helps to exhibit anti-American propaganda along the streets. Entire schools, even to the smallest children are given an opportunity to view the big bad "you-know-what." Many feel, especially among the adults, that this anti-American propaganda is being overdone to the point of producing resentment toward the authorities.

July 4. Exploding fire crackers were much in evidence this morning but they were not the symbol of freedom! Most parades are accompanied by "outriders" setting off explosions at suitable periods.

I continue to enjoy my class and yesterday was one of our best sessions. For some reason their general attitude toward their work seems to have become more sincere recently. Can this be due to a better understanding of what is taking place or one might even say, what is not taking place? I am told that a class conducted in your mother tongue, English, is highly prized above those where tongues are mixed. *("Mixed tongues" were Chinese and Russian, the officially acceptable languages for classroom use.)*

July 5. Yesterday was a cool Fourth and we had one good comfortable game of golf. This year there was no thought of an American reception. At the last count there were 192 Americans of all complexions in Shanghai; over sixty are individuals who probably have never been out of China. These comprise those who have served in our forces, even back to the First World War, descendants of service and shipping men who have made China their home and others of like nature.

The "you-know-what" mentioned above has many garbs down on the street. Clever mechanical pieces in shop windows demonstrate beyond the shadow of a doubt that he is getting the beating of his life.

If you don't believe it you have only to note the great amount of hemorrhagic paint spilled. There is some evidence that the show is being overplayed, as only the natives love to do and there are indications that some have had enough. *(The "you-know-what" was a caricature of Uncle Sam.)*

In my last, I reported that some doctors thought they saw some recovery of our "patient's" right side. I think this must have been wishful thinking and may have been only apparent movement caused by an over-active left side which pulls and pushes his body this way and that way. Of late the "patient" has not been too happy with the bed and room. Attendants must be constantly on the watch to keep insects and other vermin out. Ruthless measures must sometimes be resorted to. *(The significance of this paragraph was that the political situation in China was much to the left and that subversives were being hunted out and in many instances were executed.)*

The morning news is about what one would expect until talks begin in Korea. Here, of course, the story is that the United Nations has reached the end of its rope, hence the desire for a "cease-fire."

## 12: THE UBIQUITOUS LOUD SPEAKER

As negotiations waxed and waned in Korea over the "cease fire," loud speakers were set up all over the city for the purpose of urging the populace to greater efforts in aiding the "volunteers" in Korea. From one or more control points orators held forth all day long, relieved from time to time by recorded music and songs.

Frequently, when no speaker was available, the musical records would be repeated over and over. One that was very popular was "Aid Volunteers, Hate America."

JULY 11, 1951 TO H. S. H.)

An interesting side light on all that is going forward at the moment in Korea is the hope among natives here that peace is just around the corner and soon Americans will be returning to Shanghai to resume their businesses. A native merchant, a patient, this morning expressed himself in the above vein and added that he found it hard to understand how there could be so much anti-American propaganda as Americans had always been friends. A moderate amount of anti-British propaganda he could understand. Incidentally the populace is being told that the reason the present move is being made in Korea is because the Americans are afraid of combat and are running away. Even the well educated are not well posted on just what has taken place in Korea.

Speaking of medical schools, I had my last session with my present class yesterday and again it was most gratifying to have the students so cordial and appreciative. As the class broke up about a dozen of the students gathered around expressing their thanks for the time I had given them. In ordinary times I have never had such a demonstration. I suppose I'll be having another class almost immediately but I have had no notice.

Did you ever hear a record being broadcast over a long line of street loud speakers where the record kept repeating itself every few lines? That is what is happening just now and some one is bound to have his "hero" status reduced. It is good we can get some variation and a certain amount of amusement out of this blasting of the air. But perhaps you don't know about our "hero" system? Anyone who shows unusual ability in his line is made a number 1, 2, 3, 4, or 5, "hero" and has increase of pay and certain privileges. Herewith we initiate the new aristocracy!

Now at 9:30 p.m., the loud speakers are finally quiet, but when you know that they started at eight this morning and have carried straight through you will realize how full of music (?) we are. On exceptional days everything starts at about 5 a.m. At that we are better off than some of our friends who live near early bugles. The bugles are always in the same location, but loud speakers do move after a month or so.

July 12. Our wind has gone from the east to the south so it should be clearing away our rain. This kind of weather is hard on my golf but we do enjoy having it cool, allowing us to close some of our windows thus reducing our "musicales" to some degree.

There has been some apprehension in the minds of a number of my foreign friends lest too much be given away in Korea, but I was glad to find from this morning's overseas broadcast that many people are alive to the possibilities. There is no doubt about the desire on the part of some we could name, not too far away from where you and I used to live to the north, to use the present situation to their own advantage. Only a strong line will be appreciated. *(The place where we used to live was Peking.)*

July 13. If you find the subject matter of some of my paragraphs a bit mixed, be advised that this is not unintentional. Feather beds sometimes hide more than the springs! Of course one always hopes the beds are not made too lumpy. The sensible man does not make such an institution the repository of sharp and breakable objects or those whose breaking might cause an objectionable odor. You may remember a number of years ago our children were given a small book of musical records suitable for the nursery. I think there were four in all but I am not as clear concerning the number as to the number of times a day they were repeated. Not far from where I sit the same thing is going forward out on the street to the south. It would be interesting to examine the psychology of senders and receivers of this repetitious exploitation of the air about us. I am told this is the method of instruction so popular these days. I know that sound waves of the 4096 frequency exploding over suitable periods will injure the internal ear. My guess is that this repeated low grade frequency stuff goes inside and causes serious softening between the two ears! *(At times it was felt wise to mix subject matter in a single paragraph as well as make it somewhat cryptic.)*

Sunday, July 15. I have just come from church in Philadelphia via New York. The jammers were out in force tonight so we had the same effect which is present as I write with loud speakers blaring away down on the street. It only takes a little more concentration. It is not too difficult to believe in the act of prayer when one realizes that here, half the world away, we hear the instant a word is spoken in New York. As of today the old Union Church goes on to services in the Chinese language. As a matter of fact, the only English service is the one at the Cathedral.

JULY 21, 1951 (TO H. S. H.)

It is one hot Saturday morning! Our rain seems to have stopped after about two weeks of daily showers. I think golfers are more conscious of the weather than most other people. We shall get some golf now but it must be done in moderation. We have a postponed competition for tomorrow. At least we hope we have; some soldiers getting ready for Korea are using the grounds for practice. Something will have to be done about this or we'll have to give up the course.

July 22, Sunday. It is starting in as another hot day and a good one for our two-ball foursome. Also some word seems to have gone out as the course was entirely free of those practicing yesterday.

Our loud speakers have stopped sounding off in these parts. Perhaps the records were worn out and vocal cords need a rest! You may be sure something else is being hatched. It is possible that someone realizes that the thing is being overdone or that the natives can stand only so much.

I understand the Shanghai Club is on the point of closing. One would not think the British community could carry on without this bulwark of their prestige; excessive taxes can make such feelings secondary. The lemon is being relieved of much of its juice. Our cousins are not as happy in their semi-recognized position as they used to be, and more and more are leaving.

Renewed home leaving is causing much deep thinking. I am told that family visiting is virtually at a standstill and where there are small children about, little is said. A friend told me some time ago that "if it were permitted to talk freely we could talk ourselves out of this one." Can you imagine any of the groups you have known in China who could wear the muzzle for long? *("Home leaving" referred to above indicated increased executions for subversion.)*

July 24. Our city is unusually quiet these past few days. It may be something or nothing. Something new may break out at any moment as the system demands that the ball be kept constantly in motion. As I sit here, high above the city, it is hard to believe that the millions underneath these roofs can be intimidated to the point where they cease to think for themselves. And yet they say even a worm will turn. Plenty of mutterings but no action! If the dike were to break the waters would rush through madly.

AUGUST 1, 1951 (TO H. S. H.)

I have just been called by the man at the British Consulate who is in charge of Americans. Another of our aged Americans who has no other home but China is passing. As the only American doctor I am asked to give advice. Gradually this group is becoming smaller and I am afraid many are going due to malnutrition. We have a committee which attempts to deal with this problem but funds are pretty low. Attempts have been made to get some of these people home but most have no home ties and they would have to go into charity institutions on arrival. This woman of eighty and a man of similar age, a former member of the American Church Mission who passed away last week, have been cared for by Chinese friends who can ill afford to do so.

August 2. I think your estimate of our patient's chances for immediate recovery or even change in symptoms is quite correct. When I was home last my niece in Illinois told me that the Montgomery Ward Catalogue is known as the "wish book." So it is here, many wishes are made as pages of history are being turned but as yet we are far from realizing any of the good things of life. But make no mistake, there is plenty of wishing!

Should you feel inclined you might write to the "Voice of America" for me to say that more voices like Elmer Davis, Edward R. Murrow and Dick Shepard are desired with us. There are others that we could dispense with. On the whole, it is remarkable how well we receive

# THE UBIQUITOUS LOUD SPEAKER 87

broadcasts in spite of attempted jamming. They can't cover all the frequencies.

August 4. Some of our friends are leaving today by boat for Hong Kong. One must be ill or have a record of recent illness to be allowed to go this way. But it all indicates a lifting of some of the restrictions. Obstructions at the mouth of the River are not mentioned any more.

As far as I could make out, as I walked down the street last night all our loud speakers have been removed together with practically all the animated anti-American cartoons.

August 5, Sunday. Down on the old French Club tennis grounds we are seeing much soft ball. I am told that this is a new move by the authorities. If so it would seem to me to be a good change. One gets tired of singing and beating a drum. Also, last night we had one of the new innovations in the form of a campfire. This was in an empty lot next door, and seated on the ground, in regular groups of course, were some hundred or more boys and girls of the fifteen to eighteen age class. A good-sized fire was kept going for an hour and a half during which time there was singing and the usual bed time (?) stories which were probably "enjoyed." It may be as I suggested previously that someone is finding that the constant "ding donging" is being overdone and even the young must be given a rest or at least a change. "Rest" is not the right word. It is remarkable how feverishly they keep at things. *("The bed time stories" were always for the purpose of indoctrination.)*

A ball game is in progress down on the French Club grounds just now and the crowd is working up some real enthusiasm. It sounds good to have some normal spontaneous shouting! It sounds so different from the hysterical regimented business we are so accustomed to. I see these boys walking off the field as their game has finished and not one is in Communist uniform. It is also a good thing to get them into ordinary every day clothing. Something happens to a man when he is put into a uniform. They don't seem to be able to think for themselves. Perhaps that is the reason for the uniform. Just lately there has been great relaxation in this matter so one sees very few uniforms on the street. It may be a good sign. It may also be that the blue suit is too hot for summer use.

AUGUST 9, 1951 (TO H. S. H.)

We are in the midst of a most unusual typhoon. It started two hours ago with a good old-fashioned thunder storm which came in from the north, a most unusual direction, but now at 4:30 p.m. the true character of the storm is apparent with high wind and driving rain. And still off in the distance there are rumblings of thunder and flashes of lightning. I wonder what is happening to the tall boardings on Nanking Road with their brilliantly painted signs glorifying the "wonderful great productivity" of farm and industrial plants with here and there a downright slanderous anti-American bit of business. Usually our big winds come from the south and billboards are braced to take it from that direction but this coming from the north can show up some weak points.

I am glad if the "Shanghai Soap Opera" does show continuity for to me my letters seem at times most disjointed. They probably have one thing which holds them together and that is that they all are from behind the Bamboo Screen. Some time ago I asked D. to keep my contributions from this end so that I might refer to them later if I needed to. If you think it wise you may do the same. We live in such a changing world that it is easy to forget details which were only too poignant at the time. Some of these things I have recorded in my letters to you and to him. I am gratified that the Clan continues to find my way of life interesting.

In spite of three types of jamming, one of which I call the "dental drill," I had no difficulty in getting all that was sent out this evening. I sometimes wonder if they get as good reception behind the Iron Curtain; if they do, anything and everything can get through. I was glad to hear the frank and firm speaking tonight. A deep game may be developing behind the Iron Curtain but I am sure no one will fall for it. Deeds not words are to count! General R. is making the proper stand in Korea from my point of view as well as from an oriental point of view, and native friends say he will win out.

August 10. If you were to suddenly plop down in Shanghai you might think we are a city of accidents with all the ambulance bells and sirens going off at all hours of the day and night. As a matter of fact there were a great many ambulances left behind by our people. Trucks and jeeps also carry similar signals and frequently all these means of transportation are used for "individuals who must leave their homes for shorter or longer periods." Among other things this rushing through the streets would seem to serve an educational (?) purpose: "Be good or else—." *(This paragraph refers again to an increase in the number of executions and arrests.)*

August 11. I am just back from the British Consulate. This is my first visit to the Bund for weeks. It looks more run down than ever with the streets and sidewalks in considerable disrepair. Also in spite of all the wonderful productivity of the country as depicted by poster and newspaper there are more mendicants on the street than I have seen for some time.

I noticed this morning that while we still have plenty of anti-American posters about, some new anti-accident ones are going up. Some of the boys driving the chosen few through the streets in big American cars should take these to heart. They are always in a hurry!

AUGUST 15, 1951 (TO D. & H.)

You have seen laborers waiting for something to happen to bring re-employment back to them. As I go through the streets of this big city I get the same impression, of people just waiting for something to happen to bring prosperity back to the city. We know which way they are looking for relief and it is not to the northwest!

August 16. I am enclosing a copy of a statement which I have been asked to submit to the British Consulate for transmission to our State Department. I am not too clear as to just why this is wanted. The statement speaks for itself. The one thing they want to know, I believe, is whether or not we have asked for an exit permit.

"To whom it may concern:

"I have made no request for an exit permit and have no immediate plans for doing so. My son, John A. Dunlap, who took his discharge from army service to complete his high school work in Shanghai has also chosen to remain with his parents in order to be of assistance to his mother who is a semi-invalid following a fracture of the spine more than a year ago.

"There have been numerous personal problems entering in to make us decide to delay any effort to return to America. Among other things it has seemed wise not to have Mrs. Dunlap attempt such a difficult trip so soon after her accident. Also, the fact that native help in the house makes for easier living has been a factor.

"One of the most compelling reasons for delaying our departure is the fact that I am now the only American or British physician in Shanghai. I remain also the only foreign nose, throat and ear specialist.

"It has seemed to me, therefore that there is a service which I can render to those who must remain when and if they may require my special knowledge. The fact that fees for such services as are required do not allow me to meet my expenses does not, as some have urged, relieve me of some responsibility for this special care of the community.

"I seek no approbation in this matter and feel it is a service I wish to continue as long as I am physically and financially able to do so. I fully realize that no man is indispensable but that at this juncture I may be helpful."

## 13: REGIMENTATION OF DOCTORS

Early in 1951 the Government started to secure control over all hospitals and clinics in Shanghai. A large number of new hospitals and clinics were established; many were built as a result of a ruling that all factories and business houses must provide medical care for staff. There were rumors that five hundred-bed hospitals were to be built in the various parts of the city, but up to the time we left Shanghai none had materialized. It is probable that there were not enough doctors and nurses to staff them.

It has been estimated that there were about thirty-five hundred well-trained Chinese physicians in all China before the Communists took over. A Chinese colleague stated in the summer of 1952 that he did not think there were more than twenty-five hundred still active at that time. Many had escaped from Communist China and were in Hong Kong or abroad. Under high pressure of work, some had come down with increased blood pressures, a condition not normally found in the Chinese. Some committed suicide.

All hospital fees, private office charges, and outpatient registration fees were reduced by an official order. While outwardly this may have been done to provide cheaper medical care for the populace, it had the result of greatly reducing the number of patients entering private offices. Private hospitals also found it difficult to meet their overhead on fees they were allowed to charge even when they were extremely busy.

Many physicians were therefore compelled to enter institutional

# REGIMENTATION OF DOCTORS

work on salary for a part or all of their time. Most men found their private practice so unproductive that they gave up their offices and devoted all their time to Government hospital service.

The authorities went all out not only to provide medical care for the people but public health matters were pushed as well. Perhaps never in the history of the city were the inhabitants so completely immunized against small pox, cholera, diphtheria and typhoid. In addition, the health authorities attempted to wipe out prostitution. Almost immediately after "liberation" the long lines of amahs, who frequented certain areas, each with her gaily dressed and painted prostitute by her side, virtually disappeared over night.

Some five hundred of these young women were under the medical care of a doctor friend who had first claim on sufficient penicillin for their treatment. As soon as this group was disease-free another five hundred were to be treated. All prostitutes were finally to be given jobs in factories. As evidence that prostitution had not been completely stamped out, men, some young, some old, took the place of the prostitutes' amahs in soliciting rather openly on the streets while the young women remained indoors.

AUGUST 15, 1951( TO H. S. H.)

The wife of a Chinese doctor friend has just been in to invite us to go to the French Club tomorrow night. This is the man who wanted me to use his office when B.'s Chinese colleague was afraid to have me, an American, in their office. She tells me that this past year has seen the virtual disappearance of all private practice in Peking. One of our old crowd was down from there a week ago and brings this report. The impression locally is that the time is not far away when the same thing will happen in this area. New clinics are opening almost every week and doctors are more or less forced to service them, usually with little or no pay. What the end is to be is not clear but the hand writing is on the wall and it is evident that living standards will have to go down among these professionals. A year from now this man will not be able to pay dues to the French Club, let alone invite us out for an expensive dinner.

One of our 1931 graduates who was in two nights back must attend three different factory clinics daily with the result that his small practice has gone to pot. He gets only enough income from these clinics to meet two-thirds of his expenses. At that he is getting the equivalent of $125 U.S. dollars a month which is a great deal more than that received by those doctors in straight government work.

August 17. If you were to go down street today you would find that all the anti-American posters are down. This happened once before and we thought at first it might mean a change of heart. Now we learn that these are put up on contract and at the moment the contract is finished. Another one is being drawn up and we may expect to see bigger and better showings shortly. Generally speaking "instructional activities" are not too apparent just now. The meaning of this is not clear but every one is enjoying the respite. I may be able to pick up a little explanation at our dinner tonight. *(The "instructional activities" had to do with indoctrination classes which were constantly in evidence throughout the city. Early morning classes on a small parade ground could be seen from my bathroom window.)*

August 18. We had a most interesting time last evening with Mr. and Mrs. T. at the French Club. He still continues his practice but since he is connected with St. Luke's must spend a great deal of time helping to solve administrative problems.

Lately we have had fewer parades and bands (drums), but more soft ball games. Now down below me in the French Club this morning there is a group of women and men doing gymnastics on parallel and horizontal bars. All this is to the good even if it is in part for show. We have been pleased to see so many soft ball games in operation today. You probably know that an order has gone out that students must spend more time in school and less in parading. Doctor P. says this does not mean that there is a change in policy but simply that they want to get a little more real education going. Political education will be done in the schools. He feels that it does not mean that the left side of our patient is any less active. *(The soft ball era did not last too long. Apparently someone discovered that it was an American game. Russians do not play baseball.)*

AUGUST 21, 1951 (TO D. & H.)

Your letter of August 7 came in two days back and as it is a typhoon morning with high winds and rain and many streets flooded, all of which will keep patients away, I'll get a letter started. I do have to go out this afternoon to do two tonsils at A's hospital but I have some good rubber boots to keep my feet dry. It is interesting to watch a typhoon from our ninth floor. Usually we have been in places where outside fences have been a problem, and when blown down, an expense. Our place out on Columbia Circle is being farmed by our old fence man and the soldiers and he is expected to keep the fence in repair.

Later, same day. My operations on the two boys under ten went along very well. Coming home I thought I would try a new bus route but found my street was well covered with water when I got there. A wave set up by a passing truck went over the top of my boots so my boots and pants had to be taken off in the bath tub!

AUGUST 22, 1951 (TO H. S. H.)

Shanghai is going wild over a new carom game! It is played on a three-foot square board with corner pockets and with checker sized pucks which are struck with a wooden cue. My guess is that there is not a home, shop or street corner without a game board. I'm glad to see this enthusiasm joined with the soft ball league as it all tends to make our young people more normal. I get a great deal of pleasure hearing their cheers down below in the French Club when a game is in progress. They are not shouting something they are reading from a paper and neither is the prompter there who usually calls the slogans to be shouted ... There seems to be nothing so uncertain in this world as the mind of man! I sometimes wonder why the good Lord could not have made our minds more nearly alike just as we make motor car engines, so that reactions to outside stimuli might be somewhat the same. I realize this would make for a pretty tame world and probably not one we would like to live in. Just the same we would like the other man to think a little more as we do!

August 24. L. dropped in on us this morning. I have not seen him for years, I think since P.U.M.C. days. He has been on an inspection trip for the Government to Hangchow and on his way back stopped off in Wuhu at which time he wanted to write to you but did not have your address. I gave it to him and you may be hearing from him later, though as a rule Chinese do not write to their foreign friends abroad. In Peking, they wanted him to act as the dean of one of the colleges but to date he has avoided this by explaining that his Chinese is not good enough. He is far from sold on the present order. *(P.U.M.C. is Peking Union Medical College.)*

For the present P.U.M.C. has the old staff and everything is being kept just as clean as it once was. It is used as a show place. There is great shortage of professional staff but salaries have not been cut as yet. There are now about five hundred beds, most of which are being used by the Government. The Government staff have salaries just half those of the old crowd. He believes it will not be long before all staff salaries will be "voluntarily" reduced. Contrary to other reports a number of men like J. H. are continuing to carry on private practice. In general he described a state of affairs which coincides with what we learned is taking place, in the rear of any curtain. There is much unhappiness but there is nothing that can be done about it.

AUGUST 29, 1951 (TO H. S. H.)

A good friend was in this morning and said her father was a little happier now as he is having more business and does not have so much time to think. He makes no money, however, and this is the usual story. Work and long hours but no profits! As she says, everything is on the surface. The patience and art of waiting are being sorely tried among these people!

Later, same day. I can't remember what I could have said which would have encouraged Mr. C. to think he would be able to visit Shanghai. I am certain that he could get in if he came well supplied with "what it takes" but he would find it most difficult to leave until the lemon was dry. I don't think anyone from the West has "visited" us since we were "liberated." I am sure I shall not see him in Shanghai, if he knows what is good for him. Only substitute money bag holders can come in. *Many of those who remained in Shanghai were in effect used as hostages to guarantee that their firms or organizations would continue to send in solid currency to pay local employees and maintain western-owned buildings and equipment. None of these hostages could leave until after his replacement had arrived in Shanghai.)*

Much has been said lately about the San Francisco Treaty with more details as to what is being proposed. A friend who was in this morning said that the Chinese are afraid of the rearming of Japan. This matter is being played up and one is led to believe that Japan is to be made stronger than ever before. I think I was able to reassure our friend but the masses are convinced that something very bad is happening.

There are some here who have been refused permission to leave. I play golf with one frequently. Yesterday I had a patient who got as far as the train and was pulled back.

Out here we are all hoping the free nations will be hard boiled in San Francisco. As some of my friends who have come orginally from the "Northwest" say, "call their bluff." Incidentally many of these White Russians have left Shanghai for freer areas. Down on Avenue Joffre where whole sections used to be made up of their shops, it is rare now to see a single one. They knew what would happen long before other people.

SEPTEMBER 9, 1951 (TO H. S. H.)

Your letter written August 26 and mailed on the evening of the same day came in yesterday. I let out a little California air in opening it!

You are quite correct regarding the sampling and we are fully conscious of the practice which is more frequent with some individuals than with others. *(The last sentence refers to the possibility that some of our letters may have been censored.)*

I can think of no place where medical education is more needed just now than in China. The amount of public health and hospital service being put on by these people is bound to work the doctors into an early grave, if they don't soon get help. All of our graduates are carrying heavy loads. One of our graduates came in from Tientsin this week and reports that while the medical firm of P.U.M.C. graduates, of which he is a member, is carrying on with their practice, they are now getting ready to start a medical school. All members of his group have been to the north for varying periods usually about three months apiece. Apparently they are assigned to base hospitals, but do not actually get into Korea.

At six this morning I heard the finals on the San Francisco affair. This is very good news and should make some people we might name sit up and take notice. It will be interesting to see what effect it will have on this area. My guess is that until there is a change of heart by "brothers" there will be no alterations of present trends. While the marriage between M. and S. is not too satisfactory, even to members of the family, the ties that bind them as one are pretty strong. The economic situation within the family is far from satisfactory since father is taking advantage of mother's possessions and while some of the children gnash their teeth there is little they can do about it. *(This paragraph has reference to closer union between China (Mao) and the Kremlin (Stalin) and the increasing export of products such as beef and pork and other food stuffs to Russia from a China which could ill afford to supply them.)*

There is no word as yet with regard to what happened to our land. The regulations apparently are not very specific but we have until the end of November, I understand, to make final registration. I am sure there is a squeeze game of some sort on as that is the order of the day.

Living up so high above the ground we have had practically no insects the entire summer. It has been an especially dry summer and that also has been a help. As far as I can learn this entire locality recently has been comparatively free, even of the biped sort. I am told that at a greater distance this sort is more in evidence and there is some indication that some are nearer at hand than we know. Certainly, the exterminators are out in force these past few days. *(The last half of this paragraph refers to anti-Communist guerillas around the Shanghai area and the fact that patrols were being sent out to control them.)*

When the history of the present period is written it may be clear that the greatest stimulus for the betterment of mankind has been the anti-Christs of this age. San Francisco certainly demonstrated how thinking people react when attempts are made to push them around. I see it here in some of my oldest friends. Under present conditions they must remain inarticulate but I am sure there must come a day of house cleaning and then some I could name who have "licked boots" will be cast out.

SEPTEMBER 15, 1951 (TO H. S. H.)

I have written you previously about the recent death of Doctor James Maxwell, one of China's oldest missionaries. Mrs. M. got away yesterday by boat, a special dispensation due to her age. We had her out to dinner night before last. It is remarkable how mentally bright she is at eighty. He was seventy-eight. Their recent months have not been too happy but there is no doubt but what he has made a definite contribution to the treatment of leprosy in China. He was able to get up some of the more recent drugs from Hong Kong. It would almost seem that an exception had been made in the case of these particular drugs as very little else is coming in.

September 16th, Sunday. This has been a day of golf! As we sat in the club house it was most difficult to realize that we live behind the Bamboo Curtain. There were "certain individuals" about to remind us of the realities but all were cordial. *("Certain individuals" were Communist soldiers who overran the golf course at times.)*

I was reading in a recent Sunday copy of the *New York Times* a criticism expressed by one recently out of East Germany. He was interested in radio broadcasts, which were getting behind the curtain without difficulty but which he felt should deal not so much with what was bad behind the curtain but what plans and hopes there might be for the future. We might say, Amen! We are all too conscious of the bad.

SEPTEMBER 19, 1951 (TO D. & H.)

On September 19, 1943, just eight years ago, we left Shanghai on the Japanese repatriation ship on a day when the temperature must have been near ninety. Today it has been near seventy-five. Many things have happened since that day and still are happening. One wonders what the next few years will bring. I for one don't want to know and I don't think we were even intended to see into the future. I am confident, however, that sooner or later there will be more free air in the world than at present.

It is fairly settled weather now and we'll get some good golfing days for the next two months. A friend and I went out for a walk tonight but the streets are so crowded that it is not a pleasure to walk. The chestnut stoves are coming out and everyone is buying nuts. This is a sign of fall. They are bad on the waist line!

SEPTEMBER 21, 1951 (TO H. S. H.)

We have had another sudden death in our community, Mr. Harry Morris, the owner of the *North China Daily News*. You got the last copy of his publication to be issued and since that time he has had a most difficult situation on his hands. As a "lemon" for squeezing he had no equal and was being relieved of everything in sight and more. He died of a heart attack. This is one way of getting an exit permit over which man has no control. In this connection, with the exception of a young girl of fifteen, no American citizen has had an exit permit for more than four months. It looks as though we are all staying for the time being . . . While there is always the possibility of dire things happening, I think with very few exceptions every foreigner here lives a fairly normal life. There seems to be a consciousness of some restraining hand which will prevent things from going too far. On top of that there is the loyalty of old friends which is most heart warming.

September 24. The word this morning regarding the King of England is not too reassuring. If he has had only a lobectomy there still may be hope. My impression after listening to the bulletin is that the condition is much more serious than the doctors are telling the world. Incidentally we are having a little more difficulty in our reception these days. Apparently there are various kinds of jams to be had on the market. "Bear brand" is by far the most popular but I think there are some local makes as well. *("Bear brand" refers to Soviet jamming of our radio broadcasts. Local attempts to jam our reception were also made.)*

Later—same day. I had to go down to the British Consulate this afternoon to open an ear drum of one of the children and was interested in seeing that practically all anti-American posters are down. This may be because October 1 is coming up and something entirely new will meet the eye. I believe we are to have a big show as this is the important day of the year. *(October 1 was Communist China's founding day.)*

I was interested in the way our new traffic police are controlling pedicabs and other transport on the street. Men who are driving cars say there has never been as good control. In the first place there are many more men doing this work. In each block besides the men in charge of the light there are three or four more helping. Also between crossings there are two and sometimes more who keep the pedicabs close to the curbs. It is really a good show and very necessary now that motor transport has been reduced and pedicabs greatly increased.

Bus passengers are also controlled. We all stand in line and go one by one into the cars. This was started by the Japanese and it is still carried on. A conductor goes along such lines selling tickets. This is most necessary as the buses are so crowded no conductor could possibly sell tickets inside. I was in such a bus tonight and I think I would have been held upright even had my feet been knocked out from under me. It is remarkable the number of people coming and going by all means of transportation when one knows that profitable enterprise on the whole is at a very low ebb.

September 25. We are beginning to get in some real fall weather with cool nights. This is the best season of the year in China. It is a shame that the freedom enjoyed by the birds of the air cannot be carried down to those who are supposed to own the earth!

The ten year old son of the British Consul General has just gone home by himself by plane to enter boarding school. It was his brother I operated on yesterday and his mother told me she was relieved that he could be away from the daily passing of so many who are "leaving home for indefinite stays." The sight is more than some adults can stand. Some day the tide must turn and something other than $H_2O$ will flow in greater volume. It is questionable as to whether or not the millions upon millions can be compressed by the present ideology for too long a period.

Later, same day. I had another trip down town today to see my small patient and I must hand it to our improved bus organization for the way their transportation is carried on. The city is now covered pretty well with bus service so one can get most everywhere with a short walk and a bus. We have practically no taxis on the street. Gas is cheaper now and there is more of it, but I suspect they must still need a high charge to make it a paying business. In any event the bus seems to be the answer. *(The great expansion of bus routes throughout the city was made possible by the perfection of a gas producing apparatus carried on a two-wheeled trailer hooked on behind each of the new buses. Hard coal was used to produce the gas. The new buses were built on big Dodge truck chassis, trucks left behind when the Nationalists retreated. The man who perfected the gas producer was made much over and was given the title of "Number One Hero."*)

SEPTEMBER 27, 1951 (TO H. S. H.)

Late this afternoon after I had seen my patient at the British Consulate I walked west on Peking Road to the St. Elizabeth Hospital where we were to hold our first clinical meeting of the Shanghai Medical Society for the current season. As I went along I remembered the time when I brought you there for city experience after teaching you how to drive my old Hupmobile. You wanted to return west via Peking Road rather than Nanking Road and as we came along, driving on the left side, you almost took the handle off a wheelbarrow. It did nothing to the car but scratch a little paint off the fender and after looking daggers at the coolie (you may have used strong words but I don't remember) we drove on. Let that happen today and you and I would still be languishing in the police station hours after the accident. We would be severely lectured on the rights of "the people" and especially the common man. Our car would probably not be available for our use for another forty-eight hours and only after paying damages and a fine.

There are so few foreigners in the city now that I found I was more of an object of curiosity on this street little used by foreigners than in so-called normal times. But perhaps the only people who really paid much attention to me were the small children asking alms, sicked on by adults who remained in the background. Lately more of these people are arriving as winter approaches. Grain for India! *(At this time, the Peking Government announced shipment of relief supplies to starving India, without reference to starvation inside China.)*

September 28. Every morning as I shave I look down on some thousand or more young boys and girls doing mass callisthenics in the open space below. While this is in imitation of "brotherland," it is all for the good of these children, many of whom have never before participated in any physical exercises.

Just now we are practicing for the October 1 celebration which takes the place of the old "Double Tenth." Perhaps you think that bugle and drum bands do not need much training. In that you would be wrong as such music (?) is most scientific and requires long hours of patient repetition to which our ear drums can attest. In the evening after work (they used to do this sort of thing in working hours) small bands can be seen and heard practicing marching and playing their one and only tune. I don't know what would happen if they had to play a second! A typhoon is approaching and it is likely to be a wet march unless its course is changed.

Our medical meeting at St. Elizabeth Hospital last night was not too comfortable as we had to compete with drums, a piano and a loud speaker in the next room. I marveled at the apparent placidity of our Chinese chairman and other members of the hospital staff in the face of such extraneous noises but they have learned the hard way not to interfere with any activities of the "people." For instance, out on the golf course our caddies cannot ask those in uniform to move off a green or fairway. A green is a favorite place to sit and play cards and one's rest or pleasure must not be disturbed! *(The military contingents in and about Shanghai were frequently changed and some of the troops near the golf course were very difficult to control. Others were very cordial and helpful, but one always had to be considerate of a soldier if he wished to make use of a green for the purpose of an afternoon game of cards.)*

We did get through our meeting after a fashion but I for one will object to going there again. I had to give a report but made it short. Incidentally, our Chinese colleagues are most anxious to continue these medical meetings. It is about the only outlet they have for English language reports.

Night before last an Englishman of seventy-two and one of forty were in to dinner. Both had the same point of view: all is lost here. This means of course, in their opinion, that all business of the future will be nil. They did go on to say that they agreed that there can be no turning back from the present state of things. The squeeze play is just now being placed on the British similar to what occurred to all American business men months back. "Never" is a long time and I for one am not ready to admit the die is irrevocably cast. I see many signs about me that in certain quarters the natives have not entirely given up hope. One does certain things because it is required but precautions are taken to preserve "this and that" against a possible day of change.

## 14  DAY-TO-DAY LIVING

After almost two and a half years under the Communists there was little doubt in the mind of anyone, Chinese and foreigner alike, as to what the new regime had for its objectives. They had been extremely busy consolidating their position and the entire country was organized under committees down to the smallest village. Every person was required to have a residence certificate issued by the police. No Chinese could travel to another city without a permit.

So far as Shanghai was concerned the authorities had worked along with little fanfare except for the gathering of subversives. Virtually all the colleges and universities had been reorganized and had come under Communist control. Business conditions in the city were bad; many were finding it difficult to make a living.

OCTOBER 1, 1951 (TO D. & H.)
I'll get this letter started while I wait to be called to lunch. This is a national holiday for the Communists.

October 2. We were all very much in our homes most of yesterday as there were many parades moving about with all transportation off the streets from 6:30 a.m. until about 2 p.m. Today is also a holiday and all shops are still closed. My staff must be given a holiday as per the rules so I am having no office. If anyone comes in S. will act as my office boy and nurse.

OCTOBER 3, 1951 (TO H. S. H.)

Our three-day holiday is over and we are getting back to work, or what passes for work. I was talking to R. of Bill's Motors last evening and he was complaining of the long holiday. "But," I said, "you don't do any work when your office is open." To which he replied that the daily pin pricks were sufficient to keep one interested in one's job. When the history of this period is written it will be found that the business men who have been required to "hold the fort" have developed super abilities in patience and tolerance.

I have just had the old man in who looked after my Pearce Road property before it was "reformed." It was supposed to be divided between the families but he tells me someone is building a factory on the place. In this act you can detect some of the ancient and perhaps more modern working of the grasping mind. It would seem that "the people" may be in the process of taking secondary seats. Apparently the pattern is the same all over the world.

Today we are having a nor'easter with plenty of cold rain. It will probably wash out all the week-end sports. It was a good free day for me to go down to my dentist. From where we live it is a 1,000 JMP ride (this is the equivalent of five cents in U.S. money), and you should see the paper bills of these denominations: they are so much like bits of old newspaper. I was almost ashamed to pass out my bill this morning; it was held together with a piece of old newspaper. We have little these days under five or ten thousand JMP bills, that are at all new.

We are getting more and more taxis on the street and all I have seen are being run on charcoal. The trunk of the car is being used to hold the burner. The lift-up door is partially cut away and a wire grill inserted to let out the heat. It has a very neat appearance and does not extend out beyond the normal back of the car as so many do. I saw a motor car of an older vintage this morning which had everything on the back including the proverbial "kitchen stove" as a gas generator.

When one gets together with friends and tries to evaluate his surroundings, I find there are many variables. It is most difficult to arrive at a sane conclusion. One might enumerate some of them as follows: a good or bad night, pressure or lack of pressure by members of one's staff, increase or decrease of taxes, exit permits or none, many or few investigations, reading too much of the vernacular or not enough, hearing too much or too little of external news, faith or the lack of faith in the future of mankind, belief or the opposite that there is something in the depth of native beings which will rise up, whether or not you think right will come out on top in the end, and finally which way you were swayed by the last man you talked to. This is a time when it is pretty essential to have faith.

October 7. Last evening I went up to see A. and for a short look around. I usually walk and on my way I met an old patient who is stateless. I think he came originally from the Baltic area. When I asked him when he was leaving he shrugged his shoulders and said that new status papers had been lost in transit and there was nothing that he could do. Shanghai has a large number of such persons now and while they are not wanted here, and in fact have been given only a short time to get out, they have no place to go. Hong Kong will not permit them to enter for processing. No one who is without means of support can stay here.

Just as we were a city of loud speakers (on occasion we still are) we are now one of megaphones. Every traffic policeman carries one to help him direct pedicabs to keep behind the line on crossings or to the side of the street. I have wondered if what they say as they yell into the things can really be understood, as to my ear it is mostly a roar.

Later, evening. We have just heard a wonderful half hour of music from St. Paul's Cathedral, London, over the BBC. Nothing like the clarity of this music by organ and choir is produced by the "Voice of America." In some two hours we shall be listening to a church service from New York, but I shall turn down the choir music as anything but pleasant. The organ and sermon come over clearly. We also had a half hour of United Nations this evening, mostly about oil. I hope they can get that bit of business settled.

OCTOBER 9, 1951 (TO H. S. H.)

I am not sure I was able to satisfy you with my second letter regarding our problem of departure. Words are such poor instruments at times with which to try and convey the realities of a situation. It may be that you are thinking that a barrier has been placed in the way but as far as I know such a thing does not exist. It might appear if a move were made, as some friends suggest, but that would not be known without a try being made. I think I have no illusions regarding the increasing difficulties which attend anyone moving out of the area. It is not, therefore, with any thought that if we wait long enough we may move with more of our possessions intact. Restrictions have greatly increased and will increase more.

The prices are fairly steady, though some things, like razor blades, are four times what they cost in America. All imported things which have been in stock for some time are also in the same category. One of the notable but understandable inconsistencies of our time and place is the great desire on the part of "some we could name" for big American cars, while at the same time a strong anti-American attitude is preserved. On several occasions I have tried to sell my 1942 Chevrolet, but no models older than 1946 are worth anything. My car is well preserved, but that makes no difference. I was offered the equivalent of five hundred U.S. dollars some weeks back, but if it were a 1946 it would have brought upwards of ten times that amount.

There are plenty of large American cars still about and if you were to hear suddenly, as we do, excessive "horning" down on the street you could expect to see a long line of rapidly moving vehicles with all traffic regulation for the time being set aside. It is a wonderful life if one is in the swim! I hear a "cavalcade" going to someone's party just below, and how they love to blow those horns!

I am rather concerned for the health of some of our former graduates and staff. They are giving long hours to their professional work and in addition must attend long hours of "lecture." China needs all the physicians she can get and some of these men are not likely to last long. Some may go the way taken by L. K.

October 11. Have you ever had your morning newspaper smeared with "bear brand" jam? Until you do you will not appreciate the clean sheets offered you each morning for your edification.

October 12. Patients got in the way when I arrived at this point yesterday. I passed up the "jam" this morning as I missed the eight o'clock radio news from America. I am under the impression that there are some local brands on the market as short distances are also smeared. Be that as it may, anyone desiring to read around the "jam marks" can always see all that is necessary. For some reason Australia butter and "jam" are never mixed. This may be because the butter is set up between the earth's poles. *(To my knowledge Australian broadcasts were for some reason never jammed by the Soviets.)*

When the history of this period is written it will be found that some new and rather clever practices have been instituted for the purpose of getting "juice." There is a "heads I win and tails you lose" bit of business which is beyond belief. If you ever come in contact with a business man who has gone through the "extraction mill" out here you'll hear some unbelievable facts. Sir R. gives me some every now and then. Levies on losses are most common and at any time the rules may be changed and you'll be caught up. The old "good as his word" no longer holds. One wonders what kind of a foundation is being made for the future by using slippery methods. (There goes another cavalcade.)

October 15. Yesterday was an entire day of golf, a field day for golfers and their friends. This old man got a prize for one of the best scores over a two-hole course using a single club; a bottle of whiskey which I could not use so turned over to my golf partner. You would be interested in the people who turned up. Every one from the British Consul General to some of your old friends were there and for once soldiers kept entirely off the course. If home folk could have seen us they would not have believed their eyes, having in mind the severity of our situation. I should think we had about a hundred and fifty people out, four of whom were natives. The country boys, the caddies, were overjoyed. One only has to see the narrow margin on which these people live to appreciate what a good day of working as a caddie can mean to them. If no one else will fight to keep the club going, these boys will.

"Bear brand" jam is all the go just now and I can't remember when it has been so popular. I am interested that only an English twist and not the native tongue creates a desire for its use. When one is too full of "jam," Australian butter is a great relief.

OCTOBER 18, 1951 (TO H. S. H.)

Your letter of the 7th came in last evening making its usual time out. Yes, I do see *The New York Times* occasionally but not regularly. I have not seen the article to which you refer. Since writing you some exit permits have been given to Americans of varying faiths and complexions but not to any of Shanghai's regular business or missionary groups.

And speaking of marriage, we have had some illuminating descriptions of the civil ceremonies which all must go through before getting down to the business of the church wedding. The bride and groom, together with their best man and maid, enter a room and take their seats on a long backless bench facing the marrying official as he sits behind a plain table. Just use your imagination, draw on it for all the funny questions likely to be put to the contracting parties and you'll have a pretty fair picture of the ludicrous and anything but impressive affair. All remain seated and the official does not remove his Communist cap. Three and sometimes more "marriages" may be going on at the same time. One bride we know told how shocked her marrying official was when she was kissed by her maid before him.

I am not sure but I think the cost does not run the equivalent of one U. S. dollar.

A friend was telling us the other day of a party which he had attended the night before where one of the games was to illustrate with a picture cut from a magazine one of the Amateur Dramatic Club shows given here during the past year and a half. One group came up with a cutting showing a shop window full of solid silver for the bride, this stood for "You can't take it with you." And you can't, not more than twenty ounces per person and it makes no difference whether you brought it into China with you or not. *(When we left China we were allowed to take out only 25 ounces each.)*

The world seems to be getting into more messes and one wonders just how these things in the Near East will end. It may be about time for some one to wave the big stick. One can imagine how "some one we know" is sitting back smoking his big pipe and chuckling. It was with considerable relief that I read one man's opinion in an October issue of *Time,* which would seem to indicate a move away from the left. You may be surprised to know we see such recent issues but such is the case; I am about eighth from the top of the list of those who get a look, a look which is some twelve hours in length. Again the Chinese Post Office is wonderful!

I have thought that sometime I must tell you of the interesting kinds of jam we can pick up on occasions. It is simply wonderful, the great variety. We have both local and imported kinds. The "Bear Brand" is probably the most popular and sometimes it is foisted on one to the exclusion of all others. When that happens, as I have said before, one must move over and take another seat. (Just now I've had Tokyo on and the thing in Egypt does not look very comfortable. It would be good for British reputation out where we live if she used a little strong arm business just now.) Perhaps you never realized it but "jam" can remind you of other experiences and objects in every day life. Such things as dental drills, chirping of birds, groans, lawn mowers, typewriters and possibly certain voice sounds though I could be wrong in that.

October 19. I hope the fixing of the area for the Korean "cease fire" talks will hurry things along. It is my belief, however, that it will be the strong right arm stuff which will have the most effect. There is very little in the vernacular regarding what goes forward. Lately as I have indicated above, there seems to be greater attempts at blocking information from getting in, but it can't be kept out.

I am operating at the Jewish Hospital for what may be the last time if present rumors are correct. It is said to be closing out due to finances but this may not be correct. This is the only remaining hospital left under foreign control and it would be a serious blow if it goes. Something like what B. S. and I started in our first Shanghai home may have to be set up for the remaining foreigners simply because everything else is full. Of course the old Country Hospital is not full but it is very exclusive. Virtually everywhere, outside of a few private Chinese hospitals like A's, no foreign doctor is welcome. It is not because the men running these places are not willing, but because they have to answer so many questions.

October 22. I was talking to an American business man yesterday during which I gave him the news that the Jewish Hospital probably would be closing. I was rather surprised at his reaction as our business men both British and American have been most indifferent regarding our reduced provisions for the care of our foreign sick. He was of the opinion that something must be done immediately and he proposed to do something about it. He felt that home business offices as well as our Government must take a hand. I can't believe anything will come of this new move as there does not appear to be any conception of what goes forward out here by those in responsible positions at home. Our former British Consul General who went home some three months back was all steamed up over this matter and we all gave him data to use but not a single word has come back as to what he did. "Hostages" need medical care just as much as free men. Personally I intend to make my contribution here and hope in the next world my debits may be somewhat reduced.

An attempt is being made by the authorities to keep our golf course free of service men and their maneuvers. We have had to cut out whole sections of the place during their war games which go from one end to the other, using grave mounds and bunkers as cover. It is really made to order and you can't blame them but it does disturb our game to say nothing of the fact that we pay a big tax. The police promised last week to keep it clear but yesterday we had to go directly through a charge. It is really remarkable that they are willing to take this stand and the real meaning is not apparent at present. The income, and not a small one, which they get from the place is probably a factor.

OCTOBER 28, 1951 (TO H. S. H.)

I think most of us in Shanghai have been pleased with the results of the British election. It is to be hoped that a more definite stand may be taken in certain matters in the Near East. I don't think they will make any change with regard to their man in Peking. A British subject said yesterday in my hearing that there would not be any breaking away in that quarter as the British resented what we had done in the Formosa straits. On the other hand an Englishman said in my house some time ago that he fully expected relations, such as they are to be broken off in Peking. Will the new government stand for the indignities currently operating in this area? We shall see!

When one is cut off from fresh reading matter it is remarkable what one can find in the old *Saturday Evening Post* both in stories and articles. Also old *Reader's Digests* going back to 1942 provide food for thought. It is interesting to read some of the old articles in which men knew all the answers on how it should be done. It is possible now to see how far off the mark some have been. Some of the articles dealing with the affairs behind curtains written in the late forties come to life as we look about us. Apparently the chemical reaction is constant.

Locally we are seeing the effect of the termination of International Relief Organization support. There are not a few stranded here and they have been told that after November 1st all support will cease. It affects the Jewish Hospital where these people have been cared for. It will be difficult for patients and hospital alike since the hospital has depended on these funds for partial support. Do you know if anything else is being put in the place of the I. R. O.? It is a pretty serious matter out this way and suicides will be the order of the day if something is not done. All these people have been ordered out of China, and Hong Kong will not let them come there for processing.

Later, same day. We have just been to Washington, D.C. for the 9:30 p.m. church service. Again I cannot see why we do not have clear choir and organ reception when the B.B.C. has good transmissions even from such large places as the St. Paul's Cathedral. For the moment this is the only way we can get English language church services.

At the end of this service we were told that today's talk in Korea had agreed in the main on where the "cease fire" line was to be, but it was yet to be decided where the "buffer zone" was to be. To me this does not make sense but more details will probably come out in a day or so, or the usual disagreement.

October 29, Monday. I am just back from an afternoon of golf. The course is fairly free on the first day of the week as most go out on Saturday and Sunday. The course was clear of service activities today and it may mean that orders have come down from above at last.

Another meeting is to be held soon to determine the future of the place. Levies and taxes are being increased again and it is doubtful if the Club membership can stand the pressure. The old British Country Club has closed and the big one on the Bund is attempting to close. The French Club is in difficulties and everyone expects it to go under at any moment. It is remarkable how much "juice" one can get out of a lemon when one sets his mind to it!

OCTOBER 31, 1951 (TO H. S. H.)

Yesterday morning two wives of professional colleagues of many years came in to see Mrs. D. bringing in loads of fall flowers. It was like old times and something which does not happen too frequently these days because of "pressures." Our present locality and set up with the office in the apartment makes entry fairly inconspicuous. Their husbands are working very hard with many meetings added each week. One man is helping in a six months' course in surgery which every native physician of the old type must take before he is given a license to practice. This is an interesting way of dealing with this old problem. One wonders if some of these men may not set themselves up now as full blown surgeons.

As a means of preserving your youthful figure I should like to recommend Chinese shadow boxing. This morning after breakfast I looked down in the court yard next door where a young man of some thirty years was going through this slow motion exercise. It looks like slow motion films and while it is interesting to watch I do not find it pleasing. There appears to be a great element of exhibitionism in the thing and most people find a very public place for their show. I remember one woman out at St. John's University in the front of the Walker home several years ago who was doing her shadow boxing in rubber boots. You can imagine her raising first one boot and later the other to the horizontal and back to the ground, timing each to consume as much time as possible in going up and down. I think I have never seen as slow motion as in this man this morning. *(This type of shadow boxing amounted to slow motion callisthenics.)*

Most of the church services continue in former English speaking places as before "liberation," but every thing now is in the vernacular. A certain amount of time in each, as address period, must be devoted to present progress of the new order. If the minister is not qualified to do this someone is especially assigned to assist him. Such an atmosphere does not keep the old membership from finding other things to do on a Sunday. One man said, "Well, we did have a bit of devotion in the final prayer." My secretary rarely goes to church, but last Sunday she did and learned from one of their "assistant speakers" about "infected" dolls, which are being dropped to children in Korea. The human brain is certainly a fertile place in which to hatch some of the most remarkable things known to man!

I had an occasion to go down town today, the first time in over a month, and I was impressed with how much our water front is coming to resemble up-river ports as I remember them forty years ago. The shops seemed to be well filled with goods but did not appear to be very busy.

November 1. We go over to the Cathay Mansions this evening to a Chinese meal and are looking forward to seeing how the place is now being used. It has been taken over and is now a great meeting and eating place as well as hotel. Visitors are usually put up there when they are here in connection with the new order. C.E. was a guest there, put up in a two room apartment all by himself. I'll give you our reactions.

November 2. We had a very comfortable Chinese meal last evening next door. The place is being kept up very well and must cost a great deal more than is being taken in. The subsidy must be made up from some of the high taxes I am paying! I pay the equivalent of five hundred U.S. on my Columbia Circle and Lincoln Road properties. For these properties this is extremely high when you know that the Columbia Circle property is being used also by the communist soldiers for a vegetable garden. There is nothing like having your cake and eating it! I noticed yesterday that the little red flags which indicate land reform are stuck in the fields as far in as Warren Road on Lincoln Road, not far from your two-mu piece. I believe it will not be long before all areas outside the railroad will be taken into the land reform movement.

A letter recently from America indicates that two of our missionary doctors who went home sometime ago in very bad health are now going strong. Apparently the U. S. does something to people and I wish we might try it. Some days we cave in more than others, and this day of heavy levies is one of them. I have been advised to let your property on Lincoln Road ride for the time being. Under present conditions there is no way of protecting it with the present system operating. It may be recovered at any time up to three years from my last payment which held things up to January 1, 1951. If this thing now in operation goes on for three years and more, land is no longer of any value, and if it does not, its status is assured. I did not get my notice for the first half of this year's payment of five and a half million, and now I am warned that I shall probably have to pay a fine.

November 3. They seem to be getting a little nearer a first agreement in Korea but at this rate it does not give much hope of an overall settlement. In the meantime we continue to give "in aid." *(By this I mean we continued to contribute heavy taxes used for the prosecution of the war.)* . . . High taxes may be a Government device to keep inflation from taking place. For that we are thankful, as we have no desire to figure in astronomical sums again. We would like it if living costs would come down in relation to exchange rates . . . Within a very short time all measures here are to be limited to native or metric standards. All other measures, including inch rulers, must be handed in for destruction. We are wondering what happens to milk bottles!

This looks like a good day for golf and I hope to have some. At a meeting held three days back the Club decided to try to carry on. Each member who can is supposed to pay a million toward the excess profit tax which the club is being asked to pay on money it was compelled to bring in from Hong Kong to meet expenses. "Can you top this?"

Later, same day. We are having our neighborhood evening show down below in the next yard. Every worker on this place will attend "or else." It consists of speeches, music, loud speaker, the same three or four songs repeated over and over ad nauseam. These affairs go on for hours and I pity the people who sit immediately in front of the loud speaker.

NOVEMBER 6, 1951 (TO D. & H.)

We are turning our eyes toward the United Nations general meeting in Paris these days. It is to be hoped that something big is in the wind. They are talking about a new move for world peace which is to begin within the next few days. Unless a more reasonable attitude is shown by the Soviet Union I can't see how anything can be done short of brute force. It may be that the weight of the United States Defense Production may be sufficiently great to begin making an impression.

Later—We have just listened to Truman's speech which anticipates the resolution to be put before the United Nations by the three powers, regarding a way to bring about peace. It will be interesting to see what comes of this move now that the free world is stronger. It is not easy to see how the Soviet Union can take advantage of this situation, unless she is convinced that this is her last chance. Real peace is what we all are after and what a grand thing it would be especially for China!

November 9. I was interested in the Soviet reaction to the proposal at the Paris United Nations meeting for reduction of arms. It is too bad the poor man Vishinsky could not sleep because of his desire to laugh. What he needed was a grain and a half of phenobarbital to control his laughter. Of course it should be the Parke Davis brand. I can imagine the cartoons and wise cracks which are going to be prompted by this reply to a pretty sound proposition. If it had to be rejected I am glad it was done in this asinine manner as it gives just another indication for measuring the mentality of the men with whom one must deal. In spite of this first reaction, I am sure that we are likely to hear much more about this proposal. *(D., the recipient of many of these letters, is a sales representative for Parke Davis and Company.)*

NOVEMBER 10, 1951 (TO H. S. H.)

The air waves tonight bring the first play on the Paris "laughing business." There have been no details in the vernacular regarding the three-power proposal but Vishinsky was played up big. He was greeted in the United Nations with "thundering applause," "believe it or not." I'll bet before this thing is finished Vishinsky will be sorry he laughed.

November 12. Over the week-end I have been getting a Chinese letter written to the Foreign Affairs Bureau to inform them that I cannot continue to pay my land taxes and asking for their assistance. At the moment, the land tax man is in my office talking to my secretary. He is very much disturbed that I can't pull money out from somewhere and pay up. When the lemon is dry it is dry but it is hard to convince them. The mind is single tracked! I'll let you know later in the day what I find out down at the Foreign Affairs Bureau.

A little later. Just as sometimes March "comes in like a lion and goes out like a lamb," so it was with the above-mentioned tax collector. He was very hard boiled on arrival but went out much softened and I could see no reason for it excepting that he was pleased to find that we both had a connection with St. John's University. I gained the impression that he would like me to pay what I can, when I can, with no fines for late payment. Of course he does not have the final word. In any event, my secretary and I shall make a visit to the Foreign Affairs Bureau after lunch.

Later, same day. My secretary and I went down to the Foreign Affairs Bureau this afternoon and when they saw we had a letter setting forth all we had to say, we were told we need not wait. Apparently they wish to study the whole matter before coming to a decision. I am advised not to sign over anything but let them take it. It may be that a small amount each month, without fines, will control the situation. In any event, I feel I have taken the right course to get this burden of taxes removed ... As I moved about down town today I was struck again by the many posters and plaster of Paris doves, with red bills and red feet, which are seen everywhere crying for peace. If America would only stop her aggression all would be well!

November 13. This is certainly a "chop suey" letter. All I can say for it is it reflects our daily happenings and indirectly may give you a picture of what Shanghai is like. I was impressed with the cordiality with which I was greeted in my native contacts down town yesterday. Just take the "pressures" off and you will see true colors again. I have the greatest sympathy for those who must hide them now. In the privacy of my office we always see the true ones

## 15: THE PRICE OF AUSTERITY

In the autumn of 1951 there was every evidence that the Government was beginning to feel the need for more funds with which to meet the expense of the war in Korea. Economies were being instituted on every hand. Shanghai, with its great profusion of neon lights which are splendid for spelling out signs in the Chinese characters, was usually a show place. Now, as austerity advanced, the city became darker and darker. Each night all but a few street lamps were turned off at nine o'clock. Viewed from the elevation of our ninth floor apartment, hardly a light was to be seen, and the city had the appearance of a sleeping country village. This was not the dark before the dawn, but the dark before the terror soon to come.

NOVEMBER 15, 1951 (TO H. S. H.)

Our steam heat is on for the first time today and this reminds us that at least we shall keep warm this winter. I am being allowed to meet my share of the heating as I can. Mine will be just under two hundred U.S. dollars equivalent at this unrealistic exchange of twenty-two thousand JMP to one U.S. dollar. In this connection all prices on the streets are excessive when considered on the basis of twenty-two thousand to one. For instance, a locally made shirt comes to sixty thousand JMP.

I learned yesterday that the Cathedral will probably have to be given up the last of December. They have come to the point when taxes cannot be paid. They are casting about now to find some way of "de-sanctifying" the place so it can be used for other purposes, as for instance a lecture hall for instruction in Communism. I think if I were doing it I would be more anxious about "de-contamination" later on. One of the questions raised is what to do with the pipe organ, a very good one. As I sit here I can look west to the old German Church where the cross still stands out above the highest point but it does not represent what goes on beneath. I do not subscribe to such phrases as "the last time," "never again," and similar ones used in connection with the closing activities of our old orders but believe that history teaches that sooner or later the sun will shine again on a free China.

November 18, Sunday. Just before dinner I went up for a word with A., who leaves in the morning for the North. He is being urged to head up a medical school. After spending a week going over the school situation he will go on to Peking for a conference. The whole thing is a bit sudden but he feels there is nothing else he can do but play along. As things are going now it is unlikely he will be able for long to keep his own hospital going here. Everything the hospital takes in, just about meets staff expenses and taxes. He gets his professional fees but there is a ceiling on what he can charge. No major operation can go over two million JMP, or an equivalent of about ninety U.S. dollars and most are much lower. It is the hope of "the authorities" that at some future date all hospitals, both public and private, will be under one control.

November 20. In connection with this new post for A., it is suggested by the E.N.T. man in charge, that I should be asked to go up for a three-months period as a visiting professor. Can you imagine it? Not only would it be impossible from many points of view but it would be unwise from mine.

With the increased "pressures" on the medical profession, greater emphasis is being placed on the training of the two-and-a-half year "physicians." Perhaps I should have said "doctors." They are to be trained in public health and general medicine. Some of the institutions are going in strong for this sort of thing presently and teachers are being sought everywhere. I doubt if anything more than glorified health inspectors will result but I know what will happen once they get their licenses. No private practice will be entered under present controls, but should they ever be relaxed, these men will set themselves up as full-blown physicians.

I saw W. P. on the street the other day and was shocked at his physical appearance. You may remember he is one of the six I took home in 1916 from the old Harvard Medical School of China and who later entered Harvard. He is working very hard, giving long hours to the teaching of eye diseases. Income is not what it was and the belt must be taken in. This is not an uncommon picture and it explains why the incidence of tuberculosis is greatly on the increase among men of this group. In this connection it should be noted that high blood pressure is also more frequent than I have ever known it to be with these men and some are having cerebral accidents. One has only to see the great pressures under which they work to realize how these things can happen . . . Doctor S. went over to see one of our old colleagues this afternoon about his back and found that he has given up his office practice since he must spend so much time in institutional work. This is all just part of the same picture.

You have watched a colony of ants running about, all busy at something, but what it is all about is not apparent. So it is here. I see it down in the Club next door where young people are being trained in gymnastics. One group was at it all day with their lunch served to them on the field. There seemed a bit of nervousness about the whole show. When rest periods come, apparently no one is able to sit still for long. For instance, when they sat in circles during the lunch period first one and then another would jump up and run to get more food. (It is the running that is noticeable in this picture.) If one is so full of life and the "joy of living" as one must be in this state, one must run and always remember to smile!

November 21. As I have said to you before we are a city of megaphones now, and you would be surprised at how much volume can be produced by a bunch of men down on the street directing traffic with these things. Like a small boy with a new popgun these police officers dance around in all directions shouting to the poor pedicab men who haven't the slightest notion of what they are doing incorrectly. We can hear them way up here on the ninth floor.

NOVEMBER 23, 1951 (TO D. &. H.)

Everything goes on much as usual with us. Tomorrow I go down to the Foreign Affairs Bureau to consult them about my land. I cannot continue to pay taxes. The Pearce Road land has already been taken and divided and what happens to the rest is most uncertain. Many people are in the same boat, both natives and foreigners. These matters will have to be left to the future for final settlement. Here's hoping our own Government will back us up when the time comes. We must also register all our holdings by the 30th of the month. We must turn in our old Consular deeds and a receipt is probably all we'll get in return.  There is no other way of dealing with this matter at present.

NOVEMBER 28, 1951 (TO H. S. H.)
Yesterday I went down with a friend and registered my Columbia Road and Lincoln Road properties.  We had a very kindly man take care of us and had no difficulty.  I have been advised to lease the Lincoln Road piece for a small factory so as to get some income from it as well as to protect it.  There is no water on that road and that may prove a difficulty.  Also it may not be in a factory area.  I have been advised to let yours rest without registration as calling attention to it now will mean further taxes.

Field day exercises have been held in the old French Club grounds.  They are interesting to watch as they include such a variety of events.  Of course there are the races usually seen at such gatherings but to these are added jumping the rope, some form of dropping the handkerchief with people in a circle, leap frog, tug of war, throwing a small stick, throwing a small heavy ball and, of course, the usual broad jumping.  Great emphasis is now being put on physical culture.

November 29.  Last week we had a medical meeting at which I was asked to preside in place of T., who has gone with A. to the Northwest.  We had three papers presented on "tissue transplantation," the new thing which has come out of Russia.  I am wondering if this has reached the United States and what is thought of it.  Tissue is taken from animals and placed in a refrigerator at low temperature.  When it is to be used it is taken out and autoclaved to sterilize it before inserting it under the skin, usually just below the ribs.  All sorts of "cures" are said to be obtained by this treatment.  Scar tissue is especially susceptible to tissue transplantation and two cases were presented the other night to demonstrate.  Asthma is supposed to be cured in some people.  Chronic gastric ulcers and leg ulcers are supposedly cured.  Some of the actions suggested what I believe has been found in the A.C.T.H. treatment.  There have been many failures of course, but the good results make one inquire into it a bit.  If it does nothing else with some it does help pay the office overhead!  You can understand how a thing of this sort would catch on with the natives.  *(This "tissue transplantation" treatment continued for a time in Shanghai and then because of many failures lost its popularity.  A Soviet colleague told me that he thought it had been started in Russia to make up for the great lack of medicines, and this certainly could explain its popu-*

larity in China as well, although we understood that a definite directive had been given that it was to be used in China.)

6 p.m., same day. Please thank the Clan and especially Dr. MacDougal for their generous expressions of appreciation in regard to the "serials" which come along from time to time. I must call attention to the fact, however, that no record can be properly reproduced unless the amplifier is of the best quality and for that they will agree I have a mouthpiece of the first water. I am sure they do not under-estimate your interpretations and I for one would enjoy hearing them. *(H.S.H. served as "amplifier" by reading the serial letters from Shanghai and interpreting them to the assembled Clan at their weekly luncheon meeting.)*

Field days are all the rage just now and it seems to me that much of the students' time must be taken up in this manner. There is no doubt that much is to be gained by increasing the physical well-being of this group but one would like to see the calories of some other groups increased. Diseased conditions incident to the undernourished are causing concern.

I have just had a long session with the tax man who thinks we are farther back on our tax than our records show. He is willing to reduce a bit on properties which the army used, but for the rest is hard boiled. He says all Americans have money but I tell him here is one who does not. He gives me a week to think of a way to produce fourteen millions. I told him he could have my reply now which was that I did not have the money and he could confiscate the properties. But they don't want this property. If I could just sell everything and get out with nothing but what we stand up in, I would be happy. Sorry to end on this sour note.

DECEMBER 11, 1951 (To H. S. H.)

A. came back from Peking a week ago and I have seen him briefly just once for a talk. He states that the Peking Union Medical College and Hospital are being kept fairly clean but the place is crowded not only with patients but students as well. Many short courses are being given and the staff is working very hard on reduced salaries. They are all supposed to "work more and eat less" he says. I'll get a more complete picture from him within the next few days.

December 12. As we looked down upon the city some months back it had the appearance of a lighted Christmas tree. In some ways it reminded us of San Francisco when viewed from the east. Now we must reduce lighting, and also the use of our refrigerator for part of the

# THE PRICE OF AUSTERITY

day. The city is not so brilliantly lighted as there is some difficulty, I believe, in getting enough coal into the city for the power plant. There seems to be enough, however, for heating.

I had a long conference with the tax man yesterday afternoon at a time when I had expected to play golf. He was very nice and I think I finally convinced him that my only chance of meeting the tax demands is to rent my properties for enough to provide sums to do so. It is an interesting state of affairs when one hopes to get just enough out of properties to pay taxes. We parted on a friendly note as he described to me noises which he has in his ears and I agreed to give him a complete examination the next time he comes.

December 17. All the news I can pick up from the radio gives only slight hope for a better world, but some signs of unrest about us are indicative of something which may not be entirely to the liking of those on top. A deeper austerity is operating now than at any time. The need for funds must be growing steadily. *(The above refers to the growing popular resentment against Communists.)*

DECEMBER 19, 1951 (TO H. S. H.)

I tried to see A. last evening but he was caught up in a meeting, possibly something in connection with his proposed move to the Northwest. He will go again in the spring for another study and then if all is well will move up in the summer. He appears to be getting a bit fed up with the "pressures" in this area. He will try to rent his hospital, which interests me since I have placed certain equipment there. And speaking of hospitals, our one remaining foreign-controlled hospital is closing very shortly. The British Community Interest Committee is arranging to lease an entire floor in one of the best run of our private Chinese hospitals, the Tah Wha, and I am supposed to have something to do about allocation of beds. We are to have eight to ten beds. It is remarkable how we keep fighting to preserve some facilities for the remaining few.

Waiting, waiting, waiting! For what? Shops full of electrical appliances, garages full of stored cars! Numerous small dealers with their places jammed with cars for sale. Hotels empty; their staffs stand around doing nothing. Doctors in private offices playing chess to pass the time between patients. Foreign big business men killing time with a good book or a game of cards. Streets full of people just walking but not buying. All conversation usually coming around to "wishful thinking." What of the future? *(Doctors didn't play chess long. One by one they were forced to assist in "State medicine.")*

When one is in the forest only the trees can be seen and so it is with us, both native and foreign. We hang on our radios and any bits of news which can throw light on what is passing and what might come to pass. I suspect we are more urgent in our searching than many of you who have free air to breathe each day . . . I am told that Sunday, Christmas services are to be conducted in at least three churches and that there will be a Christmas play at the Community Church. One wonders if the latter will be straightforward or warped. There is no evidence of Christmas on the streets, with the exception of a very few trees at flower shops and an occasional Russian store.

December 21. There is some hope that I shall be able to rent the Lincoln Road property for enough to pay taxes. It is remarkable that all one can get in rentals must go out immediately for other "people," a state of affairs which is not alone confined to my properties. This in part shows why some hope for the new day. Incidentally, some of Shanghai's biggest structures are being rented only for taxes and upkeep. The American School property and buildings are on that basis. Big business houses will be compelled to do the same thing . . . As I came along the street last evening I saw very few Christmas trees about, and those few looked very lonely!

December 22. Saturday and a very rainy day and no golf! Unless the wind shifts into the north we are in for a wet week-end. Therapeutic doses of golf will be missed by any number who need weekly amounts to keep them on an even keel . . . I examined a young woman of 38, a native, who is pretty near the breaking point following the final departure of her husband from this world through no desire of his own. *(It was in this period that "pressures" on individuals and organizations began to be intense. As a result there were many executions and suicides.)*

I took a walk last evening over to Bubbling Well Road and up past the old Bubbling Well Cemetery. I was primarily interested in seeing how much Christmas spirit was about. Here and there a few shops had timid decorations and along out by the Cemetery wall were several hundred trees, mostly in pots or with roots instead of the usual branches fixed up on a wood base. Belatedly, the shops near at hand on Avenue Joffre were putting out Christmas things, probably following the lead of some courageous soul. Christmas cards are not in evidence but a number of local ones from natives came in this morning along with yours. People whom we have not heard from for months, sent cards. Also eatables, in the form of chicken and cakes, are pouring in. This is where some of my free patients get a chance to express their gratitude.

A native friend was lamenting yesterday that the usual family and friend visiting among them is not being done any more. Incidentally, much of the social life in the homes has disappeared. Children and servitors provide quick transmission to the sources of all control. *(Children and servants were questioned by the authorities regarding matters discussed within the family circle.)*

As I went along last night I was impressed by the large number of second hand shops which have opened up recently. Most of their goods were household possessions not so long ago. *(Shops of a similar nature were found all over the city; they were called "Consignment Stores." Articles were left there to be sold at a price set by the owner plus a mark-up for the storekeeper. If no customer would buy at that price, they were taken back into the owner's house. During this period there was a great need on the part of the population for funds to purchase food stuffs.)*

December 24. And still Christmas cards keep coming in! It appears that the Day is finally approaching, with the tree set up in the living room. Outside a special point is being made to keep people at work. My crowd will take not only this holiday but anything of a legal nature which comes along.

DECEMBER 24, 1951 (TO D. & H.)

S. finally got a little tree and it is now nicely decorated out in the other room. Around it and near it on the mantelpiece, above an artificial fireplace, are packages and cards sent in by friends we have not heard from for months. Patients who have been treated free during the year are sending in small remembrances. It is all very heartening and shows the Christmas spirit has not entirely left the city.

Later, same day. It is after a Christmas Eve dinner to which two of S.'s boy friends were invited. We had some good pheasant but the apple pie was terrible. I think our cook served an English mistress too long. And now our living room is loaded down with fruit, cakes, flowers and cards but no chocolates. Why? They cost too much. A pound of sweet chocolate was priced by a friend at the equivalent of six U.S. dollars. A pound of chocolate creams ranges from five to ten U.S. dollars. This is an imported item which is not coming in and if one wants chocolate he must pay for it. As a matter of fact, all prices are up.

Christmas Day. Lunch and the tree are over and someone did send in a two-pound box of chocolates! There is fruit and cake enough to last a month and much of it from patients whom I have seen without charge ... I had a long talk with my tax man yesterday who finally agreed to settle my taxes without any fine if I can pay before next Tuesday, the first day of the New Year. Since the rental of the Lincoln Road property probably will take a month longer to arrange I must borrow to meet this deadline. I think I shall be able to do so. It is all miserable business and it hardly seems worth while to try and hold on to the property when one knows that if the "present order" holds, it will all go in the end. *(As a matter of fact, I was compelled to pay taxes and would not have been allowed to leave Communist China without doing so.)*

The big day for the "new order" is coming on New Year's Day—not the old Chinese New Year but the calendar New Year. Very little is being done in the way of preparations. There is an austerity program on just now and everyone is expected to conserve. Even the tram company is feeling it as many people are walking short distances instead of riding.

## 16: IDEOLOGICAL REFORM AND SELF-CRITICISM

Up until the fall of 1951 the colleges and universities in China had been permitted to carry on with little interference. Suddenly an all-out campaign was started to convert all educational institutions into political centers and technical training schools. In order to accomplish this it was necessary to destroy freedom of thought among the teachers and indoctrinate them with the Communist ideology.

Educational institutions in China had been centers for liberal thought and progress and teachers and students had been in the vanguard of all recent revolutionary movements. Now the Communists had turned on them with the avowed purpose of destroying all independent thinking.

A mass meeting of several thousand professors and instructors was addressed by Chou En-lai in Peking in late September, 1951, and they were told what their "attitude" should be toward the new ideology. Following this meeting the educators were required to read Communist literature and hold discussion groups. These discussion periods laid great stress on criticism of others and self-criticism. Many hours were spent in such meetings and many lasted late into the night. It was at this period that every staff member was required to write out his life history beginning at the age of eight. These histories had to be complete and it was evident that these histories gave the Communists information about some individuals who were later to be eliminated.

Many educators who had been warned by what had happened, first in the universities of North China, were able to escape to Hong Kong.

Others, however, especially those in administrative positions, were helpless and had to submit to criticism which in some cases resulted in their dismissal or arrest. The head of one large university was publicly accused by his own daughter of having "been a hypocrite" and a "faithful tool of American imperialism." This man is believed to be under arrest at the present time, if he has not been executed.

And now these same tortured minds were introduced to the "three anti's." This movement was started in August, 1951, in Manchuria, for the purpose of rooting out the three evils of "corruption, waste and bureaucratism in the government." The "ideological reform" had been planned to run for only four months, but because of the resistance some educators put up against being "reformed," the three anti's movement was invoked to force them to submit.

When this campaign struck, virtually all university activities came to a standstill. The professors with the "help" of their students devoted most of their time to denunciations and confessions. The students took the initiative in this affair and many were out to pull down administrators and staff members who could be accused of "waste," "corruption," or being offensive in office. The charges were usually fabricated. Much hysteria was evident in the students' accusatory meetings.

Many accounts were current regarding public and semi-public denunciations. Prominent educators were humiliated before their accusing students and in some instances, were spat upon. It is little wonder that some of China's best known teachers broke under the strain and "confessed" to faults of which they could not have been guilty. Nor is it surprising that some committed suicide.

It is not to be concluded that the Communists have completely "reformed" the institutions of higher learning in China. The "pressure" of the two campaigns, "ideological reform" and "three anti's," has been relaxed for the time being, but since there are many educators who are merely giving lip service to the "reform," it is certain that another attack will be made upon them.

It is also possible that the educational institutions were left only partially "reformed" because of the urgent need to institute the "three anti's," expanded into the "five anti's," which were directed specifically against the merchant class. The grave financial situation consequent on the Korean war required funds which could come only from China's shopkeepers.

DECEMBER 29, 1951 (TO H. S. H.)

I am just in from down town where I was able to secure my last six millions for my taxes. Now we are going ahead, bending every effort to secure a good paying tenant for Lincoln Road. If we are able to do this, the "pressure" put on me by the tax man will have been a good thing. As usual the gardener who has been on the place for several years is demanding an exorbitant price for moving off, even when he has had a goodly part of the place for ten years to farm free of all charges. Squatters rights! The courts are always on the side of the "people" so we must make a deal.

As I passed along the Nanking Road this morning I got the impression that anti-American propaganda is getting tired. There is not nearly so much of it and much less attention is being paid to it by the natives. Very little is being done to prepare for the New Year's holiday which is almost upon us. The present austerity program is having an effect. It is possible that this move at this time is for the purpose of steadying the currency.

I was out to T.'s last night for an executive meeting of the Shanghai Medical Society after which he gave us what he called an ordinary meal but which as usual was far beyond anyone's ordinary capacity. It is remarkable how we continue to keep this Society going. With us last night were men of varying thoughts regarding the "present order" so conversation was rather restricted.

December 30. The news in our community this morning is that three Texaco Oil men, the last remaining here, have been given their exit permits and are probably leaving immediately. I have just had M. on the phone and he thinks they may be getting away within two weeks, providing his staff does not put up an objection. Some have been stopped at the train on some pretext. As more and more of our important business men leave, one detects an uneasiness in the minds of some natives over the severing of ties with the West. When one sees how flimsy the thread is which binds them to the Northwest, this is easy to understand. If a householder sees all his supplies going out with little coming in there arrives a time of concern over the future. Some natives think that this state of affairs may not be far off. There certainly are some very unhappy trade people about.

December 31, Monday. The last day! And still there is little indication that a New Year celebration is to take place. This may be due to austerity which is being pushed very hard just now, as I said above.

A German business man was just in as a patient and when I asked him how his business was, he said that they were doing nothing and he saw no possibility for the future. Government owned organizations including wholesale and retail establishments are driving all others from the field. It is probable that this period will see many shops closing. A most unhappy people!

January 1, 1952. I had intended to send this off yesterday but neglected to do so when I went up west to see an old Chinese friend who is soon to have an operation. I had not seen him for many months but when he sent word by his daughter that he would like to see me, of course I went. He did not seem so cast down about the present general situation but it may be that along with many others he has become resigned even when their hatred of it is intense. He said that he did not think austerity played any part in the lack of interest in New Year celebrations but people were too apathetic to care. This year the holiday is to be only one day as against two last year and three the year before that. He feels the business situation is very grave. His people will be more interested in the old Chinese New Year that comes the 27th of this month.

After this visit I walked back along Great Western Road and dropped in on Sir R., who incidentally is trying to close out his business. He has already applied for an exit permit. He told me he had not placed an order of any sort for imports since early October and since he must bring out three hundred pounds a month to keep his staff and office going he must watch his step as there is very little at home that he can draw on. When it is certain in the minds of his staff there is nothing more to be had, he'll be allowed to close. This experience has been repeated time and time again, not only by foreigners but native business organizations as well. "When it is dark enough you can see the stars," wrote Charles Beard and one could conclude without going very far afield from where I sit that it is certainly dark enough just now but as I have said to you before the only stars we can see are colored. Perhaps it must get even darker before we can see the bright ones, but for the sake of these people I hope their appearance will not be too long delayed. If a bright star appears over Europe you might expect to see changes out this way.

JANUARY 3, 1952 (TO D. & H.)

With the closing of first one and then another foreign business it is remarkable that so many people continue to hang on. We are losing three more American business men next week. They leave behind them properties worth hundreds of thousands of dollars, of the solid sort, to what end no one knows. In the long look ahead it must be clear even to the extremists that sooner or later traffic with the West will have to be renewed. One of the greatest handicaps to present business is the inability of the country to secure raw materials from abroad.

January 7. Russian Christmas. I have just had a Russian patient who because of her contact with the West indulges in Christmas on both the 25th of December and the Russian date. Last night as I came along there was a last minute rush for trees by our remaining small colony of White Russians who now number about three thousand as against thirty thousand a number of years back.

January 8. We were out to a tea party held last evening for the Canadian Consul General who is leaving shortly for home following the closing of their office here. I doubt if there are more than a half dozen Canadians left. Incidentally, the overseas Americans are down to about thirty in the business community and an equal number in the missionary group including Catholics. It was interesting to see the type of persons still here. Of course most are British, some of whom have been allowed to come in within recent months. Three Americans are leaving this morning by train for Hong Kong via Canton. *(With the closing of the Port of Shanghai all persons leaving Shanghai went by rail to Tientsin. Later, when the through railway to Canton was completed, this route was used.)*

I have been most interested in the reviews of the year just passed and forecasts for the future which have been coming in from overseas by air. England's No. 1 thinks there are "solid" hopes for peace and said so in Washington. I hope he is right. On the whole it would appear that the free world is building up strength at a fairly rapid rate and the chances of a real dust up do not seem so near. Unless the other side is a bunch of utter fools one would not expect them to attempt anything.

JANUARY 7, 1953 (TO H. S. H.)

Your letter of December 23rd came in night before last. The Clan seems to have been indulging in our favorite indoor sport—that of trying to find areas of peace and hope. When he arrived in America I was glad to have Churchill say that there were "solid" prospects for peace in 1952. It seems to me as I listen to the reviews from both sides of the Atlantic that the areas of strength which Acheson has been recommending are beginning to have effect. It may be that some of the effects are being witnessed out this way. It is not easy to put one's finger on such things, but those of us living within the forest see some of the trees bending a little more to western winds.

A native friend who moves freely about said to me the other night that peace in the northeast, that is Korea, is greatly desired but "pressures" are great from outside against it. The new austerity move may be a deeper thing than we realize. *(He meant that the Reds in Peking wanted peace but the Soviets did not.)*

Only Arabic numerals appear on our locally made desk pads for 1952, together with Chinese characters for months and days instead of the usual English. I must renew my acquaintance with Chinese characters. It is of interest to see billboard advertisements where the former trademark was mostly in English. Now since all must be in the vernacular, the old trade-mark also appears but with thin pieces of wood nailed in an X across it or two lines of the paint brush making an X, supposedly cancelling it out but placed on with sufficient care to preserve the real character of what lies beneath. The first time I saw this I thought it was a mistake but its recurrence in several different parts of the city indicates its real nature.

I picked up an old *Time* magazine for January, 1949, after lunch today and read some of the comments which a number of former missionaries in China had made at a missionary conference. They would be amazed at how completely some things have changed since their words were published three years ago. One man was most realistic when he said "I've got more hope than I've got faith." Our old Community Church members are now "urged" to sign a promise not to associate with Americans. This is interesting in view of the fact that virtually every cent which went into the building and Sunday School came from Americans. You may remember that in all prayer books there is usually an intercession for the Chief of State. We can stand that from our preachers but when to it is added a request that help be given for the purpose of combatting American imperialism and aggression, then some walk out.

Mencius says: "It is better not to have the Book of History if we believe everything in it." One wonders what things the historians will pick up during this age to describe what goes forward. Some things certainly will be hard to believe. In searching the records, however, the historians for this period should have an easy time since the pattern in all "liberated" areas of the world has been the same. I am impressed with this fact as I read articles written two and three years back covering situations such as ours but located in Europe.

JANUARY 11, 1952 (TO H. S. H.)

Your letter of December 30th came in yesterday with flap poorly stuck down but still intact and undisturbed as far as I can see. All recent epistles from overseas still contain their original atmosphere.

The B.B.C. radio said this evening that beginning February 1st all letters in and out of China would be searched, presumably for currency. You may be seeing some disturbed flaps shortly as a result of this. I'm not clear as to who is to do this searching. Until one sees where this leads I must be as innocuous as possible.

JANUARY 15, 1952 (TO H. S. H.)

I must start a letter to you on my birthday since you have helped me celebrate a number of them in the past. I am also reminded to write to you as Mrs. Z. has just brought in a big basket of the famous honey oranges, and just as she was leaving she wanted me to send greetings to you both from Z. D. and herself. We had not seen her for months but have understood how difficult it is for them to get in. Mrs. Z., like all other wives of physicians, is required to do a great deal of district work.

January 17. I was told last evening that A. may be leaving for the northwest in March. I was not able to see him as he was in a meeting. This has been the case twice lately when I have tried to talk with him and I am told that much of his time these days is so spent. When the history of this period is written "meetings" will play a prominent part. "Cerebrum washing" is an important matter in putting over any project. I'll be interested in what happens to A.

January 18. S. went down town yesterday, his first trip in weeks and on his return said that the thing which struck him was the few foreigners about. We get more over in this part of town, where the Russians live. A Russian friend told me yesterday that only about twenty-five hundred Russians still remain. They are all very much worried just at the moment as virtually all of them get their support directly or indirectly from British and American firms. Some are afraid of being sent back to Russia. Some must be in pretty poor condition as an unusual number are mendicants on the street. *(Most were, of course, White Russians.)*

Austerity is gradually darkening our city lights so that when we look toward the business quarter from this height it is no longer pleasing. From other points of view it is also not pleasing.

JANUARY 24, 1952 (TO D. & H.)

Chinese New Year comes next Sunday, the 27th, and it would appear that more preparations are being made to celebrate it than the recent holidays just past. There will be three days' holiday, after Sunday, the most that have been taken for a long time. It seems to me that there can be seen in this renewed interest an attempt to bring back some of old China at a time when so much is being cast aside.

You will be interested in the test being given the motor car drivers in our fair city. A rather strict physical is first given. The most frequent stumbling block being the hearing test. This is done entirely with a watch. If a man is not able to hear the watch at one meter he is out. Lately I have had two men who were thrown out in that manner. I did audiometer tests and found that one man could not possibly have heard a watch at any distance since he had wartime traumatic deafness for the 4098 frequency. However, for all other frequencies he was perfectly normal. With my audiogram, he was able to pass the second time. A second man had a very similar defect but I have not heard if he has passed on a second attempt. They say the driving test is also rather hard. Many native drivers will fail on the hearing test alone. No license will be given to a man wishing to start driving after fifty-five. Some beyond that age can get an extension of one year when they already hold the license but must pass the test.

This evening I go to a medical meeting and dinner down at the old French Club which I can see from where I sit writing. The Club is a hollow shell as far as activities are concerned and would like to close but the staff will not permit this move. This is the usual story, as everyone knows now, since even if one does get good severance pay, it is soon gone and there are no new jobs. It is a most unhappy situation! Our medical society has a mixture of all nationalities. One, a German, is having his last meeting with us tonight and in a week or so starts off with his family for Canada, where he has a teaching post in pathology.

JANUARY 25, 1952 (TO H. S. H.)

We had a very fine meeting of our Shanghai Medical Society last evening over at the old and almost defunct French Club. There were eight foreign doctors, one French, two German, four Russians and one American. The four Russians were of varying tints but mostly white. Two very good papers were presented which showed among other things that our young men are keeping abreast of the times. One very appropriate paper was on coronary thrombosis which lately is on the increase. The man reporting thought the present nervous tensions might have something to do with the present increase. Certainly we are having more high blood pressures and cerebral accidents than anyone out here has ever seen before. We are attempting to keep this society going, especially for the English-speaking young doctors. They want it very much and need it. It is a shame that men who have so much to contribute to modern medicine must spend so much time in political discussions.

The "third movement" of our great symphony is now being played and it is being received with great pleasure by everyone. In it the singers, both soloists and choir, join in a mighty "confessional" anthem which is truly remarkable in its far-reaching effect. I don't know if you have this record in your collection but should you turn it up you'll be interested in playing the first two movements again. The first as you will remember depicted the populace as bringing their silver and gold to the King in order to make possible the future all were wishing for. The second was very similar to the first but entailed the holding of the resources of the populace in a safe place for future use. The choruses covering these various acts were brilliant and done in superb harmonies. Please do a "Malik" on this paragraph. *(A "Malik" meant to take the opposite meaning. The "third movement" had reference to the "three anti's" movement which was soon to merge into the "five anti's.")*

Later, same day. It is 10:45 p.m. of a Saturday night, Chinese New Year's Eve, but as yet the usual firecrackers have been few. I suspect it is the austerity program and not any regulations which cause this silence. We have just had an hour and a half of good speeches and other things over the "Voice of America." Acheson was in good form regarding the "point four" program. I know some people around here who hate to be left out of this. It is hard to see how wordy promises in posters of a period of plenty just around the corner can long sustain those in need. Many are to be seen here and there is great need of what it takes to sustain life. Fortunately it has not been too cold at night for sleeping out of doors.

January 30. Your letter of January 21st came in late this afternoon, making good time. Your new envelopes do not have their flaps well caught down excepting for about three inches of the top. Microscopically it can be demonstrated that the closing is virgin. There just does not seem to appear to be enough salivary secretion in the original sealing. The stamps are also not well stuck on. I think it must be the paper which refuses the glue.

January 31. Things seem to be getting back to normal on the

street after the four-day holiday. It appears to me that people let themselves go in celebrating as best they could in the old way. There is a desire to retain something of the old whenever possible. This I consider a part of the turning tide.

FEBRUARY 4, 1952 (TO H. S. H.)

We are having most difficult reception from the U. S. just now and the schedule has been so rearranged that as yet we can't catch up with it. The atmospheric conditions at present must be very bad as only nearby stations can be heard. We get everything we want, however, from BBC via Singapore to keep us up to date. Some progress seems to be coming out of Korea but it is very slow.

I have been making a study of termites lately but my reference books do not give me all the information I want. Perhaps you can help me. I want to know if the termites which build the high ant hills seen in some countries are the same as those which attack wood. Is there any data on the number of ants in a hill? I am interested in finding out what situations may arise which will make the colony leave the ant hill. Is there ever any conflict between the various members?

These questions arise out of a discussion which I have had recently with a Chinese friend. He remembers from some courses which he had in college in the U. S. that on occasion individual ant hills might be completely destroyed by internecine conflict. An observer notes that what was apparently a harmonious whole suddenly begins to show disintegration. From various exit points dead ants appear as they are expelled by the living from within. He suggests that these discarded members of the colony had attempted to get more than their share of the common stores. He is confident that the entire colony can destroy itself in a matter of months. I would appreciate any light you can throw on this matter. *(The above two paragraphs were wholly cryptic because they referred to difficulties in the government and pressures which were taking place with regard to some of its own members. In other words a purge which preceded the "five anti's movement.")*

In one of your letters you were asking the date of our first arrival in China. It was in July, 1911, just three months before the birth of the Republic and the disappearance of the queue. I remember so well riding along Great Western Road and looking into the wide open barber shops where queues hung on the wall in rows. I think few monarchies have passed with as little bloodshed. History has a way of repeating itself and I know many who think the "cap" can go the way of the queue. *(The Communist "cap" is meant. The queue, of course, refers to the long braid of hair worn by Chinese men before 1911.)*

And speaking of "caps," I am interested that some of my patients who wear the ubiquitous uniform of this day which includes a specially designed cap, find it most difficult to take it off in my examining chair. Apparently it must be worn at all times. It is rather a nice looking uniform if it is not worn too long.

Later, same day. Up to this point you will note that all the stalks of my thoughts, like those of a field of wheat, are bending in the same direction. I think that it is a natural habit of some of us these days. Perhaps we have single-track minds or perhaps it is just wishful thinking. Time of course will tell but I am inclined to the thought that tides can also be in operation near at hand. *(At just that period the situation for Chinese on the mainland seemed so dark that there were widespread hopes that Communism would lose out.)*

February 6. And again wind with rain in the east, no golf—terrible! . . . Suddenly last evening our signals from the "Voice of America" cleared and we were brought up to date on home-side opinions. I was especially interested in the summing up of things accomplished in Paris. I trust the tide will set in with full force.

February 7. Shortly after seven last evening we had the news of King George's death. It comes as a surprise as last reports seemed to indicate that he was making good progress.

Dr. P., S., and I went to a movie yesterday, my first in over two years, and saw a very fine troupe of jugglers and acrobats sent to Russia from China and filmed in color. It was one of the best shows of the sort which I have ever seen. The whirling saucer men put on a show which was probably an eye opener to the audience. I can just imagine how popular such a show would be in America if it could get there, I mean if the troupes in fact would give their shows in New York or Chicago. I don't think I should want to play to such an audience as those we saw in the film, they were too stiff.

FEBRUARY 10, 1952 (TO H. S. H.)

We have broken out into clear sunshine this Sunday morning and I am living for my game of golf this afternoon. We were out yesterday afternoon and found the course a bit wet but it should be much better today. The number of players is being constantly reduced and it is a question as to how long the Club can continue. Certain business interests are helping when it comes to overhead in order to provide a place of relaxation for their men still in Shanghai.

I have just had Tokyo on and there seems to be some indication that talks in Korea may be showing some progress. The firm stand is the only one which will make for a solution. Egypt looks definitely better.

February 11. I don't remember if I have used an envelope like this one at any previous time. My secretary bought them some time back but I have preferred the regular ones. I trust the dove will carry this letter safely and that it may stand the strain of inspection. *(This was an air mail envelope in which the red dove of peace was imprinted on the outside, an emblem which was appearing everywhere on shop windows and billboards at that time in Shanghai.)*

Down on a flat roof several stories below where I sit writing, is a discarded piece of stove pipe which is being blown first in one direction and then in another by a high wind. At times it goes almost to the coping surrounding the roof, but I am interested that it repeatedly comes back to the center of the roof. In some ways this is a symbol of what one sees these days in China. The low retaining barrier of the coping, which prevents the piece of pipe from rolling to final destruction, might be likened to the deep-down moral fiber of a people which prevents a truculent wind from having its way. We can observe such a coping in operation and pray it will stand the test!

Just before Chinese New Year we were on the point of getting a renter for our Lincoln Road property, which would have given us enough to meet taxes and have a little, a very little, left over. Now with so much self-evaluation going on no one has any mind for such matters. You remember a time when land was a good investment. Now it is a liability. One wonders if it is necessary to destroy in order to rebuild.

February 12. There was once a Great Personality who wished to have a bitter cup passed from Him. In talking to A. last evening I gained the impression that he also dreaded the approaching hour of decision. It is his hope along with some others about him that some alteration in things may occur so he won't have to go north. He does not sleep well at night.

This has been quite an office day. I have had seven patients; the final and total income from them will be 50,000 JMP, or the equivalent of roughly two and a half dollars U.S. A colleague told me yesterday that more than half his patients were free. It is remarkable what "austerity" can do.

I wonder if you have ever read the article in the March 18, 1950, issue of the *Saturday Evening Post* on the Sheltons: "America's Bloodiest Gang." I have just been reading it tonight for the first time. Gradually I am devouring everything between the covers of our old issues as nothing recent is coming in. You probably remember that my home was in Central Illinois and so this gang affair was just south of where I was brought up. I was rather impressed by the harmony of the two groups which first made up the larger gang and how later they began fighting between themselves. I suspect that is true of all gangs but fighting starts earlier in some than in others. It is just possible that some near at hand may be showing signs of internal unrest but again this may be only wishful thinking. *(There were signs at that time that there were disagreements among the ruling class in Communist China.)*

February 13. Your letter of February 3rd with virgin flap came in this morning making the usual good time.

We listened again to the "third movement" of the great symphony, number 52. It is truly a soul-stirring affair and carries one out of this world—many before their time. If you have not as yet listened to this "movement" or do not have it in your collection you should make an attempt to turn it up somewhere. It is very popular with us at the moment, I suspect because it portrays the current vicissitudes of merchants of this day and age. The horn work is especially good though a bit windy at times. It is like a great stream down which strains of music come out of the remote past, with every intention of going on and on. But at regular and irregular points in the stream cross currents appear in an attempt to check and finally change the old stream for one entirely foreign in tempo. I have not as yet heard the "fourth movement," perhaps you have, but I think we shall find that cross currents have not been successful in changing the theme with which the "third movement" was started.

February 14. I have just reread this to see if it is clear enough for you to make it out. I have come to the conclusion that it is like an imperfectly cracked walnut and you will have to take a pick and sometimes a "malik" to get the meat out. Knowing your ability I am sure you will succeed in getting most of the nuts.

## 17: THE FIVE "ANTI'S"

As early as December, 1951, a meeting of merchants in Shanghai was called by the authorities to advise them that a drive was being made to eradicate some of their corrupt practices and urging any of those guilty to "confess." In January, after a speech by Chou En-lai in Peking opening the propaganda attack against business men, a public appeal was made to the people to denounce "cheating" merchants and industrialists. Denunciations were to be sent into a central committee and informers were to be protected. Boxes were also attached to official billboards throughout the city to facilitate the collection of denunciations. The campaign had the five-fold purpose of being anti-bribery, anti-waste, anti-bureaucratism, anti-tax evasion, and anti-stealing of state property.

A vast number of denunciations came in and were analyzed and studied in preparation for the attacks which were to be made on the business men. In the meantime clerks, shop assistants, and workers were being trained for their part in the campaign, that of interrogating and harassing shop owners, proprietors of business organizations, and factory managers. At the same time all business men were warned not to leave the city or alter their books in any way. Business was completely stopped, but all staffs, many of them in the interrogating group, had to have their wages paid regularly.

Toward the end of March 1952, Mayor Ch'en Yi of Shanghai formally endorsed the campaign although it had been in operation for some time. There was great fear that the merchants would be eliminated just as had been done with the landlords. The Mayor assured them that this would not be the case and urged them to "confess" if they were guilty of any of the "five poisons." The merchant was expected to "confess" to one or more "poisons" and ask that suitable punishment be imposed upon him.

And then the interrogators really went to work. Once a man had freely confessed, usually to things of which he was not guilty, a report was sent to a central committee and there the matter rested until he was notified of his fine. Most times it was so enormous that it took his entire cash reserves and properties to meet it. The man who resisted came in for some rough mental treatment. He might be kept awake for hours by relays of interrogators repeating over and over the same accusations until he finally "confessed" or committed suicide perhaps by jumping out of a window. Some of our friends went that way.

During all this time scurrilous propaganda posters appeared on our walls and shop windows, replacing anti-American posters of a similar nature. Also, there appeared in show windows papier-mache effigies of merchants, usually with bulging waist bands and money sticking out of their pockets. One such effigy had a foot on the neck of a kneeling clerk.

It has been pointed out by one who was familiar with the Communists' schedule for reorganizing all China that this attack on private enterprise was not supposed to come until at least ten years after they had gained control of the country. It was his belief that the schedule had been revised due to the Government's need for solid money to prosecute the war in Korea. It was an open secret that the Chinese populace, almost to a man, had hidden away silver dollars, gold bars, gold bracelets, gold rings (even our servants had some), and American bank notes. It was such solid currency and gold that the Government was after in making its drive against the merchants. It was a clever and diabolical scheme and it worked in this manner. Shanghai was a commercial city and everyone in it was directly or indirectly connected with its various enterprises. When the merchants and industrialists were accused of business irregularities and fined such astronomical sums that all visible cash and sometimes their properties disappeared in payment, the currency left in circulation was almost at the vanishing point. We saw it in private practice when patients brought in chickens, eggs, and other produce to pay for treatments. The inevitable happened. People had to have money with which to buy food so they began turning in their gold, silver, and

American bank notes in exchange for the Communist currency, the same currency which had been taken from the pockets of the merchants. Long lines were to be seen around the banks making the exchange, and these continued for weeks. It is estimated that tons of gold and silver, to say nothing of several millions in American bank notes, accrued to the Government without a single order on its part that it be surrendered.

Immediately after the closure of this heinous campaign against the bread winners of China, an aphorism became current among the people which clearly reflected their reactions: "They got the money but lost the people."

FEBRUARY 15, 1952 (TO D. & H.)

Your business drop is nothing like what we are having here. I don't know what you are getting in your newscasts, but it is not a nice situation. Everyone hopes for better times ahead but the dark of night is upon us at present.

February 16. We have been in a heavy snow storm since late this afternoon. The ground is covered with perhaps half an inch and we look down on roofs almost completely white. This is the best we have had this winter and if it keeps up there should be a fair fall by morning.

Today S. and I went over to Bill's Motors to look in our stored car to see if we could find some old papers. It is the first time I have inspected the car since it was put up. I was surprised to see how well it looked. There is absolutely no resale of cars now. R. has over a hundred stored in the place waiting for the day which never arrives. At the rate austerity is going at present there will never come a time in the very near future when cars in any considerable number will be put on the street. And you talk of getting a new '52!!!

February 17. We are going out this noon to lunch in the home of Russian friends. We have experienced their lunches before and shall not need any evening meal. This is a family we have known for a long time. I did a mastoid many years back on the young woman of the family who is now eighteen.

February 19. It was a good lunch in spite of the fact that this man is having a most difficult time making ends meet. He told me that if he could get his family out with just the clothes on their backs he would go. He sees no future. If you are following the papers you know even the native merchants have no future. It is a most difficult time for everyone. Our practice is down almost to free patients and few of them.

Most people when getting ready to go home are able to sell enough of their things to meet settlement expenses but Sir R. who leaves by boat the end of this week told me yesterday that he was virtually giving things away. No one is buying a thing outside of food since the present "movement" started. Six months ago my medical and surgical instruments would have brought in a goodly sum but now there is no purchasing.

FEBRUARY 15, 1952 (TO H. S. H.)

And now your letter of Januray 29 comes four days after yours of January 23rd. It does not appear to have been in any trouble along the way. The flaps seem as good as new. *(The previously reported censoring of letters seems to have been confined entirely to discovering whether or not they carried American bank notes.)*

Mrs. D. and S. went in to the Cathedral this morning for a memorial service held for the late King and tonight we have been listening to the minute by minute account of the funeral. It was very impressive and came over BBC with great clarity. At one point there was a bit of jamming but someone must have gotten ashamed as it soon stopped.

The letter which I sent off to you the other day may seem to you to be overly filled with wishful thinking. I want to say it was a recording of what goes on about one when many suicides are occuring immediately about us. Under such conditions a change is highly desired.

February 16. Our rain turned to snow this afternoon and now at 11:15 p.m. it is still at it. It is a real pleasure to see the whiteness covering up what lies beneath. Would that it could clear out the "parasites" as the Chinese farmer says it does in his field. As I listened to the "Voice of America" just now I learned that something of what goes forward with us is common knowledge but I doubt if the depths of the thing are understood. The complete story may come out presently.

Later, same day. Sir R. has just been in to say good-bye, expecting to leave by boat on Saturday or Sunday. It has been most difficult closing out his affairs and it has come finally to his virtually giving his firm over to his former staff. In fact, they consider that it belongs to them. Under present conditions it may not prove to be a baby worth holding and in fact may become really a "hot baby."

February 20. I shall be glad when I can see some late periodicals. I think there is not an article or story in the two and three year old issues which we have that I have not read several times. If this keeps up I shall think I am the author of some of some of them. It is remarkable what one can get in repeated readings. I have come to the conclusion that all politicians should be required to reread everything they have said in any previous year before saying anything new. Communism has had many elucidators. (*During this period of "pressure" against the merchants various institutions including hospitals were to have three days of intensive study of Communism. In connection with this study individuals in the institutions were required to write personal histories going back to the age of eight.*)

I was reading the other day that it is poor taste to write about the weather in letters. That may be true under ordinary circumstances but when such references are used as background, I should think one might be forgiven. Our present cold wave cannot in itself be of great interest to those living in a climate like California but the fact that it comes at a time of low morale should serve to give an idea of how feelings are being chilled, in some instances to a cadaverous status. Do you remember the quotation, "All must end"? Out here one is inclined to ask, "How long, Oh Lord, how long?"

A native colleague hits the nail on the head when he says that the important thing during these days of intense "pressures" is to preserve mental health. (*The depressing tone of the above and reference to "cadaverous status" reflects the profound gloom of the period together with the great number of suicides among merchants.*)

FEBRUARY 25, 1952 (TO H.S.H.)

I am being pushed into a difficult situation and I don't like it. I want to give you the picture, if I can, in such a way that you can understand what I am up against. If you think it proper I should be glad to have you discuss it with the Clan.

Up until Chinese New Year, when the present movement started, I was receiving enough income from Chinese and foreign patients, in addition to the monthly grant from the British Community Interests Committee, to meet my basic needs. Since that time all business, including doctoring, has stopped excepting for the barest necessities. What few patients there are, are without funds or are keeping what they have against the day not too distant when it is expected there will be considerable want. More than ninety per cent of those coming in are unable to meet a fee and for many I must provide medicine from my stock. You have to witness what is going on to realize how completely former limping activities have come to a full stop.

It may be argued that all Americans should have been out of China and those remaining for any reason are expendable. Today there are thirty-three professional or business men, forty-five missionaries and members of families and fifty-six Chinese with U. S. passports, including twenty-nine children, making a total of a hundred and thirty-four. The British have about five-hundred in all categories  It is unlikely that these numbers will be reduced much further unless there is a change in policy.

I wish to submit that those of us who have remained will some day be seen to have made a valuable contribution toward lasting friendships. The British are conscious of the need to keep a toe in the door, and are prepared to meet the expense of so doing regardless of the fact that they are under great pressures. Americans need not be so much concerned over commercial aspects of such a "toehold" but they should be profoundly interested in spiritual and cultural relationships. Sooner or later and I believe it could be "sooner" all American contacts remaining are going to be of extreme value.

In spite of the smallness of our foreign community I feel that I have a definite obligation to see this thing through. As a matter of fact, I cannot at this juncture sell any of my belongings and provide funds for the purpose of moving out. As you know the British Community Interests Committee is meeting about 45 per cent of my office and apartment rent. Since they are involved in subsidizing five rooms in the Tah Wha Hospital for British and American patients they are unable to do more. Some American businessmen tried to get funds from their firms to assist the British in this community insurance but were not permitted by their native supervisors to do so. (*Each foreign firm was assigned a Chinese supervisor who controlled the expenditures of the firm's funds.*)

The above grant was given because the Committee felt I should remain, if possible, as they wish to have a specialist in the city still permitted to do private practice and to act as consultant in medical and surgical situations. This attitude was taken after Dr. B.'s death, leaving me the only British or American physician. My function, therefore, is to advise when a specialist's services are needed, control a five-bed ward at Tah Wha Hospital and act in an advisory capacity for those seeking surgical or medical help from the native group.

FEBRUARY 25, 1952 (TO H.S.H.)

I am surprised that you have not heard the "third movement" of the symphony, as I listened to a rather faithful rendering of it by the "Voice of America" orchestra on two occasions recently. Certainly by this time you must find records in all the good shops. **It is all the rage** among the young people just now. Over page, there will be some references to certain prominent passages.

February 26. A very splendid and unexpurgated rendering of the "third movement" came over again last evening, I am surprised you have not found it playing in some of your music houses. The score of the music played in New York differs just a bit from ours as they use only fifty terminations while ours come to sixty. A daily failure of vital air in such a number is truly remarkable! I certainly hope that you can hear it. *(The "terminations" referred to relate to suicides taking place in Shanghai at that time. As many as sixty were recorded daily.)*

February 27th. Your letter of February 17th came in this morning. I believe it has a virgin flap or a great deal of cleverness is used in covering up an opening of the envelope. *(No evidence of censoring.)*

Many thanks for the Clan's contribution to my zoological problem. My friend and I have been discussing the habits of termites again since I wrote you and he is convinced that the deterioration sometimes takes place in a matter of months. I am wondering if there is any difference between the red and white ants. It is a former variety he is thinking about and I think he would agree that common effort toward colony preservation is a rule. But on occasions there is a different action which results in destruction. *(Reference is to serious purging which continued within the government, mostly of small officials.)*

The same virulent brush and paint is much in evidence which was seen before, the only difference is the subject. Soul searching can frequently be soul destroying. The merchant, big and small, is the victim. *(During this period of purging and investigation of merchants practically all anti-American pictures on the streets disappeared.)*

There has been considerable radio broadcasting regarding the possible bombing of Chinese cities. The friends of America, and there are many millions about, should never be attacked. It would set back relationships to the dark ages. And while on the subject of friends, many would lose all hope if those in Korea not wishing to go home were forced to do so. There must be no weakening. Respect for the strong stand has been built up and must not be destroyed!

I want to send you in a few days a copy of our "controlled" foreign language newspaper. It will show you how fast we are progressing **and** how much we are working for peace and prosperity, not only for

# THE FIVE "ANTI'S"

those in China but in Korea as well. If it reaches you it will be by slow mail. Do a "Malik"!

Our stores have almost been out of Jam recently, but within just the past few days a new supply of "bear brand" has been put on the market. It has more body and spreads over our bread much more completely. We are enjoying it "Malikely"! *(This referred to intensified jamming of overseas broadcasts by Soviet stations.)*

February 28. If a copy of the paper reaches you by slow post, which I shall get under way tomorrow, you can have a good laugh over the insects entering into a new life in the frozen wastes of Korea. It is really remarkable, the imagination and something else which is brought to bear upon problems of alibi and cover up. *(The above refers to germ warfare propaganda which was being pushed in China at the time. Our Chinese friends called it "the silly business".)*

We had a most interesting sleet storm today; for a time small wafers of ice sailed down, some of which were an inch long. I don't think I have ever seen such a thing before. It has been a cold, miserable day. I wish I might show you some pictures I saw with A. this afternoon; they are anything but pleasant or hopeful. The tempo of the "third movement" is being increased and "terminations" are also increasing daily. A friend was almost struck by a falling body on the Bund several days ago. *(During this period, when great numbers of harassed merchants were committing suicide, the tall buildings in down-town Shanghai were frequently used for that purpose. When one walked along such buildings it was highly desirable to keep very close to the building. Pedicab men and pedestrians were sometimes killed by falling bodies.)*

MARCH 4, 1952 (TO H.S.H.)

The weather which is sleeting and cold this morning continues to keep pace with our morale. For more than three weeks it has been dark and dreary. And so are all the thinking hours of this great city. Events move with great rapidity and each day brings a new tightening of the worm mechanism which has for its objective the leveling of all humanity.

At times I have a vision of events leading up to a reversal which might save the world from present trends. The individualism of those about us may prove to be the Waterloo of the Communists. It is a big gamble of course, but from where I sit there are indications which may be favorable to change in spite of the present darkness, so I want to stay with it if at all possible. As a matter of fact, there is nothing else I can do at present.

MARCH 10, 1952 (TO H.S.H.)

There is something new every day! My secretary, Mrs. C., was knocked down by a bicyclist a week ago, but instead of going to one of our recognized foreign trained men, she consulted an old-time physician. He diagnosed it as a nerve injury and put on a poultice and bandage. When the hand began to swell he said this was "bad blood coming out." When I saw it, I sent her along to L.S.C., who was immediately suspicious of a fracture. An X-ray revealed a fracture of the olecranon process.

Later, same day. One of our graduates of 1931 called me by phone this evening and said his youngest brother who recently graduated from a medical school has just committed suicide. He had a letter today but no details. It is all so sad and so unnecessary. I continue to act as a father confessor to a small group of our old staff and students. If I did nothing more than this I am glad to be where they can come to me.

March 13. There is little to add to this letter, and now at the end of my office hour I will get it sealed and sent along. Our envelopes as I have told you before come without glue so this business of closing the flaps is always a homemade job. Recently all yours appear to be coming through virgin.

MARCH 14, 1952 (TO H.S.H.)

Tomorrow is pay day in the city and a number of firms are in grave difficulty as funds are limited. I may have just enough to get past, but unless a few outstanding bills are paid soon, we shall be on our uppers, as the saying goes. If there were any way of selling our belongings that would help, but no one has any money to buy a thing. It is rather remarkable when you stop to think of it, that we have been able to carry on so long.

March 17th. Some of the big firms are able to meet only a portion of their payroll. We are in the same boat, with everyone on our necks as usual.

MARCH 21, 1952 (TO H.S.H.)

I am going along to talk with the British C.G. tomorrow morning in the hope of getting a little light on what our next move should be. At the moment no move seems possible, as there is no hope of selling enough things to provide sufficient funds for the purpose of paying off the eight people on my staff. Severance pay is a big item in getting out, and you can't blame most of them since the departure of their source of income leaves them high and dry. Hardly a day passes without a native or a foreigner asking me if I know where he can get work. The most I can do is to give them free treatment and medicine.

March 24th, Monday. This is a blue Monday in more ways than one! It is overcast and my staff along with every other in Shanghai is getting out of hand. Their demands are beyond my present ability to meet. There seems to have been an order down from above to get tough with the non-native within the gates. Two foreigners have already been locked up for non-payment of wages and a third has his bedding in his office ready for the move which may come as his deadline approaches at three p.m. today. In all this you see a growing resistance on both sides (employer and employee) and on top of it all is a growing fear of the empty stomach. There is a great deal of short-sightedness on the native side; the source of supply, the employer is being squeezed for all he is worth.

Later same day. Your letter of March 10th came at a most opportune moment, the end of a morning of inquisition of the female members of my staff by an individual of the same sex who is chairman of their union. It is a great lift to my spirit to know you are sympathetic with our problem. One good thing did come out of this morning when I found the younger of my two women is more loyal than I had supposed. The fact that her father is having rather a rough time at the hands of his own union may in part account for her present attitude. It is most difficult to get it through the heads of these people that just because one comes from overseas, he is not necessarily made of money. (*As one looks back on this period it is quite evident that many members of one's staff were really quite loyal, but they had no other course than to take orders from their unions in exerting pressure on their employers.*)

At the moment I can see my way for the next month, but beyond that all is obscure. One of the male members of my staff has been set the chore of seeing to it that I do not take anything out of the house to sell, and if so, it must be reported immediately to the union. What goes on in this respect with us is also true of the big firms. We had the same situation with the Country Hospital. It is a device to force foreign currency into the country just as the "third movement" is having as a by-product the surrendering of gold, silver and American bank notes at the principal banks in exchange for JMP.

Seven p.m., same day. I am just in from a short walk in the streets;

ninety per cent of the shops are closed at this hour. (*This was most unusual as many shops in the city were kept open to all hours, but it was quite evident that there was no buying or selling in any of them, and little even in the earlier hours of the day. This was a clear indication that the people in Shanghai were without funds.*)

I am sorry to have interjected my community and personal problems into your vacation. No one could have foreseen such a situation and the suddenness with which it struck. Patients I had been treating and who could pay something were without funds over night. Some employed by big firms but hired locally were cut off with little notice on the 15th of this month. These were mostly Russians who, by-the-way, seem hardest hit by the present turn of events. As one said to me, "If the British and the American firms are finished so are we."

March 25th. A side light on what goes forward is the fact that many in the city are finding it impossible to pay gas bills. I understand the Company has not decided what to do about turning off the gas in these cases. It would be a tremendous job to turn them all off.

## 18: PERSONAL PRESSURES

Street loud speakers continued to blare demands that capitalists "confess" and submit to the "clemency" of the Government. Suicides became more frequent with wives and sometimes whole families taking poison along with the head of the house.

As money became more scarce, labor unions became insistent in their demands for prompt payment of wages and increases in rate of pay although it was "illegal." It is possible that a directive had come down from above to go after foreign capitalists in this connection to force them to bring in U. S. dollars and British money to meet their pay rolls. By this means the Government could gather in more solid currency.

Along with many others, we were caught up in this situation. Distressing days were spent fending off the demands of our staff which finally ended in our signed statement that we would submit to the "law" of the land. As will be seen upon reading these letters, the Government Labor Bureau declared later that the union and staff had no "legal" basis for making their demands.

MARCH 25, 1952 (TO H.S.H.)

While my last letter was lying on the desk waiting to be mailed, four union officials walked in who in the past hour have put the squeeze on me. This is the week when all private concerns are being investigated and "irregularities" are to be "corrected." We are found to have used our own scale of salaries, which was satisfactory to the staff, but now these people say we "sinned" against the Government regulations and must pay what they call back payments within two days. I don't know how much I am in for and whether or not I can raise it within two days. I suspect I have only the Consulate to fall back upon. Phoning out from a private place just now I find that the whole city is in turmoil this morning, because the "squeeze" has been made simultaneously all over by teams especially trained, and if the one which visited me is any sample, especially hopped up for their jobs.

On the surface this is all made to appear as being done for the protection of the worker, but there is something else back of it. I believe it is to secure more foreign exchange. At the moment, the British Chamber is meeting to try and find a way out. I hope to get in touch with the Consul General this afternoon. After I left the room this morning my staff was told they were going to be particularly hard on me because I am an American and my country started bacteriological warfare, but to my face they said they would treat me no differently than the Chinese. The leader of our group this morning, I should say, is not far from needing a psychiatrist.

March 26. I am in the midst of it! If I do what was demanded of me yesterday, I must find eighty-five million JMP, or an equivalent of something over forty-two hundred U. S. dollars, mostly as back pay, by tomorrow. I consulted various persons who know and am told that what I have been paying is absolutely legal and no more can be demanded of me. I am going to the Foreign Affairs Bureau this a.m. if I can find someone willing to translate for me.

March 27. I have certainly been through the wringer these past forty-eight hours, but I think light is beginning to appear. I went to the Foreign Affairs Bureau yesterday and was given advice which I put into operation just now in my office. That is, to have a talk with my staff and come to an understanding to carry on as of the present. I have left them to think over what I said to them and it remains to be seen what will come of this thinking.

I am enclosing a rough draft of some new regulations which came out yesterday morning which have greatly changed our situation over night. It is quite clear now that the young men who came in from the union and badgered me were acting beyond their rights. It is this sort of thing which has been going on all over the country which has caused great criticism of the authorities. They are calling a halt to it and the city is breathing easier. One wonders if this may mean

**PERSONAL PRESSURES** 149

any turning to the right. It is too early to tell. There is no reduction in the "third movement."

The Chinese papers of March 26th contained the following eight regulations (translations by Dr. Price) governing the "5-Anti Movement" promulgated by the Shanghai Military Commission and People's Government:

"1. All private industries and business must observe the Government regulations in connection with the 5-Anti Movement.

"2. Without authorization of the Production and Economy Committee (which directs the 5-Anti Movement) and without proper credentials and arm bands no organization, group, or individual may enter any factory, shop, or business office to carry on any 5-Anti investigations.

"3. No staff or worker may initiate investigations in any factory, shop, or business, except to expose unlawful and criminal activities, without express authorization of the Government.

"4. No private organization, group, or individuals have the right to detain or arrest persons; only the Kung-an-chüe can do this with proper papers and according to Government procedure.

"5. No private organization, group or individuals have the right to search for or impound concealed articles or money; only the Kung-an-chüe with proper papers has this right.

"6. Only the authorized representatives of the Shanghai Military Commission and the Production and Economy Committee have the right to seal, confiscate or take over factories, shops, or private property. No other groups or persons have this right.

"7. In 5-Anti investigations all forms of torture, third-degree methods and persecutions are forbidden.

"8. All who take part in the 5-Anti Movement must strictly observe the above regulations. Those who disobey them will be severely punished. Any infractions should be immediately reported to the Kung-an-chüe which should seriously investigate and report to the higher authorities for appropriate action."

March 29th. At this moment I have been served with some kind of a paper to appear before the union this afternoon. They are still after me! (*It was illegal, following the posting of the eight regulations cited above, for union members to come to my office, but they could command me to appear at their headquarters.*)

April 1. Well, we had our session and I stood pat that I did not have funds with which to meet the demands still being made. The whole thing has now been placed in the hands of the Labor Bureau, which is a government organ and we may not have so much fireworks. At least, I hope there will be someone of more mature years with whom to confer. A. is helping me out with my petition and we are putting all the cards on the table. Anything you can do at that end must be held in readiness, but it cannot be brought to this area where I can be pressurized. This is the attitude being taken by everyone out here at present, as the demands have been increased. *(Evidence that one had funds abroad which could be brought in made settlements very difficult.)*

In my petition to the Labor Bureau, after placing my problem before them and asking for their help in reducing my staff, I am also asking for their assistance in closing out my office. I don't think there is much hope of the latter as nothing is moving in that direction just now. It reminds one of the last few drops which come out with the last twist of the lemon squeezer. Just enjoy your freedom among the great (California) trees a little bit for us and all your friends out here!

April 4. And still we go on in much the same way without any more "ruction," but I am anxious to get my letter into the Labor Bureau before anything more happens. A. is getting it ready and either today or tomorrow it should be sent.

April 11. Last evening I had dinner at the home of our one remaining French doctor, together with four other colleagues. We constitute what is left of the executive committee of the Shanghai Medical Society, and participate in the only activity of the Society considered prudent at this time. At our table were heard French, Russian, Chinese and English. We were brought up-to-date with regard to some things, but others were forbidden fruits, such as germ warfare. It would appear that all foreign doctors may be out by summer or early fall. All teaching is being taken over in Chinese. All practices are being reduced to the vanishing point. Business firms are being brought under control of "finance committees" so that every doctor's bill is being beaten down. One of mine is in the process. Such "committees" look upon a physician's work as anything but skilled.

April 12. Easter is upon us, but there is very little indication of the fact. The Cathedral will have a service tomorrow to which most of us will go. We shall see no Easter hats and eyebrows will be raised at anyone wearing a new suit. There are still a few courageous shops with chocolate eggs and bunnies.

After a bit of rain and wind our day seems on the point of clearing.

## PERSONAL PRESSURES

My golf has been shot to pieces by recent "pressures," but I am hoping to get some either today or the first of the week. I certainly am not playing up to my handicap of fourteen. I hope that my next letter will be a little more cheerful. We live a day at a time and anything can happen. Some of my native friends say that they "live only an hour at a time."

APRIL 15, 1952 (TO H.S.H.)

My first session with the Labor Bureau did not go very far as they wanted data that I could not give without referring back to my young secretary who is ill. We will make another try day after tomorrow. I hope after this matter is settled I can apply to close my office. I am told that as soon as the "present movement" is finished, that can be done. If this can be carried forward satisfactorily, we shall then put in for an "exit." Under present conditions there does not seem to be anything else to do. My remaining foreign colleagues are trying to do the same thing.

April 16. Unless there is a sudden change it would appear that the present "squeeze" will push out any number of people. After the summer I don't think there will be a single foreign doctor of any nationality providing exits can be obtained. Please thank Dr. MacDougal and the Clan for their continued interest and sympathy during our time of "pressures." As time goes on, I feel we shall be lucky to get out with little more than what we stand up in. We shall certainly need a lifeline the moment we can get away from behind the Bamboo Curtain.

I go again to the Labor Bureau in the morning and I am hoping to get some help from them. I certainly have a bunch on my hands with Mrs. C. going blind, Ma with a condition which prevents his presence in the small office, and now my young assistant to Mrs. C. at home with a long drawn out case of urticaria, "bad blood" coming out, so the Chinese doctor says, to which I would agree. I will write later to give you the results of the next session.

April 18th. I had a short time with the Labor Bureau man yesterday morning and he wants more information on our income and expenses for the past year. His attitude was somewhat reassuring and I have hopes of clearing this staff matter up so that when the present "movement" is over I can ask to have my office closed *(In all the investigation by the Labor Bureau as to my financial status, the primary objective seemed to be as to whether or not I had any gold resources which might be called upon either to continue with my staff or to increase pay. This was the general pattern in Shanghai at that time, for both Chinese and foreigners. The government undoubtedly was out to secure just as much foreign exchange in the form of solid currency as could be had from any source what-so-ever.)*

APRIL 20, 1952 (TO H.S.H.)

Your letter on April 6th came in yesterday making a little more than the usual time, but as far as I can make out, a virgin flap.

If your plans have carried you should be finishing your first week of visiting in the north. How we envy you! I have been told that the tempering of steel by fire is a refining process, but I don't think the steel likes it, nor do we. What useful purpose can come out of these disturbing experiences remains to be seen. I am reminded so often these days of what a native colleague said to me some time ago. He was impressed by the need of preserving mental health at all cost. Yesterday morning I talked with two British women who have native husbands, one of whom needed her own mental health bucked up a great deal. Such individuals together with their husbands are having a beastly time.

I don't think I have paid much attention to the "fifth movement" of the symphony in writing you as it has seemed to me to be a continuation of the "third." I have listened to it several times and I can't say I like the music. Time will tell but I should not think it will ever be passed down to future generations. It seems to me that there are too many jarring discords which offend the finer sensibilities of the human mind; but enough of that! (*As stated elsewhere, the "third movement" or the "three anti's" merged into what I have called the "five anti's" or "fifth movement," which was primarily directed toward the merchant class in China.)*

April 21. I had my third meeting with the Labor Bureau this morning and, I am relieved to say, got a fairly good settlement. Demands made illegally on March 25th, which required the equivalent of something over 4,200 U. S. dollars in local currency, were completely cancelled, and I was scolded for having signed a statement agreeing to pay in the first place. (*I thanked the Labor Bureau man for scolding me.*)

I replied that I had no way of knowing that the group which attacked me was not acting in an authorized manner. Now the thing is under control with a signed agreement with the bureau and union, which keeps my wages at the present level, but requires me to pay only one back yearly bonus. Instead of being required after all this

# PERSONAL PRESSURES

business to pay the above amount I need not pay more than the equivalent of eighty-five U. S. dollars. As soon now as the dust has settled, we will take the next step, which is to close the office if there is no way of reducing the staff. The difficulty of closing the office forthwith is that my income and British aid will be cut off. We are studying the affair carefully before taking the next step. If one only knew what the chances of an exit permit might be, the course to take would be more certain.

There is some talk of the "fifth movement," or the "five anti's ending on May Day, after which time one may be able to sell things, but from past experiences I an inclined to think this is a forlorn hope. It is true that at the moment there is a little pianissimo but the conductor may at any moment call for a fortissimo.

April 22. A native friend was saying yesterday that when a man is sick he cannot wait for medicines, if he is daily growing worse. The longing with which such an individual looks for relief is almost beyond belief. *(The above suggests the great urgency with which many Chinese longed for relief from the great pressures placed upon them by the Communists.)*

In going over future plans with A. last evening, I felt that he was resigned for the first time to our leaving. He has maintained that my foot be kept in the door for morale reasons. He now feels that if present trends are continued there is no useful purpose to be gained, especially when one's means of livelihood is being cut away.

APRIL 27, 1952 (TO H.S.H.)

The sun is almost down on a beautiful day with just enough clouds about to make a good sunset. It would be a relief if there could be more beauty down below where people live.

We are getting ready for our May Day, but up to the moment the drums are not beating too much in practice. An old native judge, a friend of many years, said to me the other day, "Oh, must we hear those things again?" He sees no immediate light but points to the four thousand years of Chinese history, to emphasize his contention that it will end.

Later, same day, after the evening broadcast. As one listens, one is impressed with the great number of words being used in order to keep the world on the track. I suppose that is the only way to do it, but it does seem to me that we might have a little more action at times.

One of the phenomena of our times is the great number of young lovers walking arm-in-arm or hand-in-hand down our streets. I was out for a walk after supper and it seemed to me I have never seen so many. You will be interested in our city which begins to go to sleep at a very early hour. Some of the streets are so free in the early evening that they make good roads for the beginners on bicycles.

Dr. P. has introduced me to the thirty-seventh Psalm as a help in times like these. A year ago when they were in the thick of things it was a real aid.

April 30. I am told that the May Day parade tomorrow is not to be a big one and certainly there has not been as much preparation as in the past for such affairs. Can enthusiasm be cooling? It may be that one can pick up some pointers tomorrow. A native said today "George" is taking all the money, but losing the support of the people. He says this is a definite reversal from two years ago. It may mean much or little; like a dry forest, a single spark will set it on fire, but who is to create the spark? The loss of faith in past leaders is pathetic and perhaps they must not be blamed too much for hoping that a hand from outside would start the fire. (*"George" was the Government.*)

May 1. I had the unusual experience of listening to the Tokyo broadcast this morning while watching the flags and picture bedecked parade. All sounds along the line of march came from those participating. On the sidewalks were the curious and, as far as our area was concerned, also the inarticulate. There was rain most of the morning, but it is attempting to clear this afternoon.

There is no indication that the present "fifth" is to end soon. Some have thought, and I had hoped, it would mean I could collect a few outstanding bills. I wonder if you at home can imagine what it is like to have a city where everyone is scratching the bottom of his pocketbook in the hope of finding means to carrying on from day to day. One of Shanghai's former well-to-do foreigners called me last week to say that he just could not find money to pay his bill.

MAY 2, 1952 (TO D. & H.)

The world seems to be in more trouble with the steel situation going off in America; apparently we still have a lot of free speech in the U. S. and that is as it should be. I hope they get it settled presently as some people we know make a good story out of such things.

May 4. From Tokyo just now we learned that many of your gas pumps in Detroit are dry today. I guess you will have to sit home and think of your sins. We do it all the time, but it does no good. We also know what an empty gas pump looks like: here either the hose is removed or wound around the pump in a figure-of-eight. This sign for several years has meant "no gas."

Money in our city is extremely scarce at present. I received this morning the first payment made to date of all my bills for last month's work. People call up to say they just do not have it. Some say they would have it if someone else paid them. That is the story I give my landlord. It is a vicious circle and there is nothing that can be done to relieve the situation. The freezing of funds at home and the recent action prohibiting sending pounds and dollars to this area is making an impasse.

S. and I "went" to Chicago for a ball game between the Cubs and the Dodgers. It was an exciting game with the Cubs winning three to two. Later, I will ask you to take me to a game in Detroit. Following the game we had the Kentucky Derby which was not too interesting for those of us who do not follow the horses.

May 8. Our big job will be to satisfy the people of the staff who have become too big for their pants. If you try, I don't think you can realize how much pressure the so-called laborer can put on one, especially if he is a foreigner. It does not matter that I am also a laborer. It may be interesting to look back on this period, but it is certainly not very attractive when viewed from this point. It might be good training for a younger man, but I am too old to get any profit from it. If one did not believe in the ultimate winning out of the right, many of the things we have to go through would floor us. Fortunately we are all keeping well and I am hoping to resume a little more golf at the end of this week as I think our good weather is likely to stay with us for a time now.

MAY 3, 1952 (TO H.S.H.)

Late this afternoon I had a good talk with A. regarding our future procedure. He advises against requesting closure of the office even though a satisfactory agreement would permit closing out the staff but might leave me high and dry without even a little income for what might be an indefinite period, in case an exit was refused. He thinks I should attempt to reduce staff to the end where I can carry on for the time being, with Mrs. C., my secretary. Since she is going blind she will probably leave me of her own volition this summer. It will be a complete staff reduction by steps. I plan therefore to make a request next week to the Labor Bureau to this end on the basis that I cannot earn enough to meet wages.

May 4. This is a gloomy day in more ways than one, and with the course so wet, golf is out. It is grand at times, however, to have this sort of relief and to get away from the eternal "pressures." Nothing new has come up during the last twenty-four hours. It is just the constant bearing down which is with us all the time. As my judge friend said, this is the thing which gives the "long faces" in the streets. The children and birds react to life in their usual way, but no one else does.

Later, same day. Dr. P. was quoting a Chinese saying yesterday which points out that in climbing a mountain the top can be attained only by taking a step at a time. This is a lesson we are all learning the hard way out here. He is hoping, incidentally, that something will happen during the next few months which will permit an exit for them. It is most difficult to understand what can be gained by keeping them here. Fortunately they are being allowed enough money to live on at present.

This evening no progress is reported in Korea while Churchill states that the world is nearer peace than a year ago. Out here we see only the "trees" but on the whole, I would agree with him even as regards this area. Mr. R. told me last evening that their spare parts at Bill's Motors were a little more active recently and his boys have the impression that the "fifth movement" is moderating. One becomes suspicious of "moderation," however, because of past experiences, when such apparent softening has been followed by harder squeezes.

An hour later—during which I took my daily constitutional over to Bubbling Well Road and back. It was of interest to find windows and walls back to normal with all "advertisements" of the "fifth movement" cleared away. Many places are putting on sales but there are few buyers. I can't believe that in the long run the storekeeper can be put on the shelf. He has had a severe blow, but like the rubber ball I believe he will bounce back. Is a bounce starting? Who can tell! As I walked today I was impressed, as many have noted, that we stroll comfortably and virtually un-noticed about, whereas those coming as "friends" are never seen excepting in something moving very fast and with curtains to the windows like the traditional Chinese wedding chair. Also they are not seen in public places with other foreigners. *(The above refers to the transportation of Russian "advisors" and, in some instances, Government officials through the streets of Shanghai in curtained motor cars, blue coolie cloth material hiding the occupants in the back seat. When the so-called "Russian advisors" came into the city for the purpose of purchasing new clothing on their arrival in Shanghai, shopkeepers were compelled to put up curtains both at the windows and doors in order to keep out the curious.)*

## 19: COWED MERCHANTS

While the "five antis" were not officially terminated, due possibly to the fact that there were some merchants still awaiting "punishment," the vast majority made their confessions and paid their excessive fines. Some, of course, were dead or in jail.

Now that the bourgeoisie had been purged of the "five poisons," the Government set about to secure their assistance in anticipation of the "Year of Prosperity" which was just ahead. To this end the staffs, members in some cases of former "interrogating groups," were told to cooperate with their bosses.

While merchants were compelled to conform to the new "cooperation movement," it is not likely that they would soon forget that they had been humiliated and relieved of most of their worldly goods. Nor did it help that the Government offered them loans at a low rate of interest.

This was a period when most foreigners saw the hand writing on the wall and made attempts to leave China. Along with many others we sought to terminate the services of our staff and close our office. A reading of our day-to-day struggle in this matter will show how difficult a move this could be.

MAY 10, 1952 (TO H.S.H.)

This should have been a Saturday afternoon of golf but rains came on just as we were ready to start. I will open this new "serial," therefore, and add bits as the spirit moves. As a matter of fact, the spirit is much like the weather with its ups and downs, but mostly the latter.

A little later—I have just come in from a long walk in the rain down on Avenue Joffre. One is impressed by the great number of mouths walking here and there for which someone else must provide sustenance. Many cheap sales are on with the shops apparently well supplied, but with few buyers. Some of the old landmarks, such as buildings which in your day were in apple-pie order, would distress you no end at the use to which some are put. *(The "great number of mouths" referred to the large number of soldiers seen on every hand together with women similarly dressed, perhaps Chinese "Wacs," perhaps soldiers' wives, perhaps something else. There were always a fair number of babies in arms, with others on the way. Some one has estimated that there were about ten million of these people for whom food must be provided by the farmers.)*

May 11. Some of the advantages of being in this glorified "prison" are the interesting articles which one turns up now and again in such periodicals as the *Reader's Digest* and which have been entirely overlooked in ordinary reading. Our issues of '47, '48, '49, all we have, have been read and reread and still something turns up which has been overlooked. Last evening for instance I turned up in the November '48 *Reader's Digest* an article by John A. O'Brien on "Atom Fairyland." It is perhaps the clearest statement I have seen regarding protons and electrons. I think the thing which impresses me as much as anything is the fact that the atom has so many empty spaces. His statement that "If we eliminated all the unfilled spaces in a man's body and collected his protons and electrons into one mass, the man would be reduced to a speck just visible with a magnifying glass (Eddington)," makes one feel even smaller than when reading about the new astronomical findings. One might think that with all this knowledge of the realities of the universe, "pressures" exerted by man against man would not make too much impression! I suspect, however, they will continue to get under our hides so long as we are human beings.

Evening. I am just in after a short visit with A. While everyone here would like to see Korea finished, it is his opinion that it will be most difficult as long as it can be used as a control to keep everyone in line in this area. Nothing would suit the book of some we know better than to have an attack on the Mainland. It must not happen! If what he thinks is true the talks might just as well stop. The brick wall of obstinacy which is present everywhere and is shown by those inside the curtain "is most discouraging." How wonderful world progress could be if this wall could simply disappear! Is this to happen from "pressures" from in front or from behind the curtain?

May 12. Everyone is waiting for the next "movement" but there is no indication as to what it is supposed to be. In the meantime "consignment" houses are becoming more and more crowded with goods.

May 13. Late this afternoon I went for a walk and called on my Russian doctor friend who inherited a British medical firm, and found him in a very troubled frame of mind. He cannot meet expenses and has told his staff today that he is going to close his office.

May 14. In our "bull session" today P. said that the "movements" are finishing now in favor of renewed productivity. All the "poison" has been cleared out and now everything is to be peace and harmony. Who can say!

May 16. Yesterday I got my first game of golf in three weeks. It is remarkable how many things outside of rain can prevent one getting a game these days. On Sunday we are hoping to hold a Club Day when Mrs. D. expects to join us for lunch. The Club has a new lease on life since some young people of the British firms, who are just taking up the game for the first time, have joined up on easy paying terms. This is one of the strange inconsistencies of our times . . . Our small executive committee of the Shanghai Medical Society held one of its monthly dinner meetings last evening when we got several ears-full of current gossip. It is apparent that every effort is being made to discontinue all private practice within a comparatively short time. It is expected that within a year all private doctors will be working for the state. Some day I hope to give you by word of mouth greater details of how this transition is made. In passing, one member gave us the gist of a recent lecture he had heard in which the speaker, a V. I. P., had predicted that peace would come in Korea in June. It just goes to show that one can hear anything if he keeps his ear to the ground long enough. Aside from this one item it was a most gloomy meeting.

We are discontinuing our evenings together for the time being and either we will get together again in better spirits or not at all. You will remember how medical men, especially in Shanghai, carried on their practices in connection with drug stores. From the point of view of tax this is proving to be a very expensive way of making a living. (These men now pay the business income tax, which is heavy.) I as a physician on my own with no selling of drugs from my office have had to pay no income tax.

Later. P. and I have had our usual Friday session. We have been trying to evaluate various world events in relation to our own. There are many evidences that the hand is being overplayed in these parts but where it may lead is not apparent. You write of the V. O. A. having difficulty and we can attest to the poor results out this way. I wish it could be gotten over to who ever is in control that just now much careful attention to what comes over on the waves is important. It ought to be poured in "world without end"!

May 17. This must be gotten in the mail tomorrow. If you find difficulty in reading this serial you may be consoled by knowing that anyone else attempting to do so might be completely discouraged.

MAY 13, 1952 (TO D. & H.)

Just three quarters of an hour ago at 8:35 a.m. your voice was coming into our apartment. It is interesting that it came over so well, as I was unable to get the V.O.A. this morning due to bad broadcasting conditions. Dee's voice came over well and her grandmother will live on that for days. It was good to hear from you and to know that you stand there alerted to give us assistance in case of need. One of the biggest problems is to cut free from staff and servants, who think that one must stay and support them. While I do most of the work around here, I am the Capitalist and must pay through the nose.

10:30 p.m., same day. It has been a day! First your phone call and then scattered through the day six Chinese patients, all free with the exception of one man from the country who brought a live chicken to pay for his call.

May 14. I learned tonight that we now have only two mails out a week, Monday and Thursday, so I'll try to mail on Sunday and Wednesday in order to get the best service. I suspect we have the same number of mails in but I don't know which days.

May 17, Saturday. I had my game of golf today and my brain is cleared a bit. Tomorrow I spend all day out at the Club. It is a tournament day and we hope to have a good crowd.

May 19, Monday. This is a dark day but yesterday was clear for the most part so the Club golf day could be carried on. We had 110 for lunch and others came and went during the day. Mother was able to come out for lunch.

Later, same day, 9:20 p.m. Just now an item came over from London which is of greatest interest in Shanghai. The Government here is shortly to be notified by the British Government that all British firms in China are to close immediately. In phoning to a British friend just now he said this did not come as news to the British here as they have known it for some time. These closures will make a great difference with the Shanghai foreign community.

May 21. It is possible that the British move to clear out may help some of the rest of us to get away. I don't think it will be easy for their firms to close as there are thousands of workers involved, who realize that as soon as the foreign group leaves the bottom will fall out of their incomes.

MAY 22, 1952 (TO H.S.H.)

I have given my staff notice that I want to terminate their services the end of next month, but have not gotten very far. They insist that I must keep them on until I have an exit permit. This is the usual pattern but I have pointed out that even now I cannot meet their wages as they come due. If I cannot bring them to some sort of terms I'll take the matter to the Labor Bureau next week. You can see in such actions some of the bars which keep us in "prison." I am afraid to apply for an exit permit while these negotiations are going on but it may be the only way in spite of the fact that no exits are being given to Americans at present.

May 23. Today is bright and clear and we may expect to get a little lift to our spirits. These past few dull days have certainly not helped us much in meeting our days of "pressures." As we progress more and more deeply into the affairs of these days it is astounding how completely employees have become dependent on some of us to provide the means by which they can fill their tummies. They have become so parasitic in their outlook that the source of livelihood must be held on to for dear life! Since no other source is being provided there is great fear of what is to happen. I suppose one should not blame them but it is pretty hard on some of us who must try to carry them.

May 24. Your May 11 letter with its reassuring word came this morning, just in time to give an uplift as I went away this afternoon to the Foreign Affairs division at the police station, to explain why I had not paid a tax bill. It was not too difficult an experience, not like some I have had. It was of value as pointing the way which I must take to get out from under with this land business before I get away. The milking process will continue unless I find means of prying myself free of these properties.

I think I wrote you that A's plans are indefinite as he will not go north until he has been given assistance to close his staff out. This will not be an easy matter. Many first plans have fallen through because of such obstacles. The outlook for prices in the next few months is not too good. An association out to protect "current prices" has gone on record as stipulating that they should not be raised to "overseas status." I don't think this group has government standing . . . My golf certainly suffered this afternoon due to my grilling by the Foreign Affairs group but I hope to get a game in the morning. I had a game yesterday with a man who has been out of it for three months due to "recent pressures."

May 25, Sunday. After a talk I had with a British subject as we were driving out to the golf course, I think I may have been too optimistic regarding British firms closing out. He does not think they can avoid going through what has happened and is happening to American firms, a long slow tugging away first in one direction and then in another, to sever the ties which bind. He did not think anyone who had not experienced this process could realize the difficulties. I am not sure this man is entirely right with regard to what will happen now to British firms, as it is a much larger group than the American, and they are completely fed up. Eden had his story straight and everything he described as going forward here was and is correct.

I have not seen A. for more than a week as it appears wise not to be too often together. He has been very helpful in our recent difficulties even though his nationality has been warned to abstain from giving advice to Americans. This is just one of the small things which go on and which probably indicates that the authorities are not too sure of their ground.

MAY 26, 1952 (TO H.S.H.)

While you still sleep we have just heard that the Bonn Treaty was signed some two hours ago. Of course it must be ratified but it is to be hoped that certain things are being set in motion which cannot be turned aside. The V. O. A. commentary this evening thinks the whole world including the Far East will be affected by this agreement and I hope he is right. It may help some to realize that the good friend (?) in the Northwest is not so all powerful in Europe.

I have had the man in today who is using my Lincoln Road small house and he has agreed to carry on the tax for that particular piece. I am saying to the "powers that be" that I want to abandon all the rest of my properties. I was told the other day that no American can own or sell properties but that I can use them and of course pay taxes. All land in China today belongs to "the people."

May 27, Tuesday. One sometimes wonders if it would not be better to have less attention paid to the debates of the articulate gentlemen in Washington when stimulating the air waves. We know it is not true but some get the impression in these parts that the structure of the democracy is falling apart and much is made of it. I have especially in mind what is going forward just now with regard to the appropriation for the mutual security affair.

May 30, Friday. We are in the midst of preparations for a mass calisthenics exhibition. I use the word "exhibition" advisedly for that is what much of it is. It is undoubtedly good for some of the young people who are finding some muscles they never knew they had. However, one of the important exercises is to learn to throw so that lethal objects may be hurled through the air. Races, jumping the rope, and shadow boxing are highly esteemed. One wonders when these young people do their studies. Perhaps they don't need to do so as cerebrums which are pretty much in their native states are more malleable. It is remarkable what one can do with such organs when everything which passes through is carefully supervised.

We are still waiting for our resident certificates. No American businessman has as yet had his renewed. No one can explain this delay but it becomes increasingly apparent that U. S. citizens are not in great favor with the authorities. It may be a reflection of what goes forward in Korea and Germany. Since some recent Hong Kong affairs, the British are catching some of the things constantly pointed at Americans. Just as with the calisthenics exercises, it seems to me that there is a certain element of hysteria in everything being done and said.

May 31, Saturday. Our Pacific air mass is overhead this morning and a driving rain is putting the annual golf match out of joint. It is remarkable how frequently of late the week-ends have been giving over to storms. It is a good day to remain indoors and if one could be as sure of keeping his door closed against any intruder of an undesirable character as you are, it would be a very relaxing experience. There is an old saying that "love of money is the root of all evil" and from experience and demands we can confirm this adage.

I was wondering last evening as I sampled my international diet of air waves if I might not be overeating. As one goes to the four corners of the earth for choice bits the resulting meal is not too satisfying. It is sometimes difficult to separate personal equations from seasoned studies which do not have as their objective the earning of one's salary, as is the case of some commentators. I am not too happy with some recent non-American editorials regarding Korean prisoners of war. I suspect there have been mistakes but this "holier than thou" attitude gets a bit under my skin.

I believe it is a practice when certain instruments are being tested out that someone listens at a distance in order to judge of the purity of sounds produced. If this were possible, air waves at a distance should have such a measuring. It might reveal some striking imperfections and some results which were not intended. I am sure from the point of view of one consuming this diet that the "cooking" should be more carefully done. *(These remarks refer to imperfections in broadcasts which reached China from various sources. It was quite apparant that their sponsors had not kept in mind how the broadcasts might be received by those living behind the "curtain.")*

June 1. A. has changed his mind again and thinks I should make immediate contact with two Government organs to close out my business. He does not know if it will be the correct move but he believes no harm can come from it. The thing which concerns me in all these moves is that if I am permitted to close out my office I may be held here without an exit and without any means of support.

JUNE 2, 1952 (TO D. & H.)

There is nothing new as far as our staff affairs are concerned. They continue to be firmly non-committal. When we are able to settle this affair, we shall make definite application to get away. Under present conditions I doubt if any early permission to leave will be possible . . . I think there is very little which goes on in the U. S., such as the gasoline shortage at the moment in Detroit, that we do not hear about. For instance today we learn that the usual large number of deaths took place over the Memorial Day holiday, California first, Ohio second and New York third in the largest numbers. It would almost seem that holiday motor driving is a bad thing. Of course there were deaths from other causes . . . I have already told you of our reception of your telephone call. It was of far greater value to us than might be apparent from the limited conversation permitted in the short time at our disposal.

June 4. I had a session at the tax office this afternoon in an attempt to get a bill for taxes cleared away which I have felt should be cancelled, due to the fact that the army used the property for the purpose of growing vegetables. We found a really helpful man and if we can get a police statement that the place was used as I have stated, then the tax will be remitted. It is remarkable how much time must be spent in such matters . . . This is the final day which I have given my staff to make a move but they have not done so. I am, therefore, preparing my letter to the Labor Bureau and shall get it to them within another few days.

JUNE 5, 1952 (TO H.S.H.)

We have jumped into summer days with our usual southwest prevailing winds which are dry at this time of the year. Our golf championship contest has been postponed for two Sundays but if this weather keeps up all should be well for this week-end. It will probably be a good week for the city-wide athletic tournaments for which the young people down below my window have been getting in training during the last few weeks and months. Foot racing appears to be one of the big events. If nothing else is gained from this period, China should have developed some super men and women! . . . Along with other Americans, we finally got our residence certificates this week but they are only for six months from the time they were called in. In our case, it means we go up to August 31st. It is not clear just why this limitation. I hope it means that we are not wanted beyond that time. Whether the squeezing of the "lemon" will be complete by that time, remains to be seen.

Evening, same day. I was able to get my game of golf this afternoon, playing with the man who is managing Culty Dairy. He is a Dane and is hoping that his show will be taken over so he can get out. He does not see very much chance of British firms, such as his, coming to any settlement in the very near future.

June 7. I am in the midst of trying to get freed of my land. I have come to the point when I can no longer pay taxes and have expressed myself as willing to abandon my land but while all land in China belongs to the "people," I cannot give mine away and avoid taxes. I am taking the matter up the first of the week with the Foreign Affairs Bureau but do not expect any assistance. There is only one key which unlocks all doors and that is made of precious metal . . . The first of the week I am also sending in my letter to the Labor Bureau asking for assistance to arrange a settlement with my staff. Yesterday I talked to them sympathetically urging them to come to an understanding with me regarding the payoff but I got no response. One has to see and hear at first hand this sort of thing before one can believe it. One can understand how and why one's staff will hang on for dear life when there is nothing ahead, but disloyalty of those one has employed for years is hard to take.

A. seems to be making no plans about a move north. Like many other things his affairs seem to be just waiting. He was much more relaxed than I have seen him for some time. He was describing the different manner in which Americans and Chinese attack an obstacle. The Americans simply double up their fists and with a little profanity make a frontal attack. The Chinese on the other hand say "there is no method by which to remove the obstacle," but in the same breath they say, "we'll find a way around." He says this is a deep down characteristic and always a way around is found. I replied that that was all very well but when would a way be found. There, he said "You're acting like an American; what is a thousand years to us?" You will see in this mild exchange one of the deep philosophies of our area.

You may remember the place in the Bible where the rich man was asked to give up all his wordly goods and follow Him. That is the "new movement" just starting. Make your own substitution in keeping with present trends and you will see what a diabolical move this really is. It is just starting and looks as though it may be the ultimate squeeze. It might not be so bad if those collecting these "voluntary" contributions were to use them for the commonweal instead of the wheels of state.

I can't see any repercussions as yet from the British firm affair. Outwardly there is no change.

JUNE 9, 1952 (TO H.S.H.)

The mother of a patient who has not been able to pay a fee just came in with a bottle of rum. The other day another patient brought in two bottles of whiskey. This may come in handy when we get down to our last potato! This woman brings a common story, her husband with no business and office staff of four hanging on for dear life. With no resources of any sort anywhere what is the answer? Everwhere we turn, both natives and foreigners, it is the same. Some "tummies" are going to revolt some day! P. went down the Whangpoo River the other day by boat and afterwards told me that it was absolutely dead. *(The liquor mentioned was later sold at a good price to meet operating expenses.)*

June 10. Our summer is back upon us again today. I have just come in from an evening walk, not a very pleasant one with streets crowded. As I came along Avenue Joffre the pedicabs were doing a big business as there had been a breakdown of the trams out to the west.

I am rather glad they were getting a break as their incomes have been rather reduced lately.

June 11, Wednesday. You would be interested in the different varieties of "bear brand jam" we are eating these days. Did you ever make a willow whistle as a youngster? You will remember how you could make a sliding end and produce higher and lower frequencies. So does our "jam." There are others like frogs in the pond, birds, and even domestic fowls. I sometimes think I can detect some barnyard animals. *(The above referred to the constant attempts by the Soviets to jam air waves coming into China.)*

June 12. A good day with a game of golf has set me up a bit. I am always glad of these days because they bring me in contact with men from various walks of life.

The seller of goods is now being courted, possibly in the hope he will forget recent "pressures." This reversal seems almost too pointed and one wonders what is next. On top of this I am told that some of the British firms are having an easier time than they expected in terminating services. The three members remaining in Standard Oil, all Americans, have been advised to apply for exit permits. Again there is talk that all foreigners including those in restraint may be going out in the not too distant future. There is no doubt but that there is some change in the air but what it means is most obscure. *(The reference above to the courting of "The seller of goods" relates to the effort on the part of authorities to secure the co-operation of merchants so that the "year of prosperity" which was approaching would be an accomplished fact. The staffs of merchants, who had been crucified by them, were urged now to give their cooperation and let bygones be bygones.)*

June 13. I was talking with a business man this morning who suggests that all "lemons" which have been squeezed dry may be cast out. If this is true more exit permits will be granted in the near future. We certainly will try to ride the crest of this wave if it becomes a reality . . . As I look down upon the old French Club this morning I can see workmen repairing the terrace matting and bamboo covering. I would have said their summer evening parties and dances were finished but something is giving them a new lease on life. The upper floors of the building are being used by the authorities but they pay very little rent.

Evening, same day. The boy who helps me with my translation went with me in search of the Public Health Bureau this afternoon. We finally located it after five tries and after riding all over this end of the city in a pedicab. Since it was raining hard the pedicab was a great help. Those we have are large enough for two sitting side by side.

We met a very agreeable man who set us right as to the order of closing the office. I must terminate services of the staff before I can close the office and not the other way around as insisted upon by my staff. We must now try to get action by the Labor Bureau. *(In the final settlement I found my staff was right.)*

June 14. As usual our week-end rains are on. Out at the golf club an old caddie with a sense of humor said some time ago when we were caught in a shower, "even the weather is 'liberated.'" As a matter of fact, I could not have gone out today as I must go along to see a division of the Government regarding their remitting part of my land tax. I doubt if anything will come of our efforts as I have been trying for over a year to get this rebate. The currents of a river flow only in one direction and likewise the currency of our day. In any event I am prepared with funds so that when the 21st of this month comes along I shall be free for the time being of tax claims. In other words I cannot be hung up in applying for an exit permit because of non-payment.

5:30 p.m., same day. Believe it or not I am to get my rebate on the property used by the soldiers. We spent three hours this rainy afternoon going over the situation with an official and going out to the property where eye witnesses were found to confirm our claim that soldiers had used the property. The man we had today was most helpful. The saving of the equivalent of $90 U.S. is important these days. The thing which impresses and depresses in all this is the great amount of time and talking required to get anything done. One reason may be that those in junior positions are always afraid of doing something which will get them in wrong with those above.

June 15. My office staff is the present obstacle. Apparently their union has told them to stall and to that end they will not talk. I have been advised to take this matter to the Foreign Affairs Bureau by a man who has had a great deal of experience in such matters. I am pushing to get some action before the last of the month.

JUNE 15, 1952 (TO D. & H.)

One of the difficult bits of business in getting away from here is the listing of every article taken out. There are also certain things such as silver which cannot be taken out unless foreign exchange is brought in to cover. We have very little silver but at the moment have no way of bringing foreign exchange in to cover. It works this way, one buys local currency with foreign money to the extent of the value of what one wants to take out and then one uses the local currency in paying off debts here. It is just a method of getting more foreign currency in for the authorities. *(This regulation was changed and we were allowed to take out 25 ounces of silver without bringing in foreign exchange.)*

This morning I learned that all American accounts must be transferred to the Bank of China—meaning that all American accounts must be controlled. This probably means that a limit will be placed on the amount of withdrawals each month. This will mean little to us as we rarely have much in the bank at any one time. Taken together with the fact that all American residence certificates have been extended only until August 31st, this may have some meaning.

## 20: CLOSING THE OFFICE

In the early days after "liberation," when certain missionary organizations and a few foreign business concerns were permitted to close, severance pay in some instances was excessive. There was no definite rule but some went so far as to give one month's salary for every year of service. An overly generous manager or individual who wished to get out quickly and without too much fuss might pay a great deal more. One individual paid 36 months in severance pay to a small staff. By the time we were preparing to leave, a new ruling had been made by the authorities that all staff members who had served less than ten years were to be given only three months severance pay. For those serving over ten years a sliding scale was provided. Regardless of this ruling my staff insisted that I, an American, had money and must pay more. This was the real reason for the struggle between us. Later it happened that because I was a member of the Shanghai Practitioners Association, I was not permitted to pay more than the "legal" three months.

JUNE 16, 1952 (TO H.S.H.)

I went out for a long walk over on Bubbling Well Road late this afternoon and was much impressed by the shop windows. It seems to me I have never seen them so well stocked. Consignment stores were everywhere and perhaps enjoyed the major portion of the window shopping, which was virtually the only kind of shopping to be seen. Only those places putting on excessively cheap sales showed any activity.

This evening our air waves from New York said that Peking had

# CLOSING THE OFFICE

announced that the purge of business men had been completed. All are urged locally to cooperate but there are some sore hearts where fathers and husbands are no longer around. This thing may have gone much deeper than some realize.

June 17, Tuesday. Two things have happened today. First, this afternoon I received a letter from the proper authorities finally giving me credit for the time in 1950 when soldiers used my property in Columbia Circle for the purpose of growing vegetables. Then when I got home from the office I found a request from the Labor Bureau to call on them for a conference regarding staff matters tomorrow morning. I hope to get some immediate help from them as my staff absolutely refuses to discuss severance pay with me. This is the usual way it is played so I must force their hand. I'll let you know how it comes out.

June 18. Well, we did not get very far with the Labor Bureau this morning. They say they can do nothing until the office is closed by the Public Health. Last week the Public Health Bureau said we could not close the office until the staff was paid off. Now we must begin running around in circles again! *(It will be seen that there was much confusion regarding the proper procedure in the closing of my office.)*

Not more than ten minutes after I got in from my session with the Labor Bureau three office clerks and union members of Sassoon and Company (my landlords) came in to demand that I pay my back rent on this flat. This approach is a new one! They contend that they have just as much right to my small income as my staff. Unless rents are paid to the Company (and less than forty percent are being paid) they cannot get their salaries, hence their canvas. When all is said and done, this is an indicator of the fact that Sassoon is bringing in no more foreign exchange.

Evening, same day. I feel a whole heap better this evening. I met two human beings in the Public Health Department! The young man who is helping me in translations went with me to the Public Health this p.m. and placed all our cards on the table. What I wanted was to be able to discharge my staff and carry on alone until my exit permit is given. They are going to see if this can be done but it will require letters here and letters there. The man in charge was rather critical of this morning's Labor Bureau man. This brings me to say that there seems to be an element in responsible positions which is attempting to do the right thing. Some of the men down town trying to close out are finding helpful individuals in larger numbers than has been apparent until recently. What is the meaning of all this no one seems to know, but it is being remarked upon.

JUNE 23, 1952 (TO D. & H.)

I am going to see the British Consul General this afternoon regarding aid in paying off my staff in the event I can get a settlement with them in the near future. I have just finished meeting all my taxes and a half month's rent on the flat and there is practically nothing left.

June 25. As we draw near our time of departure there will be certain bits of mail coming along to you which I'll ask you to simply hold. There is so little we can carry out but some of it can go by mail. *(It was of interest that we could send out certain things by mail but could not carry out address books and other personal documents.)*

June 30. We have been in the thick of trying to get rid of the office staff today. I have told them I cannot pay them after today. But with regard to separation pay we have not come to a settlement. We go to their union in the morning but I don't expect much in the way of results. We shall probably have to carry it to the Labor Bureau at which time the Medical Practitioners Association will come to my aid. I am refusing to pay more than the so-called three months separation.

July 1, Tuesday. We got nowhere in our staff Labor Union meeting this morning. I did not think we would as the Labor Union must always stand up for staff. Now we take the whole matter to the Labor Bureau where I shall have some help from my Medical Association. All this business is so time consuming and belittling. One does not enjoy being asked by his office boy if he is "keeping the law." But what I have gone through is nothing when compared with what some of our native friends have had to contend with.

Since writing the first part of this letter a friend has come in and volunteered to help me with an advance when I get ready to terminate staff services. I am all right for the time being but sooner or later must make plans for a larger loan. I am getting my letter into the Labor Bureau this morning and we should be having some action before too long. One gets so eternally tired of talking, talking, talking. When one is behind the curtain he takes many things which would not be tolerated otherwise.

Six p.m., same day. We made an attempt to see the Foreign Affairs Bureau this afternoon but found their office hours had been changed to the morning. I'll make another try in the morning because I must see them before going on to the Labor Bureau.

JUNE 23, 1952 (TO H.S.H.)

I had a long talk this evening with one of our former staff members of the Peking Union Medical College. Our talks did not bring to light any bright spots. He had recently visited a friend over in the big hospital beyond the creek in French Town. It made him sick to see how dirty and run-down the place is even to bed sheets. Following the grant by the Rockefeller Foundation for the building and equipment of this place it used to be kept in very good order, but now there is a "new order" in control. One sees the same low standard everywhere.

From our talk tonight it is increasingly evident that private practice for every one is soon to be a thing of the past. It works this way. A man is asked to give half a day to a general clinic. Soon pressure is used to make him give all day and no time is left for private practice. W. has been able thus far to preserve a small part of the day for his practice, but does not know how long he can do so. Everyone must be on the same level when it comes to treatment so all must take their turn in a general clinic. All the more reason why I should be closing out my practice.

June 24. There is a big move on to establish five 500-bed general hospitals in the city and it may be that within a matter of weeks I can sell my equipment at a fair price. Great difficulty is being experienced in securing the 1,000 nurses required in the city. Only one fifth of that number have thus far turned up. You can understand what such a program will do for the professional personnel of the city.

JUNE 30, 1952 (TO H.S.H.)

I am in the midst of trying to get a settlement with my staff. This morning we had a session but did not get very far. As I pointed out to you before, they hang on like leeches. I have another period with them at their union in the morning but don't expect to arrange anything. I told them today that I could not pay them wages beyond today and they need not come back but it remains to be seen whether I get away with that.

I have the backing of the Public Health Department and the Shanghai Practitioner's Association and am told I need not give them more than three months separation pay. I intend to stand by my guns, *(My staff reappeared the next morning without any intention of quitting their jobs until a complete and final settlement had been made.)*

July 1st. I had another session today with my staff in the presence of their labor chairman but without any results. I now take my affair to the Labor Bureau for final settlement. A letter is being prepared tonight and will be sent in tomorrow. I go also to the Foreign Affairs

Bureau tomorrow to tell them what I am doing. They will not give me any help and perhaps not even advice.

July 2. We are to have a Fourth of July reception at the British Consul General's home, of all places. As a matter of fact there are not many Americans here and it will not be a large party. We have a way of forgetting history at these times. You may be sure that all the Americans in the city will be there. There are not many meetings of this sort when we can get together.

July 3, Thursday. This morning I went along to the Foreign Affairs Bureau to report what I am doing in trying to close out my office. They told me that I am doing the correct thing and must first get my staff taken care of before I can apply for an exit permit. What happens now at the Labor Bureau remains to be seen.

July 4. The anodyne of these days is liberal doses of Edgar Wallace and Irwin Cobb. It is absolutely necessary to crowd out of one's mind the recurring pressures which daily beset us, for short periods at least. I would think that the businessmen of this period have never done so much "light" reading as now. Any person indulging in the classics can be put down as free of pressures! . . . One of Shanghai's former very wealthy men has just been in as a patient. He paid "what he could afford," the equivalent of $2 U. S. by the present unrealistic exchange. He goes to Palestine now with virtually only the clothes on his back. This "milking" and "squeezing" process must not only be seen but experienced before one can see how diabolic it is.

9:15 p.m., same day. Perhaps forty Americans attended the Fourth of July reception at the British Consulate General. There were also a number of friends from other countries.

JULY 5, 1952 (TO D. & H.)

It was rather a subdued group of Americans who gathered at the Consulate for the Fourth of July reception yesterday, as most of them are waiting to close up business and get out. Some have been waiting one or two years. Since B. was deported some ten days ago there seems to be a little more hope that things may be changing just a little so that others can get out. My feeling is that this is just wishful thinking but who can say. We shall be pushing ahead with our plans just as fast as possible but one must realize that only one step is made at a time. When we have this staff matter cleared away I am sure greater progress can be made.

July 8. All day long we have been getting bits of the Chicago Convention. Their hysteria sounds like some we run into now and then

# CLOSING THE OFFICE 175

on this side of the Curtain. I guess human nature is much the same wherever you find it.

July 13, Sunday. We are delighted with Ike's nomination. S. and I stayed up until 3 a.m. Saturday morning and got the turning of events just as they happened. We caught the European relay of the V. O. A. via Tangier and had everything as clear as could be. Yesterday at the golf club, as an American, I was congratulated on the outcome of the nomination by our British cousins. Native friends are also very much pleased.

JULY 7, 1952 (TO H.S.H.)

The last of the Standard Oil foreigners are getting their exit permits and expect to get away within a week. There are still some ten men in the British American Tobacco Company with C., with no indication of when they can get away.

July 8. I am beginning to receive reactions from people who are learning that we are trying to get out. They are what one might expect. "We don't want you to go but we know you can't stay." I wish it might be possible to get out quietly between two days. Of one thing we will be thankful, we shall avoid the eternal feasts which are usually given on departure. As a matter of fact we rarely see any of our old students and they do not see each other.

July 11. One of the new things is a demand by the students union that a part of our golf course be given to them for a six-to-eight-week summer camp. They want a place where eight hundred can hang out for that period. Of course they do not wish to pay anything toward land tax. I believe that this would be a first step to get a foot in the door and it would not be long before they would have the entire place on their own terms. This is the usual way it is done.

JULY 14, 1952 (TO H.S.H.)

Most of the morning, I spent with the chairman of the Labor Union controlling my staff, in an effort to get a solution. One always starts these conferences with two strikes against him. The ignominy of sitting on a hard bench and being interrogated by one who probably at one time was some one's house boy is sometimes hard to take but it must be taken with a calm exterior, otherwise one gets nowhere.

It is just over forty-one years since I came to China but I might just as well have come only last week for all the consideration that is given to my years of service to the Chinese people. I realize, however, it is the spirit of the times and many of my native colleagues have had to go through the same sort of thing. I think I did get a little more light this morning with regard to what I must do. I have been under the impression that I must have my staff separated before I can apply for an exit permit. Now I know that I must have a contract for severance pay and then services can be terminated. I must now keep my staff on until I close my office. If I can get a written contract within the next few days I shall immediately apply for an exit permit. This will give me two months in which to clear everything else away and get out . . . I suppose one should not blame my staff too much for they know that when they leave this job the chances of getting another are pretty slim. All the law allows them is three months' salary as separation pay. It will not be hard for you to imagine a fair number in this city who are in the same position. That is why there is so much of this leeching activity but in my case I am told that a signed contract will heal it and no obstruction will be placed in the way of an exit permit.

July 16. There is some question as to which department has the most say in terminating our affairs. I am to see the Public Health Department today to make absolutely sure I must carry my staff on to the point when my office is to be immediately closed and my license recalled. I would not mind closing my office since my staff takes most of what comes in but I dislike turning some of my old Chinese patients away who have been under treatment. Two are having larynx dilations and three are having ear drums closed.

July 17. Another session this morning with the Labor Union with absolutely no results! One of my friends was right, "we talk and talk and get no where" and when one feels he has had one point settled it is brought up in new clothing in the hope of getting it past.

It is most sickening business for one who has spent so much time aiding the sick in China to find such disloyal individuals in his own staff. Of course they have back of them the union which prompts them on the things they should say. I don't think Mrs. C. is too much a party to what these young people are doing but she is forced to keep still or go along with them. My Chinese friends think it is a shame but there is nothing they can do, or dare do about it. *(Mrs. C., now dead, was my nurse-secretary for fifteen years.)*

July 18. Before the others arrived this morning Mrs. C. wanted me to know that she does not agree with the others in what they are demanding. They are forcing her to go along with them but she hopes I'll not give in to their demands. My greatest concern is to get everything settled "legally" finally in a contract which cannot be violated. Anything which is down on paper and is signed is "legal"!

July 19, Saturday. This business of getting separated from one's

# CLOSING THE OFFICE

staff resolves itself into a regular stand-up knock-down verbal fight with the staff and Labor Union on one side and the Capitalist Doctor on the other. If you have any illusions as to whether or not any consideration will be shown you in consequence of your long period of service in China you must put them aside at the start. Every word you say will be questioned and frequently you will be told you cannot be trusted. Some day I think I must write it all up as it is all so unbelievable.

Yesterday afternoon I had another long session with my staff which while it cleared up some points left a final settlement every bit as far away as before. The young misguided members of my staff are grasping at every device to force me to pay out to them excessive separation pay. Fortunately I have an agreement with the Labor Bureau which will hold them down . . . One of the saddest aspects of this whole affair is that they can probably force me to turn in my license to practice at the same moment they are discharged. I asked the Labor Bureau man yesterday what happens when I am without license and a sick man presents himself at my door. "Send them away," he said. If I can't get this point cleared up I may have to keep my staff on until I have my exit permit. Otherwise, aside from the business of old patients, I will have no support and may be kept here months before an exit permit is granted.

Later, same day. The Public Health people were very nice this morning, but they said that they were helpless where doctors had staff members because the rule is that as long as you continue to work you must employ them. I asked what would be the situation if I made it worthwhile for them to resign. Then they said there would be no labor problem.

I am therefore putting two alternatives before my staff when they return on Monday. One, that they continue to work through August when I shall close my office and return my license. Two, to resign as of the end of this month with an extra month's pay plus the three legal months which is already granted and agreed to. In this case my license will be left alone until I can get my exit permit.

JULY 21, 1952 (TO H.S.H.)

A long session with my staff this morning produced no results. They maintain that a foreign doctor must be treated differently than a Chinese doctor although in answer to a question of mine the Labor Union man stated that there was no difference in the treatment between Chinese and foreigners. Also they have the belief that I have some gold hid away and they mean to get some of it. It is the old labor union squeeze game and I shall probably not get it settled until I can place it in the hands of the Labor Bureau. They are fighting to keep it from getting to that point as they know the Bureau is official and will make a final decision.

With regard to Dr. V.'s query as to what news penetrates behind the Bamboo Curtain from abroad, one may reply that a surprising lot does come in and it is passed around by word of mouth. I am constantly amazed at the up-to-the-minute knowledge which my native friends have of current world events. There are no "legal" only "moral" restrictions on reception. I am inclined to believe that the more that can be poured in the better. *(At about this time a Chinese friend who had recently returned from Peking informed me that all foreign broadcasts were monitored in Peking and after translation were placed in the hands of the important individuals in the Government.)*

July 22. Yesterday it was announced that the "fifth symphony" will be played no more and that it has been brought to a "harmonious conclusion." Page Mr. Ripley! I wish I might paint a picture of a young but not too young couple, who visited me night before last, giving me a before and after description of life as it was and as it is. I had not seen the lady of the union for months and was really shocked when I saw her in her required uniform of the day. He was incarcerated during the playing of the "fifth" and only came out after paying his share of the "playing" which was equivalent to $7,500 U.S. Can you believe that happiness is built this way? One day I hope to give you more of this picture. *(There had been many rumors regarding the final termination of the "five anti's movement" against the merchants, but this was the first official notification.)*

When you next come to China and look for "Henry the Tailor" or "Young Fit-All the Tailor" you will not find their signs. Just now all English signs must be removed and as you know in Shanghai that means not a few. All imported things coming in now must use native characters on their labels. Your "Johnny Walker" is hid behind a native label.

July 24, Thursday. Your letter written on the 13th and mailed on the 14th came in this morning making very good time. It finds us with heat returning after our recent typhoon but with cool nights. I don't know why we did not go into an apartment building a long time ago since summer living in them is very much more pleasant than in a house. I had not been in to see A. for a long time until last evening when I went up to find his household things almost completely packed ready for shipment north. He leaves either on the 2nd or 8th of next month. He is not a very happy man. In fact, I can find very few these days.

July 25. We certainly ran into a hot one this morning! The Labor Bureau man we have always talked to was most rude as we tried to get some advice from him as to how to settle my office affairs. He pounded on the table saying he could do nothing until the Labor Union acted, to which my translator replied as quietly and courteously as possible that we could get no action by the staff or Labor Union. He continued to rant (I think he has ulcers or is near a nervous breakdown) so we walked out. Then an amazing thing happened. He came along behind us before we could reach the gate and called to us and in an entirely different tone asked if I was not a member of the Shanghai Medical Practitioners Association. He knew I was because I was wearing my Association pin. He advised that I should go to the Association for "advice" and "assistance." Why he had "two faces" is hard to tell but this afternoon we went to see the head of the Association and now we know where and what to do next. *(Since our discussion with the Labor Bureau man took place within a building with low wall partitions between conference rooms it seems probable that he was under observation by a superior and was compelled to be hard-boiled. In subsequent contacts with this same man he was quite cordial.)*

As a member of the Association I am forbidden to pay more than three months' salary as separation pay. The president of the Association told us how to write an official letter now to the Labor Bureau and said that if it did not produce the desired result the Association would come to my aid as I was on correct and legal grounds. As a foreign member I must not pay any more than a Chinese member. With this backing I am much easier in my mind tonight and see a definite possibility of closing my office next month.

Later, same day. A. and two of his doctors were in this evening to look over my equipment. They would like very much to secure it all for their new school but the Government will pay only about thirty per cent of the original cost price. As you probably know, I have the best equipped ear, nose and throat office in the Far East and I don't want to see it go for a song, if I can help it.

July 28. Our air waves have just told us of the United Nations walkout in the Korean conference and their intention of taking a week's recess. I know from personal experience that negotiations mean talk, talk, talk, until some one gives in. The idea as seen in things near at hand, is to repeat over and over again the same thing so that the brain cells are turned all in the same direction. There are signs that not only students but other groups are getting fed up with this studied repetition. It is most difficult to spend the day at work, and then sit in meetings from two to three hours more.

10:15 p.m. We have listened to a most timely sermon for our special situation by a Mr. Anderson of Scarsdale, New York. He spoke of courage to stand up to things. It was most helpful. If there ever was a time when one must stand firm it is now. Any giving way will be considered as a sign of weakness.

JULY 28, 1952 (TO H.S.H.)

If you were to hear the "walla-walla" which is going on in my outer office you might think that a fight is on but it is only a patient telling his experiences in a hospital where he had a radical antrum to cure atrophic rhinitis. This is a sample of what goes forward these days. Good men, like my former resident H., are not allowed to do anything but administrative work. I tried to send him a patient day before yesterday but he could not even examine. The new order requires purity of duties. Something will burst one of these days with all these young inexperienced men pushed into surgical work before they are trained. Most have not had proper training in the fundamentals of diagnosis. It is modern medicine and surgery run wild!

At this point one of my old Chinese patients goes out weeping because I told her I must close my office within a month.

Later, same day. Somewhere I read the other day that impatience is the greatest sin. I don't know about that but I do know that patience is one of the greatest virtues. Certainly it is one we can't get along without in these parts. And it is not so easy these hot days but my native friends warn it is the only instrument to use to pull through current situations. I hope theirs will be rewarded one of these days but there are days when it seems pretty far away. I was talking to a native friend last evening who is separated from his wife in Hong Kong. He has a brand of patience which I think is beyond me. He wants the things in the North East, that is Korea, to continue "as is" as he believes it is the only way to bring sense into some of the people living in Peking. He wants them to go bankrupt.

My Russian colleague told me today that he is tired of it all and is seriously thinking of going to the Fiji Islands where they are wanting doctors. He was with the British firm and is the only one left since Dr. B.'s death. Some day I must tell you about him for I admire the way he has stood up to "pressures." The fact that he belongs to a friendly nation has not saved him, in fact, he has had more troubles because he is what he is.

# CLOSING THE OFFICE

July 30. A long talk with one of my old students last evening paints a picture of increasing gloom. The latest group to take to the act of "termination" is that of pregnant women. He feels that "termination" is on the increase primarily due to the poor economic situation. This man sees no way out. *(The "termination" mentioned refers to suicides among pregnant women who saw very little hope of securing food for a growing family.)*

I have been rereading Dale Carnegie's "Live in Day-Tight Compartments" which appeared in the *Reader's Digest* for August 1948. It is useful for those of us who must meet pressures from day to day. It was Sir William Osler who first called it living in "day-tight compartments" and considered this the secret of his success rather than "any special quality of brains." I like what Carnegie says about carrying burdens: "The load of tomorrow, added to that of yesterday, carried today, makes the strongest falter." I have to remind myself of this thought as each morning the number of things facing us to be done, in the getting away process, comes crowding into my mind.

July 31. We got our petition in to the Labor Bureau today for staff settlement and closure of the office. It has been two weeks since the Labor Union told me they would consult the Labor Bureau and give me a decision soon. It is the usual way of doing things. Stalling is their order of the day. They avoid a final settlement and try to keep the staff on. I have my Practitioners Association back of me now and we are trying to force the issue.

August. 1. I am hoping I am starting my last month of practice in China. A Chinese doctor of the old native group has just been in for another treatment in the closing of his ear drum. He is not happy about my license being taken away before I am ready to leave China. There are many other things that he is not happy about. Out of ten thousand native doctors in the city only about two hundred can now make a living. This man has come down to almost nothing with practically all his property gone.

August 2. I had one of my old students in last evening to go over my equipment problem. He would like to get everything I have for his hospital but they may not have any money to spend for it. Also the Government may be pushing all the medical schools together soon giving each only a special line to follow. I want to make a private sale if possible.

This period will be etched in my memory as that of the "racing ambulances" and "barking megaphones." With windows wide open to get all the breeze we must put up with the noises as well. Last night in the middle of the night I heard a drum corps going past and was reminded that I had not heard one for a long time. As a matter of fact we have had no parades for some time, as we are in the phase of "increased production." *(The "racing ambulances" were used not only for the purpose of transporting the sick but also for moving prisoners from jail to jail or to the execution grounds. Subsequently, during the period of large numbers of suicides at the time of the five anti's, bodies picked up on the street were initially taken to the hospitals for investigation. However, during the period mentioned above, ambulances were being used excessively by laborers and various individuals whose firms or factories were responsible for sending them to the hospital in the event they had a fever or had dressings of one sort or another to be done. The head of one of Shanghai's largest hospitals told me that this privilege was greatly abused. Since many Chinese experienced motion illness it is probable that individuals calling these ambulances were really ill by the time they arrived at their destination if they had not been so before starting.)*

## 21: FINAL SETTLEMENTS

During our early days in China, hawkers were frequently at our door selling porcelains, silks, brasses, linens, and similar wares. The newly arrived foreigner was always warned that under no circumstances should he pay the peddler's asking price. A game of bargaining must be played and an opening offer considerably less than the one asked must be made. The hawker might show disgust and even anger at your low offer while on your part you let him know that you did not intend to pay such an unheard of price. This would all be a part of the game but eventually he would come down a little and you would go up a little, step by step, until a price was arrived at that was mutually agreeable. The bargaining over, all would be peace again.

And so it was with the prolonged and at times most disagreeable bargaining between my staff and myself. They undoubtedly were asking for a great deal more than they ever expected to get, and like the hawker, were very unpleasant about it. On my side resistance to demands had to be maintained primarily because of the principle involved as well as the limitation of funds available. When final settlements were made all tempers quieted and the staff carried on faithfully until the office was closed the last day of August, 1952.

AUGUST 4, 1952 (TO H.S.H.)

There seems to be something brewing with the Labor Bureau as my staff has been called in to give their side of the claim. I hope before the week is out to get some action which will settle this. Just as

I write, the Labor Bureau phoned to ask if I am going to join another group of doctors or am I going to join a Government hospital. "No," I said, "I'm going home!"

Within the past two hours natives, one an educator and one a lift man in this building, have both expressed their sorrow that I am leaving. The latter added, "When can we have peace?"

August 6, Wednesday. I have received my call to the Labor Bureau arbitration meeting which takes place day after tomorrow. I am having the backing of the Practitioners Association and I think all will be well. If I can get my exit promptly I shall be able to manage local finances, I think, but if I am delayed for several months without the right to see a few patients, I shall be in a spot. I think I told you that I must return my license at the same time I close my office and discharge the staff. This date is August 31st if all goes well.

AUGUST 8, 1952 (TO H.S.H.)

It is almost 11 p.m., but I want to report on my victory over the staff at the Labor Bureau arbitration meeting this morning. Dr. W., president of the Shanghai Practitioners Association came to the meeting and was instrumental in holding them to the legal payment of three months separation pay to which was added lunch allowance for the same period in the amount of 150,000 JMP or the equivalent of about six U. S. dollars. They were trying to hold me up for millions but all they got was this measly 150,000 JMP above the legal three months and this was granted only as a face saving bit of business . . . Now I am free to apply for an exit permit and intend to do so early next week. The agreement which was signed by all parties this morning requires the closing of my office on the 31st of this month and the returning of my license to practice immediately. I shall use this state of "no income" to press harder for my exit permit.

August 9, Saturday. With this pressure of staff off I feel like a new man this morning. All the talking out in the other part of the flat as to how they are going to trim the old man should now stop. Just outside my door, the two people on my staff who have caused all the trouble would whisper all morning long and then later rush over to their union to see at what new angle they could set their guns. Their first ganging up in March, when they tried to get eighty-two million from me, failed when we got it into the Labor Bureau. And so it was with this last effort which was intended to send me down for a much larger amount. They were trying to use the services of my old office boy, the grandfather of the male trouble maker, to get a toe in the door of what they felt must be a richly supplied treasure house hidden away somewhere. They claimed the period of forty-one years service for old Ma, counting in the time I was in Peking and he was not in my service. The Labor Bureau, however, threw out all claims for any period before my return to China in January, 1947. A new "law" has just been passed giving special grants to men of ten years service and longer. This is why they were trying to establish such a claim. All services under ten years are terminated on three months separation pay.

August 10. I am still luxurating in my freedom from staff "pressures." I shall have problems of other sorts but these constant daily staff digs have rather got me down. I shall now hope that my step-by-step process will be less of a burden. I don't like this idea of closing my office at the end of the month and sending my license back as required by the Labor Bureau, since all my income will be cut off but I shall enjoy being free of all professional responsibilities.

Yes, all money in Hong Kong should be subject only to my order but since the staff is now under control the need for such care is not as pressing as it was. As a matter of what I hope will be a fact, there should be enough from the sale of equipment to meet my local obligations. This will not be the case, however, if I must sell my equipment to the Government at thirty per cent of its value. I think I told you that if we go by boat, and there is every possibility that we can, I must pay all fares and freight within five days after arriving in Hong Kong.

Now that it is becoming known that we are getting out, various Chinese friends are slipping in to offer help. Now our real friends show what is in them. The old "Shanghai mind" which I meet frequently can not admit that any good remains in the Chinese but I know where to find it and at times it is most touching.

AUGUST 12, 1952 (TO H.S.H.)

This is pay-off day for my staff. The two rampaging members have been much subdued since the Labor Bureau's decision. Now as we pay them off we are making them sign a statement that all my obligations to them have been met. Since my cook has given me a letter stating he wishes to have the same treatment as the staff I think we should have no further trouble.

I have been advised to wait until I get my copy of the agreement with the staff before going in to apply for an exit permit. Since I am hoping to get my Lincoln Road property leased for at least enough to meet my tax obligations I can't feel there will be anything that can hold me up.

A. gets away next Friday. There has been delay due to the disposing of his hospital, which is now closed and all his staff sent over to another Government-controlled institution.

August 14. This has been a full day! People are getting wind of the fact that my office closes the last of the month and patients, mostly Chinese, are coming in. Virtually all are without funds with which to pay fees. R. told me last evening that he didn't think I can even give my car away. All one can do is keep it and pay storage.

August 15, Friday. It has been another active office morning. An old larynx case, a boy of eighteen, got out of a sick bed to come in for an examination. His mother said he wept yesterday when he heard I was closing my office. There is no sympathy for the Labor Union which requires this move. As a matter of fact, it may be the best kind of radical surgery to cut me away from the situation.

This morning I paid off the last of the staff and now I have four statements that they have been paid in full and I have no more obligations. The house servants, I think, are under control. It is then only my land which might hold me up. My Labor Bureau copy of agreement has not come as yet but just as soon as it does I am off to apply for an exit permit.

Later, same day. A. has sent in a letter to say they go tomorrow night. He writes that they definitely want to buy all my office equipment but must first get approval. I am asking one hundred and forty million for everything and he thinks this is possible. If I can get near this figure I can clear away all expenses up to Hong Kong exclusive of ship tickets and freight charges. I have a number of parties after my equipment so may realize what I want. A. is the best bet. The big chore is to make a complete list of every single item. That is the way they work so that is the way it must be done.

August 16, Saturday. My copy of the Labor Bureau contract came this morning so I shall be applying for an exit permit the first of the week. I have been in to see my shippers this morning and I think everything will go along well when once we have an exit permit.

AUGUST 16, 1952 (TO D. & H.)

I am just in from a short game of golf, just as the sun goes down, giving us a beautiful sunset. It is good to have beauty above if one must see other things below. We are on the edge of a typhoon so our cloud effects are rather unusual.

August 18, Monday. Well, we have started the ball rolling for our exit permits. S. and I have just been down to get the forms for ourselves and Mrs. D. and they are now being filled in for returning within the next few days. I can't believe we shall have too much difficulty but one can never tell what may show up. *(Each person applying for an exit permit had to appear in person at each stage of the process. An exception was made in the case of Mrs. D. because of her extreme lameness.)*

I am at a loss to know what to do with my old 1942 Chevrolet. At present I can neither sell nor give it away. Something may open up before we finally go out as gasoline is being sold freely again and most cars may be put in use if anyone can afford to run them.

August 19, Tuesday. S. and I are just in from getting our applications in for exits. Now we must wait and watch the papers for our names to appear. In the meantime we are beginning to pack some things. Nearly every day some one comes in to look over the furniture in the hope of finding something they want. But they have little money to pay for what they want.

August 20. There is one disadvantage in these disjointed letters, they jump about with little bits of "this and that." As the days progress they are likely to be even more disjointed due to the fact that that will be the sort of life we shall be living as we get things under way in preparation for moving out. In many ways it will be just as well that I am prevented from doing any practice after the end of this month. I can then devote all my time to clearing away my office things.

S. sold his bicycle yesterday for the equivalent of $100 U. S. which is a good start at our things. He got more for it than I could get at the moment for our motor car. Changed situations have a way of radically changing prices of various articles. If we can pick up enough from the sale of old furniture to pay the back rent I shall be thankful.

AUGUST 18, 1952 (TO H.S.H.)

I spent all of yesterday going over my equipment and I am impressed with the completeness of my things. In my forty-one years of practice I have accumulated most everything needed by ear, nose and throat specialists. I have so much extra snare wire and any number of lamps for instruments, a clinic would not need a supply for a long time.

August 19. While at the Police Department this morning to put in our applications for exit permits I gave them my agreement which has recently been signed by the staff as well as the Labor Bureau. It was an impressive document to place before them. I doubt if I have enough land left to cause trouble. There is belief that all American land will be taken over within the next six months. Much depends upon how the present regime develops.

August 20. This has been a day! In the morning I had twelve patients and in the afternoon an operative nose case. Everyone came rushing in because my office is closing at the end of next week. It is remarkable how fast this news of closure gets around. It would be helpful if these last minute patients could pay a proper fee but many are without funds.

Some of my experiences with patients these days, especially Chinese, are most touching. They don't want me to go, but when I explain, they realize it is impossible to carry on. Not a few blame my narrow-minded staff and the Labor Union which demand the closure of my office. The man I operated on this afternoon broke out in his poor English in the midst of the operation to try to convince me that China needs me to stay. I think he was stimulated by the fact that I had just removed a man-sized polyp from his nasopharynx and was breathing through his nose for the first time in twenty years. There are a number of my students who could have made the operation.

AUGUST 27, 1952 (TO H.S.H.)

Your letter of August 14th arrived last Sunday, the 24th, and found me in bed with a virus infection. I have never had anything just like this before and don't want it again. It is taking a long time to get back in the swing of things and it is necessary to get back as I am in my last week of office practice and am being rushed with patients who want to get in before the door closes. I am even having to have appointments after office hours.

SEPTEMBER 1, 1952 (TO H.S.H.)

Our big news here this past twenty-four hours is that the P's are on the Sunday exit list. They go now on Wednesday to pick up their exit permits if all goes well and no one has put in an objection. I can hardly think there will be any as their case has been investigated so long. After all this time one would feel that all objections should have been exhausted. If everything is cleared they plan to get away in about ten days.

This is my first day as a free man; free of an office. My license went back this morning and I have a sign on my door saying in both Chinese and English that my office is closed permanently. I think most people know, as I have had no one attempting to get in. I am trying to get a paper from the Public Health Department which will allow me to advertise in the newspaper that I am closed. The amount of red tape is truly remarkable!

You should see my office at the moment. It is filled with tables on which all my equipment of years is spread out. A's chief of Ear, Nose and Throat is going over everything piece by piece making a list which must be placed before the purchasing agent of the Government. A's people have already said they will buy but it must be approved finally down here.

Your letter of August 17th came in yesterday. It finds me, as you can guess, in the midst of many things but still limping along from my virus infection. I shall be relieved when I can get this equipment business out of the way. We shall then begin to sell off bits of furniture here and there and reduce things to the point where it will not be too much of a chore to get away. The packers will take much of what we want to send out down to their warehouse where all the packing is to be done.

September 2, Tuesday. Our lists are all made and now the debate starts regarding what the Government Purchasing Department will pay. I am insisting on a blanket amount.

September 4. I did not get this off yesterday as I had no immediate good news to give you regarding the P's exit permit. When they went to pick it up yesterday they were told it was not ready and when it is they will receive a telephone call. They are taking it very well but it is a disappointment when they thought everything must be clear inasmuch as their names appeared at last in the newspaper. That is the way it is, any small thing or thought by someone may stop the thing cold and one rarely knows what it is. · It is to be hoped that theirs will be cleared away shortly.

Yesterday, I was informed that I must make a complete list in English of everything I am selling. It has been a big chore but we are getting it completed this morning. We are really in the hands of the Government Purchasing Agent. No one else can buy and they can decide what will be paid. It does not matter what I want as I can sell no place other than to a similar institution which would then have to transact everything through the same purchasing agency. I'll be lucky if I can get enough to meet my debts. I would be willing to walk to a ship tomorrow with only the clothes on my back.

A colleague was in the other night who described to me the general plan of medical education and hospitalization now going forward here. It is probable that in no other place in the world can a man or woman begin to remove tonsils after two and a half years of medical school training. The emphasis is placed on specialization and the control is compulsory consultations between specialists whenever a major procedure is proposed. All our old crowd are getting out of private practice and into institutional work. They must, if they are to eat.

September 5, Friday. I am getting used to sitting in my office without patients and I think I like it. Some do not understand that I can no longer practice but they will come to it. I hope all this is going to push me out of China fairly soon. We shall begin to look in the papers at week ends. *(A listing of exit permits was published in the Sunday newspaper.)* There definitely seems to be evidence of a little easier movement of people outward now and we may get in the stream. We want to leave Shanghai by steamer if possible and I think it will be possible because of Mrs. D's difficulty in walking. She could not possibly do the walk in Canton of a mile between rail points. More people are going out by steamer from time to time so I think we shall have no difficulty.

Later, same day. A friend came in today to read us an item just received from a San Francisco paper in which I am described as attempting to get out . . . A man was sent in today from the purchasing department to look over my instruments and equipment. He confessed that he had never seen special instruments before yet he is to decide what my things are worth!

September 7, Sunday. Wonder of wonders! Our names are in the paper this morning for exit permits. Now we wait three days and if no one has anything against us, we pick up our three exit permits.

Now we have or will have when we really have our exit permits, two months in which to get out. We shall plan to get away by the end of next month. Our phone is ringing every five minutes by people wishing to congratulate us on our luck. P. called at seven a.m. We really don't get hot and bothered until we have our exit permits in hand and like many others will not really feel we are away until we are fifty miles out at sea.

Now will come the big business of making lists. Everything one takes out including books must be listed in Chinese. Names of books must be listed in Chinese. P. has just learned this as it is a new ruling and became big business with him as he has many books to take out. We shall discard just as much as possible. This is a time when sentiment must be cast aside. We shall try to sell off our piano and furniture but don't expect to get much for it.

# FINAL SETTLEMENTS

SEPTEMBER 8, 1952 (TO H.S.H.)

This has been a day of heat and showers. In between the morning ones I managed to go down town and make my peace with my landlords so they won't put a crimp in my exit permit. I am hoping to be paid for my equipment by the end of the week and should be able to clear everything away easily. Then I went along to make reservations for the boat to Hong Kong, the last of October. In the event we secure permission, we shall be leaving here about October 21.

Our packers are going to be very helpful. They will take everything to their storage and pack our lifting van, which incidentally we have kept all these years since we last came out from America. A lifting van is about the only way one can protect his things from being broken into. The thefts between here and Hong Kong or in Hong Kong are beyond belief. I am advised to ship directly to San Francisco but while my van will have to go via Hong Kong I will not have to bother with it there.

September 10, Wednesday. We have just come in from the exit permit office where S. and Mrs. D's permits were forthcoming promptly but mine was withheld for some two hours while they were getting information regarding some back taxes which I had paid more than three months ago. The coordination between some of the departments is not too good. We now hold our exit permits and begin tomorrow to move things. The first will be our rugs out to the cleaners and then on to the packing company.

SEPTEMBER 13, 1952 (TO H.S.H.)

My letters are likely to be even more disjointed than usual from this point on. We have been packing hard all day or rather sorting out and getting things ready for the packers who come Monday morning to take the first load away. I'll not try to get a letter out to you tomorrow as I sent you a brief note on Wednesday saying we have our exit permits in hand.

I hope to have a final word to give you regarding the sale of my instruments after Monday. These people have been taking almost two weeks to come to an estimate of my equipment. I have only one desire and that is to get enough to meet my debts and to pay for all my outgoing expenses up to Hong Kong. It is like passing on to the next world: "You can't take it with you."

September 15. People are beginning to wander in to see if they can pick up various bits of furniture for a song. One can't blame them as few have any money. It is still the 1942 Chevrolet which is giving me concern as I don't want to keep garaging it after I leave. As near as I can find out there is absolutely no resale value. I can't sell it even for junk. All this shows most clearly how little there is in the private home with which to buy anything but food.

The amount of running here and there which we must do these days for permits for this and that is beyond belief. For instance we must go down town one day next week to be vaccinated and then in two more days our arms must be inspected. A friend is loaning us his car so these trips should not be too bad. Some of my Chinese colleagues, many of whom I have not seen for months, are expressing themselves as being "very unhappy" that I must get out. I think they are really disturbed at having the last link with the American Medical fraternity severed.

September 16. Dr. P. has just been in and we have held our usual "bull session." Some activity since Monday by the Foreign Office may signify efforts to clear away the last remaining obstacle to their leaving. He and I have a wager which goes like this, the first to arrive in the United States is to give the other a bang-up meal at such a time as our paths cross. It is still not impossible that they can beat us out of here. *(The P's left China before us.)*

September 17. This has been a day of happenings! First, my equipment sale was completed a little after twelve and I was able to receive a check for 130,000,000 JMP, which is very near what I was hoping to get. Second, just this evening I have been informed that funds are lying in Hong Kong for us when we are permitted to reach that city.

## 22: DAWN OF THE "BEAUTIFUL FUTURE"

The year 1952 was ushered into China with austerity and gloom as the Communists made their drive against Chinese merchants. Then came the period when the authorities wished everyone to be happily together again, to forget the cruel days of early spring and cooperate in making China more prosperous.

The early morning indoctrination lectures to workers in banks, factories, and similar organizations, were the same: Everyone must cooperate and "work hard" for the "beautiful future," which was just around the corner. In that "beautiful future" work hours were to be reduced, food would be in greater abundance, and material blessings would be available for everyone.

SEPTEMBER 19, 1952 (TO H.S.H.)

Just nine years ago today we started out of here on the Japanese repatriation ship. They certainly were not very kind to us and I remember it was an extremely hot day, much unlike today which is seventy degrees . . . Today I have been down in the city paying debts in the amount of 50,000,000 JMP. To date I have spent 75,000,000 of my 130,000,000 JMP . . . My office is still a mess as the instrument packers are not finished. They expect to finish day after tomorrow and I shall be glad to have Communist-minded individuals out of the apartment.

Our plans are not too definite after arriving in America. I want to have the pleasure of meeting the Clan. In any event, we shall keep no schedule and will let things work out as we go along.

September 21. The other broadcast system has not come through to anyone as far as I know. The V. O. A. is pretty bad as no one can catch up with their frequent changes. If they would simply take five minutes a day as the BBC does and give their schedule it would be helpful. Our native friends complain of too much Ike and Stevenson news. They crave news of this area as well. *(The other broadcast system was the voice of Free Asia, a privately supported organization.)*

We are getting tuned up for our October 1st celebration and loud speakers are at it hot and heavy. One over in the French Club grounds is pointed this way and one is best heard if he yells into the thing! I cannot carry on a conversation in this room with a window open because of the noise and the songs, the same old ones! They are played over and over again until some of the records are far from perfect. The French Club is being decorated on top with flags. We'll probably see a show there tonight.

SEPTEMBER 21, 1952 (TO H.S.H.)

While out for a walk this evening I dropped my letter to you for tomorrow's train in a mail box and now as I wait for the evening meal to be served I'll start a new progress note to be sent the middle of the week. This I do to the "practicing of drums" down below my window. Also in the distance under red, white and blue colored lights, on the roof of the French Club, the new social dancing is in progress.

I have been watching these antics with glasses and they remind me of what used to take place in my part of the world when I was a child. These people make up in energy what they lack in grace! All this new social dancing is to prepare our young people for the "beautiful future" which is "just around the corner." Incidentally American dance music is always played for these exercises but no American words must be used!

September 23. Dr. P. told me yesterday that the authorities were in all day checking on the furniture and equipment of the mission house in which they live and that they are moving into the Cathay Mansions next door to us tomorrow. I feel that this is the last stage with them and they will soon be getting their exit permits.

Not only are we working for the "beautiful future" which lies ahead but we are to wear our best clothes now that many visitors are coming to Peking for the conferences soon to be held. Every effort must be made to put one's best foot forward. School children returning north following vacation have been instructed to bring back to school all their best clothes. For my part, I am taking out virtually nothing but

# DAWN OF THE "BEAUTIFUL FUTURE"

old clothes. It is rare to see beautifully dressed young people on the street now but I understand all this is to be changed as soon as our guests arrive. *(The "peace" conference was about to be held in Peking and numerous efforts were being made to show visitors from the Communist areas that China was prosperous and happy. Orders had gone out that marchers in the October 1st parade were to replace the usual Communist uniform whenever possible with their best clothing. Men were to wear foreign business suits with colored ties while women were to wear good looking dresses. Flowers were to be carried by some and bright ribbons in the hair were in order. The object of all this finery was to provide suitable subjects for colored motion pictures, later to be used for propaganda purposes. Above everything else, paraders were advised to smile!)*

Letters in this morning from Hong Kong from friends offer two more places for us to stay and a car for our use. As a matter of fact we shall be so relieved to be in Hong Kong that we shall be glad to stay anywhere. I think we are doing this business in a slow and serene manner but along towards the last it may be more of a rush. Much depends on how we go out.

September 24. We are just back from putting in our request to go out by boat. As usual we are not to get an answer until four days later. Everything must be referred "upstairs" and it would never do to have anyone give an immediate answer!

Our midday temperatures still are pretty high but nights are nice and cool. It looks as though it will be good weather for the October celebrations. There is much practicing, including much talking, but not a great deal is known about the parade excepting that it must stop promptly at 12 noon so those participating can go home and rest for the afternoon and evening. The whole night may be used in feasting. After noon, especially, everyone must dress in his best and men must wear ties. The "beautiful life" begins at this time. Can't you imagine the "beautiful propaganda" pictures we are going to be producing shortly? . . . We are getting fed up with so much in the way of political round-up from home. A little goes a long way out here. This does not mean that we don't want to know what goes on but we don't want to hear it repeated over and over again. We also want to hear about other things. We want to know how we look to the rest of the world. This I write on behalf of some of my Chinese friends.

SEPTEMBER 25, 1952 (TO H.S.H.)

It is Thursday and we have much of our remaining freight out of the house. The more empty we become the better I like it. We are giving things away right and left but also selling a few. It does not take long for word to get around that there are things to be had for the taking. I have been down to the British Consulate today to get my application forms for our Hong Kong transit visa. We are supposed to know when we'll be leaving Hong Kong but an exception will be made in our case.

I had Dr. P. on the phone just now and find they are still in their house waiting to have it taken over. He thinks now tomorrow will be the last day and they will move next door to us. Everyone thinks this is a final cleaning up of things for them and before long they may have their exit permits.

September 27, Saturday. "Believe it or not" we sold the old car for the equivalent of three hundred and fifty U. S. dollars. In getting rid of the car I am also freed from providing storage for an indefinite period.

I am up early this cool morning and as I write at 7:30 I look out on young people practicing for the "great day." A new dance apparently is to be made popular. As one looks down upon them one is reminded of the Mexican jumping bean. It may not be that it is a larva inside but certainly they act like they have "ants in their pants." What about the ladies? We all wear pants out where we live! One gets the impression that there is a great element of mass hypnosis in a great many of the things going on.

Later, same day. It is now 11 p.m. and we are just in from a regular old time home dinner with native friends of long standing. W. and Z. and Mrs. Z. were there and talk was very free. It was like old times without present "pressures."

The big news today is that the P's were called in this morning and given their exit permits with instructions that they should get out by Monday. This gives them just two days to make ready but they are prepared for it. I believe the time limit placed on their going is to avoid any more blockage by anyone. Also that their house is being taken over and they have no place to go excepting to a hotel. They will probably get out of China a month before we do and he will probably contact you as he goes through San Francisco.

September 28. The P's were in to evening meal and told us everything is progressing well towards their departure on tomorrow's train. It has been a mad rush but everyone, including the officials, has been helpful. Good golf today!

# DAWN OF THE "BEAUTIFUL FUTURE"

September 29. We are just back from getting our "yellow card" which is given in connection with vaccination for smallpox. No injections are required at this time. In three days we have to go back to have our arms inspected. It is most interesting that one must be vaccinated to go out of China. I suppose this is because some must go by train . . . On every hand preparations are going forward to make this the biggest October 1st yet. It is the year of "prosperity" and everyone as I have said must wear his best clothes in the parade and smile. All night on the first is to be devoted to "happy participation" in parties and dancing. We have ringside seats to two "parties and joyful celebrations" down in our garden.

P. M. same day. We got it! I was handed permission about an hour ago for all three of us to travel to Hong Kong by ship. I went immediately to the shipping company where I was told that we must be ready to go any time between the 18th and 23rd of October. It is a great relief to be able to go out this way and have all our baggage examined at one place. The "year of prosperity" and "smiles" may be altering relationships. They were very friendly with me at the exit office!

SEPTEMBER 30, 1952 (TO H.S.H.)

It is the night before October One and the city appears to be resting up for tomorrow. Unlike last night there are no blaring loud speakers. In the distance one can see some fireworks but the big show comes tomorrow. Parades are to come in the morning and each section of the city is to have its own. This is the year of prosperity and all must show it. All must keep smiling! This I want to see and shall make it a point to go out for a short view of how "prosperity" looks and later I'll give you my impression.

Today was a wonderful day for golf and I had a game. I did not play too well as my own clubs are packed but I got plenty of fresh air in good company. Near one green we had to detour as soldiers were practicing the new dance which in part looks much like our square dances.

October 1, Wednesday. It is six a.m. and things are starting! Early trams will soon stop after they have helped people get to their collection points of marching. I am up early as I suddenly seem to be taking after my paternal grandfather and am wide awake at this hour. Perhaps it is also the daily planning I must do to get things moving towards our departure. In any event, I see the sun rise and I see the sun set. It is going to be a beautiful day for the parade and all the beautiful clothes with bright ties are going to film well!

The motif in all the decorations this year is the "dove of peace." New posters on the walls look only upon the bright and happy side of life. It is rare that one sees anything implying hate, such as anti-American or anti-germ warfare displays. We are in an era of "smiles" and "prosperity." You will know that a "Malik" is being perpetrated by decree.

Six p.m., same day. It has been a good day for parades. I don't think I like a parade without bands; drums do not give the right atmosphere. It may, however, give the kind of reaction wanted here. Now as night comes on everyone is making ready for the night of "joys." Loud speakers over in the old French Club are just starting. One wonders why they must have such volume! A man speaking just now can be heard certainly a mile.

It was just as had been predicted, the women wore their best and merchants their foreign suits, otherwise there was little change from past years as far as I could see as the parade passed. Also there were not too many smiles. I'll hope to give you more details when I see you. I'll be glad when it becomes cool enough to close the windows as this noise is almost beyond the point of tolerance. There must be many traumatic eighth nerves near the speakers. One might almost agree that the loud speaker is an invention of the devil.

October 2, 5:45 a.m. "Believe it or not" the loud speakers have just gone off and the last of the crowd has gone from the French Club. Now, at sunrise, everything is quiet. I'll bet there never were so many amplified words spoken in a matter of twelve hours in the history of the world. There must be a lot of very tired loud speakers this morning! The three or four records which have been repeated over and over must be worn out. The party down below in the garden of this apartment building all seemed so very artificial.

We had a grandstand seat for the fireworks over at the old race course and they were really beautiful. I don't know if I told you that the race course has been converted into a people's park and square. I approve of the park. The Hardoon Garden should also have been converted into a park but it is being divided into building lots.

October 3, Friday. We have been in to have our silver sealed by the Bank of China this morning. We are each allowed to take out twenty-five ounces. We also are allowed to take out fifty U. S. dollars each for which we must get a permit when we have our tickets in hand.

## 23: LAST DAYS

The business of moving one's home from one locality to another is never an easy matter for the average person. Our move from Communist China was complicated by regulations and red tape applied in such a manner that they could serve no useful purpose except perhaps to harass the departing foreigner. Most individuals were given two months in which to leave after receiving an exit permit and at least this much time was needed for making the necessary arrangements.

OCTOBER 8, 1952 (TO D. & H.)

As I look out of my window this early morning, 6:30, the first batch of people are doing calisthenics over in the old French Club. Later, a much larger group, probably students, will come on. Setting up exercises are an important part of every morning in all walks of life. Now this group is doing the new square dance. I'll try to demonstrate it when I see you.

I have been looking over my memo pad covering the things I have had to do, beginning several weeks back, in order to get out of China. They go something like this:

1. Secure separation of staff and closure of office. (Accomplished after innumerable meetings, letters and running first to one office and then to another.)

2. Apply for exit permit. (One trip to secure application forms, second trip to hand in and answer questions as to why we want to leave China.)

3. Go back to secure exit permits after name appeared in paper. (Waited two hours until they could straighten out matter of land tax payment before receiving permits.)

4. Secure doctor's statement regarding mother's physical condition in order to make application to go out by boat. (Secured statement from doctor who knew her condition without having to go to the hospital.)

5. Presented doctor's statement with letter making application for all three of us to go by ship. (Had to return later for answer.)

6. Go back after five days for answer regarding going out by ship. (Given with apparent pleasure. Approval noted on exit permits; must return again with letter from shipping company when they have tickets so that ship and sailing date can be entered upon exit permits.)

7. Move small pieces of furniture and trunks to storage go down for packing.

8. Secure "yellow book" of vaccination. (Two trips, one to be vaccinated, one to have arms inspected.)

9. Have silver weighed and sealed. (Secured 25 ounces for each individual.)

10. See about sealing documents to be carried out by hand. (Finally decided not necessary to seal since we are being allowed to go out by boat.)

11. Secure certificates regarding our old lifting van, which came from abroad when we last arrived in China. (Finally decided that inasmuch as new timber had been used in reinforcing lifting van, foreign exchange must be brought in before it could be permitted to go out.)

12. Secure transit visas for Hong Kong. (Secured with one visit.)

13. Secure permission to take out $50 U.S. each from Bank of China, when steamer tickets are in hand. (Later permission was given on presentation of tickets.)

14. Secure doctor's letter regarding Mother's general health for shipping company. (Later secured.)

There may be other "runnings" but the above is enough to show you how it goes.

OCTOBER 9, 1952 (TO H.S.H.)

Thursday. I am still basking in the glow of last evening when friends of long standing came in for the evening meal. I have just arrived in my office at 7:30 a.m. in time to see the second group arrive for their usual morning callisthenics. Much of it is devoted to foot work of the "jumping bean" variety. We had some very amusing descriptions of the new dances last night. Much of the callisthenics was approved, for the young, but they drew the line at "silly dances."

Last evening some were lamenting their inability to get any satisfactory program over the V. O. A. in English. I caught it at 10:45, at the end of which it was announced that the next program in English would be at 7:30 tonight. Nothing apparently comes over during the day. It seems to me that this is poor policy as there is great demand for English programs and they carry much less jamming than some of the others just now.

October 10, Friday. As I sat listening last evening to an old Shanghai hand set forth his ideas of the present situation, it occurred to me that it really is not strange that the people at home have uncertain views of what goes on when various individuals locally size up the situation differently. I have come to see that the personal equation plays a very large part in one's reactions. If one could take all our opinions and throw them into a machine which could turn out the answers perhaps the resultant would not be far wrong.

October 11. The ship we are to go on was in port yesterday leaving early this morning so she is on a schedule which will bring her back in about ten days. We are likely to get out, therefore, about the 24th.

OCTOBER 13, 1952 (TO H.S.H.)

A letter came in from Dr. P. yesterday from Hong Kong describing their trip down. On the whole it could pass, but he had one anxious fifteen minutes just before going over into free territory when he was severely questioned. They were met in Hong Kong by many friends and are seeing many more daily.

Today must be another one of "running" for both S. and me. Mine is to the dentist and the customs, his is to the tax office to try and be relieved of a fine for the improper cancellation of tax stamps. I think this particular bureau must be credited with more ways of catching people in the "wrong" than any other in the world

Later, same day. S. is just back from the tax office and after an hour's talking was let off without a fine. I, therefore, save over a million JMP. It seems that in cancelling these stamps in the first place S. had neglected to carry his cancellation mark onto the document on which they had been placed. He was accused. therefore, of using previously used stamps. We were fortunate, however, in finding the man who gave us this particular document and he went along with S. to bear witness that S. had used only new stamps. It is one thing after another!

Our apartment becomes more empty every day. We are trying to get rid of as much as we can either by sale or giving away. A doctor friend will come on Saturday to take the last of my medical supplies. Inasmuch as this apartment is paid for until the end of the month we shall keep as much as we need of the furniture and kitchen things until we go, and then Mrs. C. can help close things out.

October 14, Tuesday. As no letter has come from you at the regular time I suspect you assume we are on our way. You will learn from my letters that our boat has been delayed and we now expect to leave not earlier than the 24th. I have been down to the shipping company this morning where I was told that we must have all of our lists of things in the trunks and suitcases in their hands by the 21st. This will be three or four days before we close our suitcases so we must know what is going into them, as once the lists are made nothing can be changed.

We went over to have private documents sealed but were told that those going out by ship do not have to go through that formality. We have plenty of other things to do! We shall know in a few days whether or not all our things are passed by the customs. One never knows what they will turn down. After everything is all packed it must again be all unpacked and inspected at the custom shed. I am being required to bring in a little foreign exchange to pay for my old lifting van.

October 15, Wednesday. It is 6:15 a.m. and I have just had Tokyo air waves on, it being our best bet at this hour, when we get ten minutes of the latest news.

We were hoping to pay our one last visit to the small Lincoln Road house but it is a day of rain and must be put off or given up. So many going-away lunches and cocktail parties are coming along that we are likely to find ourselves a bit rushed at the last. Our deadline for all packing lists is the 21st so we must be pretty well organized at that time.

OCTOBER 15, 1952 (TO D. & H.)

I have just signed an agreement this afternoon with a Chinese who will take over the Lincoln Road property and provide a home there for the amah, Yen Nai-nai. We have been concerned over what we should do about her and had even considered an old ladies' home but this will give her just what she will like with little or no work attached. This man agrees to give her spending money on top of all living expenses. I am leaving her a little money so she should be well taken care of.

August 16, Thursday. I am preparing certain slow mail letters to you, one containing the above mentioned agreement, which will be sent off to you after I leave. Just put them away in a safe place and

# LAST DAYS

I'll pick them up sometime or you may keep them with your own private papers.

October 17. I am just back from down town where I was told our ship is already turning around in Hong Kong and is starting back today. This means she will be in Shanghai Monday and we shall sail on perhaps Wednesday the 22nd. This is going to produce some last minute rushing as our heavy baggage must go in by 3:30 p.m. today.

October 18, Saturday. We finally got our trunks off yesterday afternoon and now must pack our suitcases with lists prepared to go in early Monday morning. A later word we have says the ship will probably not sail until the 23rd, that is Thursday.

We had word from the packers late last evening that our lift van had passed customs with only a few things removed All the rugs passed, I am happy to say.

OCTOBER 17, 1952 (TO H.S.H.)

This will be my last letter from Shanghai as there is every indication that our ship is making a quick run back to Shanghai and we shall be leaving on the 23rd. We have been warned to be ready and are doing last minute packing and "listing." I hope I never see another list!

Later, same day. Now at 4 p.m. our big trunks are going out. We will live out of our suitcases for a few days. Monday should be busy with tickets to get, money to be certified as to amount which can be taken out, exit permits to have name of boat and sailing date stamped on them and finally our residence certificates returned to the police.

We are finding that one of the things which takes so much time, in addition to packing, is the visiting of people who must have a last word. I think now with these trunks off and nothing but hand baggage to prepare and list we should be able to do it easily. I shall not draw an easy breath, however, until we are moving out into the Whangpoo.

October 18, Saturday. It is 5 a.m. and my planning brain is working early. I think it must be the great number of needed actions in connection with the red tape of leaving which makes for shorter sleeping hours. It cannot be worry as I am completely resigned to walking out and leaving many bits of business, such as the selling of the last stick of furniture, entirely in the hands of the people who are helping us get out. I am only interested in getting out from under "pressures" and free of debts. In the matter of debts, I am leaving with some dozen people owing for professional services. Some cannot pay but others can but will not, knowing I am soon to be out of their hair. I shall be glad to be away from professional charging at last, for human nature is a raw affair with some people.

October 19, Sunday. 6:30 a.m. It is going to be a beautiful day for our last in Shanghai and our "going away" luncheon at the Golf Club. I go out with one of my partners for a last game this morning. My last list is finished and only those of Mrs. D. and S. remain. Chinese friends come in this evening bringing the evening meal with them and will come in sufficient time to help in making out the Chinese translations of the lists.

I'll be writing you next from Hong Kong, probably next Sunday or Monday.

## 24: HOMEWARD BOUND

It is most difficult to explain to one who has never experienced the pressures within a political state the lifting of spirit which comes as one passes the barrier into the free world. Our release came on October 23, 1952, when the S. S. Yunnan flying the British flag left its wharf at Shanghai to return to Hong Kong. The actual release came when all ropes were cast off, although there were a few anxious moments when our ship almost fouled the lines of a Communist boat tied up ahead of us as we moved into midstream. An accident at that point might have delayed us for hours or days during which an investigation would have been carried on.

This was the second time in less than ten years that the three of us had been compelled to leave China because of political unrest. On September 19, 1943, we had been repatriated from Shanghai by the Japanese and had taken that long round about sea-voyage to New York. Then as now, there was a finality about the whole affair which was most disconcerting. Then as now we were leaving behind many life-long Chinese friends.

As the time neared for our departure many Chinese colleagues, students, and friends, came to bid us goodbye. Many were concerned over possible reactions in America with regard to the anti-American propaganda which had been foisted upon them. Almost in identical words they asked that a message be brought back to the American people to let them know "the Chinese do not hate them."

During the summer of 1954 there were widespread floods in China, which were inevitably followed by famine in many areas. The Communist hierarchy in Peking does not admit the existence of the suffering and hungry millions. To them this is the "period of prosperity," and posters throughout the country show smiling Chinese in the midst of plenty surrounded by all the modern inventions of industry and transportation. What does it matter if the population of China is reduced by several millions?

For many years America has come to the aid of the starving millions and would do it now were it not for the callous rulers in Peking who can interpret such assistance only as a means of subverting the people. There are multitudes, however, living today only because America sent ship load after ship load of food to those in need. Memories in China are long and the people know that the Americans sent food to them out of the goodness of their hearts and not for any subversive motive. The masses have not been swayed by anti-American propaganda. A smaller but more important number of Chinese who have had the advantages offered by American educational facilities both in China and the United States, will never forget what they owe to those institutions. Under present conditions there are some who are forced to give lip service to the new order, but as one of them said to me, "we speak with our lips but not with out hearts."

In this period of world tensions it is well for Americans to remember that the old and traditional friendship which has bound the Chinese and the people of this country together over the years still exists even if it is not articulate. It is not easy for those without firsthand knowledge of China to understand how completely the present masters of China are hated by the people. That the officials are conscious of this antagonism is borne out by the fact that Russian advisors and Communist officers travel from place to place in curtained and speeding motor cars.

China may be typified by the old Yangtze River as she plows her way to the sea. She may at times have her course deflected by outside forces; but sooner or later she rights herself and flows serenely forward. A culture such as the Chinese have had, which stretches back more than four thousand years, and has withstood many pressures through the ages, some as great in magnitude as the present one, will again emerge and China will take her place beside the free nations of the world.